THE OLD HOUSE CATALOGUE

THE OLD HOUSE CATALOGUE

2,500 Products, Services, and Suppliers
for Restoring, Decorating, and Furnishing
the Period House — From Early
American to 1930s Modern

Compiled by Lawrence Grow

BONANZA BOOKS
NEW YORK

Library of Congress Cataloging in Publication Data

Grow, Lawrence.
    The old house catalogue.
    Bibliography: p.
    Includes index.
      1. Historic buildings—United States—
Conservation and restoration—Catalogs.
I. Title.
TH3411.G76   1982 728.3′7′028802947   81-21788
                                    AACR2

ISBN: 0-517-371618

h g f e d c b a

Contents

Foreword

Assembling a volume as complex and detailed as *The Old House Catalogue* has been a long-range effort. The idea for the book, and its title, were first proposed in 1973, a time when it appeared that there was not a sufficiently large audience for such a publication. By January of 1975, when a final decision was made to undertake this large project, the preservation movement had grown measurably. The National Trust for Historic Preservation had nearly doubled its membership in the preceding five years, and other organizations such as The Victorian Society in America and Friends of Cast-Iron Architecture were reaching out to many thousands of persons. The recent recession has proved what preservationists have been saying all along: the rehabilitation and restoration of period structures is an idea whose time has come.

Numerous readers, advisors, and editors have made contributions to *The Old House Catalogue*. From hundreds of sources have come suggestions and material on the products and services that might be included. And the flow of information continues to this day. The first edition of *The Old House Catalogue* is just a beginning, a modest first step toward meeting the real needs of old house owners and those who would like to take part in the growing movement to retrieve the livable past.

Anyone seriously interested in the technical aspects of building restoration and preservation should become acquainted with *The Old-House Journal*. A monthly magazine, it is a very helpful, highly intelligent source of information for the home craftsman and decorator. Although we share a very similar name and interest, this book is not related to the magazine. The journal also publishes a *Buyers' Guide* to restoration and preservation products. This is an unannotated compilation of listings (without prices) primarily in fairly technical areas. It includes advertisements. *The Old-House Journal Buyers' Guide* will be published each year, and it is a wise purchase for the professional or gifted amateur. Similar regional buyers' guides are being prepared by preservation agencies and societies; a group in Wilmington, Delaware, has just issued its first edition. This publication and many others on the subject of home restoration are included in the bibliography to be found at the end of this book.

It would have been impossible to pull together so much disparate information without the participation of hundreds of companies and craftsmen. While many large firms, particularly those in the home decorating field, have been indifferent to our appeals for material to evaluate, the small entrepreneur, in the true American spirit, has responded with eagerness and keen interest. It is to them that *The Old House Catalogue* is dedicated; for not only have they helped us, but, by their imagination and commercial daring, they have created alternatives for all who are tired of the general shoddiness and bad taste which seem to afflict much of the commercial world.

Several people have been of particular assistance in assembling the book. Martin Greif, my partner in The Main Street Press, has spared even minutes that he has not had to read through submissions and manuscript material. James H. Burke spent valuable time compiling information for several sections. Allen Chambers and other members of the Historic American Buildings Survey staff in Washington, D.C., provided useful historical material. Norman Wiltsie aided in the early work of contacting suppliers. Among these, Adriana Scalamandré Bitter of Scalamandré Silks, Inc., New York City, and Murray Butler Douglas and Joseph D. Moore of Bruschwig

& Fils, Inc., New York City, were especially helpful. Their interest and sympathy has been greatly appreciated.

Special thanks are due, too, to Gilman Park, president of Universe Books, New York City, for his steadfast friendship and belief in this project, and to Terry Morton and Diane Maddex of *The Preservation Press* of The National Trust for Historic Preservation, Washington, D.C., who encouraged publication of the book at a time when no one else would listen.

Lawrence Grow

Introduction

Americans love to search for *the* old house, *their* old house. As a child on family outings, I used to try to spot the old from behind the asphalt siding, the overgrown honeysuckle, the pile of rubber tires. Each Sunday we drove to the big city, Chicago, and along the old Lincoln Highway were any number of broken-down farmhouses; the streets of the West Side were jammed with sagging tenements. "Now, if you could just rip off that porch." "Look at that ornamental iron railing!" "It's too bad they let it get so run-down." The story was always the same—one of neglect, of not caring, of being surrounded by more and more trash. But we were never ready to give up this search for the perfect old house.

The Little House by Virginia Lee Burton was my favorite book, a story about a modest dwelling abandoned by its owners and engulfed by the crude commerce of the city. I knew many like it. A very human house it was, its windows having become soulful eyes, the front door a saddened mouth. It had started life on a gentle hill in the country surrounded by flowers and lovingly tended by its family. This was not the home of Dick and Jane who lived in that pretentious and boring brick thing down the street, but a comfortable cottage with shutters, a house with a cheerful pink coat of paint. How truly sad it was, then, to watch it die.

But the house was saved—at the last moment before the demolition squad was due to arrive. The house-mover declared, "Sure, this house is as good as ever. She's built so well we

could move her anywhere." These were the days before urban homesteaders, before it was fashionable to "redo" that tenement into a proper row house. The little house was moved back to the country, to open land. The cycle was about to begin all over again. I wonder where it is now? Surrounded by sprawling buildings once more? Probably.

There is no escape in this world from the steady pressure of population. I know that someday the old house I live in will be surrounded not by a grove of hemlocks but by ranch-style houses. New York was once a good two hours away; now it can be reached via the interstate in little more than half that time. But give up? Not on your life. If I had been raised in the city, I would feel the same way, despite the threat of default, despite the very real terror of the neglected streets. Only an inability to support a family, to carry the crushing property tax burden so unfairly imposed on the urban homeowner, would force me to flee. And then I would search again for the old rather than the new, the well- rather than the jerry-built, the real rather than the plastic. I'll take three rooms of the former rather than eight of the latter.

Why? Unlike Mr. Blanding, I need a dream house with roots in the land, in a community—and I won't give up restoring the old. I need the past, a history that makes the present and the future more interesting. I like the fact that people lived here before I did, that they left initials scratched on the window glass, a name etched in the pointed stone of the toolshed. I enjoy the unevenly hewn timbers, the imperfect fit of the floorboards. It all has a very human quality, something which cannot be instantly fabricated by machine.

Perhaps you will say that this is a mere nostalgia, cheap sentiment. I'll admit to a certain amount of overindulgence: this can be a comfortable way in which to live. But it can also be an extremely practical means of surviving this decade. It needn't cost an arm and a leg *if* you are willing to give up some of the luxuries that you probably don't need anyway. Have you noticed how an old house is sited on its land? It sits snugly in the ground, protected from harsh winds in winter. Mature trees shade the dwelling, and windows are designed to open, to provide cross-ventilation in the summer. Central air conditioning is really a waste. In addition, the house will probably have at least one fireplace, if not an opening for a Franklin stove. You will discover that you can save considerably on your winter fuel bill by burning wood or briquets. Both inner and outer walls are secure and well-padded; you don't need to insulate them against noise.

What then of the rotten beams, the termites, the leaky plumbing, the puttyless window-panes? You'll find them. Some old houses were built as badly as new ones today. Others have so fallen into disrepair that not even the wealthiest patron can afford to resurrect them. But of every one such structure, there are at least five more in the city and the country which can be used again, which can be made liveable and enjoyable at a cost less than that required to start anew.

The Old House Catalogue is designed for those who want to give it a try, who have found or are still searching for their old house —in the city, in the suburbs, in the country. It is for the hardy band not intimidated by the realtor's lament: "You want to live in a *used* house?" It is a book of dos and don'ts, of gentle advice for making the best of a difficult undertaking. Hopefully, some of the real excitement, the deep pleasure of making an old house your own, will emerge in these pages amidst all the warnings.

The Old House Catalogue is a sourcebook of products and suppliers—2,500 in all, in ten different subject areas, from structural needs such as doors and siding to minor appointments such as weather vanes and clocks. A surprising number of these products can be purchased from national suppliers or through retail outlets. As more and more people discover that not only small—but old—can be beautiful, business moves in to satisfy their needs. Increasingly, too, there is a need to sort out the best of these products. Lamps made from butter churns and sofas fashioned from buggy seats are not recommended within these pages.

The term "old house," like its first cousin "antique," can cover a multitude of sins. "So you bought an old house," my accountant's wife told me. "What is it? Ranch style?" God knows it could be if you read only the pages of building-supply magazines. The landscape is increasingly dotted with new structures which combine French Provincial, American English Colonial, and Swiss Alpine in true ersatz "style." Some even like it. An institution as prestigious as the Smithsonian recently devoted one of its major galleries to an approving display of structural kitsch. Many architectural critics who should know better willingly accept this Venturi-esque put-down of sound design principles as a valid artistic expression. Perhaps they do not realize that it is a cruel joke, especially on those who find themselves trapped in flimsy bi-level houses with walls that can be punctured with a fork and surrounded by 1001 gadgets that break down daily.

The term "old house" is used within these pages to mean almost any structure built before World War II—from French, Spanish, and English Colonial in style to 1930s bungalow-modern. Because no two human beings are exactly alike, neither are two dwellings. Mount Vernon has been copied from coast to coast in America; Scarlett O'Hara's "Tara" pops up time and time again. You will never find, however, an *exact* copy of either building. Structural elements have been mass-produced in America for many years; the Victorian cast-iron fronts so valued today were stamped out in New York, St. Louis, Philadelphia, and in other cities; yet each is used in a unique manner. It is difficult, then, to recommend any one style, any one product, for such a diverse constituency. What is appropriate or fitting for a California Mission-style town house in Los Angeles is hardly to be suggested to the owner of a Cape Cod saltbox.

For purposes of categorizing products, four of the most basic North American architectural styles are referred to throughout the catalogue—early Colonial, late Colonial, early Victorian, and late Victorian. Products suitable for early twentieth-century buildings are included, but it is impossible at this stage to group them together with any consistency. The owner of such a dwelling will find that a visit to a junkyard or a salvage depot will often provide him with many of his structural needs. In addition, he should know that for the first three decades of this century, home furnishings remained essentially the same—late Victorian in syntax. When it comes to furnishings, the 1908 Sears, Roebuck catalogue is almost identical with that of 1927. Buildings of this period are infrequently considered

worthy of maintenance, not to speak of restoration. Within another ten to fifteen years, however, a large-scale reproduction industry will have developed to supplement the dwindling supplies of the junk shops so necessary to the owners of these "period" houses.

With the assistance of the Historic American Buildings Survey, a National Park Service archival service, it has been possible to outline and broadly explain the four different building styles. An understanding of the basic architectural elements helps greatly in defining both exterior and interior old-house needs. Documentation of the visible and invisible history of a house is of immense value in planning its proper future use. If great houses are always given such attention, there is no reason why the owner of a more modest dwelling should not attempt the same thing. A bibliography to be found at the end of this volume contains any number of books and other publications which will be of great value in the work of documentation. In addition, information on such valuable institutions as the Historic American Buildings Survey has been included.

Such terms as Colonial and Victorian are imprecise at best, but their usage is so prevalent that there is no way to avoid them. In an article for *Historic Preservation*, the National Trust magazine, members of the HABS staff state that "for the preservationist interested in identifying, enjoying, and defending the architectural assets of a community, the real need is to understand the broad stylistic movements in American architecture." This is exactly what is attempted in the eight pages which follow. The reader should understand, however, that little but general characteristics can be conveyed through the use of extremely broad terminology. These characteristics are best understood in high-style buildings of the sort chosen to illustrate early and late Colonial and early and late Victorian styles. Again in the words of the HABS writers, "the designers of such buildings would most consciously have adhered to the dictates of fashion. These structures also served as models for simpler buildings."

Early Colonial

The Joshua Brooks House
Middlesex County, Massachusetts

built c. 1730

The New England clapboard-sided farm house of the early eighteenth century is one of the enduring classics of the New World. It has been reproduced time and time again and is found today even in the tracts of suburbia. It is a modest, simple, direct architectural statement well-suited to the still-heavily-wooded North American environment. Ornament, at least on the exterior, is minimal; the interior contains more high-style elements, but these are restrained.

NORTH ELEVATION

The measured drawing outlines the basic elements of early-Colonial farmhouse styling—a shingled gable roof with simple wood cornices and boxed eaves; six-on-six windows, fluted window heads or caps, and straight sills; a six-panel door with four lights framed by a pedimented head with dentil course in the cornice and fluted pilasters at the side; a central chimney of bricks. The foundation walls are stone below grade, brick above. The wall construction is of wood frame measuring overall 36' x 75' 4".

The house as it existed in 1961. The shrubbery obscures the almost perfect symmetry of a rectangular, central-hall Colonial. The clapboard siding has been replaced over the years. Did the house have shutters? Many country houses of the period were not so adorned, and there is no structural evidence to suggest that this house employed shutters. There is a full basement divided into two areas by the fireplace foundation of stone and brick. The first floor contains an entry and stair hall, two formal front rooms, a winter kitchen, and a modern kitchen in what was formerly a buttery or bedroom. An addition added on to the house at the back now includes a laundry, storeroom, and garage. The second floor of the main building also contains four rooms, two bedrooms, and a bath and a storage room. The latter two smaller spaces were once combined into what was known as a kitchen chamber. The attic floor completes this most economical and functional dwelling.

The winter kitchen makes use of a paneled room-end fireplace wall, the long supporting fireplace beam handsomely defining this utilitarian space. The fireplace wall contains a brick oven with chamber below. It is seen here to the right with a wood door cover. Storage space is above the fireplace. The hardware is of the most basic sort—H and HL hinges and wood knobs. To the left can be seen a corner cupboard and horizontal wainscotting of a simple beaded variety. The flooring is mainly of the modern 4″ wide wood strip sort, although some original boards, 10″ to 17″ wide, remain. The ceiling is unadorned plaster; the beams also have been plastered over.

Credits: measured drawing, Terrence A. McCormick, HABS; exterior and interior photographs, Cervin Robinson, HABS.

Late Colonial

Cliveden
Philadelphia (Germantown),
Pennsylvania

built 1763-1767

Jacob Knor, master carpenter
John Hesser, mason

A masterful example of late Colonial Georgian domestic architecture, Cliveden was the home of the Chew family until 1972. It was then acquired by The National Trust for Historic Preservation. High style in almost every respect, the structure incorporates elegant appointments in its exterior facade and interior spaces. An appreciation of classical architectural elements, only modestly stated in the early Colonial period, is here fully expressed.

SOUTH ELEVATION
SCALE 3/16"=1'-0"

The measured drawing illustrates the essential forms of the Georgian building style which were shaped by the principles of Andrea Palladio. These had been enunciated in English translations of the sixteenth-century Italian designer's illustrated treatises, and in books devoted to English country houses built in the Palladian manner. While there are no Palladian windows to be found here, pediments, pilasters, elaborate cornices, and stone urns on brick pedestals define the classical style as interpreted in the mid- to late- eighteenth century in America. These elements are used in both the main structure and the two side dependencies, the one on the left having been joined to the central block in 1856.

Cliveden as photographed in 1972. The fine ashlar finished cut stonework of the main facade is clearly in evidence. The side walls are of scored and stuccoed rubble. The structural framing throughout this center-hall Colonial is of oak. A two-story ell extends from the rear of the building, and the walls of this section and of the two side buildings are of stuccoed rubble.

The heavily pedimented Doric entryway, the twelve-on-twelve windows framed by three-panel shutters on the first floor, the elegant cornice and bracketed eaves, the shingled gable roof with front pediment, and the Gothic sash dormer windows with side consoles—these combine to form a gracious and rich late-Colonial style appropriate for a rising class of urban merchant princes. The employees of these gentlemen were more than likely to continue to dwell in early Colonial style houses for another half-century or more.

The interior of Cliveden matches the exterior in splendor. This is the parlor which centers on a marble-faced fireplace. The facing is surrounded by a large egg and dart moulding. Above is a mantel shelf in the form of a classical entablature supported by brackets. The chimney breast above is surprisingly simple in its tabernacle form. The chair rail above a plain dado or lower wall section is similarly restrained as is the ceiling moulding with its Troy dentil. Paneled pine is used in many of the interior doorways. Ceilings are unadorned plaster and wood; floors are of random-width pine boards. The parlor is one of thirteen rooms on the first floor. The second floor contains eleven, and the attic, six.

Credits: measured drawing, C. Stanley Runyan, HABS; exterior photograph, Jack E. Boucher, HABS; interior photograph, Cortlandt Hubbard, HABS.

Early Victorian

The Hermitage
Nashville, Tennessee area

built 1818, 1831, rebuilt 1834

builders, Joseph Rief and William Hume

Greek Revival in form, Andrew Jackson's Hermitage is not considered Victorian in a textbook sense. It is included here because it departs from Colonial precedents and because its interior space, gutted by fire in 1834, was most decidedly reconstituted along early-Victorian lines. While Victoria had not yet come to the throne, the series of architectural revivals which were to follow one another—Greek, Gothic, Renaissance, Romanesque, Tudor—were underway by the second decade of the nineteenth century in America.

Only today are we able to view the Victorian in terms of its multitude of styles, from the airy expanses of ante-bellum ironwork to the heavy timbered interiors of the robber barons, its intense love of glass, richly printed papers and fabrics, and fine workmanship in metal and wood. The Hermitage has something to say about these varied elements.

This photograph, taken in 1972, captures the monumental proportions of The Hermitage. The figures on the right approaching the building suggest the immense, the romantic scale of the building. The window sashes in the center structure are the twelve-on-twelve pane forms found in high-style Georgian structures, but they are surrounded by rather simple frames. The shutters are horizontal louvers rather than paneled affairs.

The measured drawing devotes as much space to the Corinthian columns as it does to the brick south facade. The columns of wood with cast-iron leaf decoration, a second-floor gallery, and the overarching cornice combine to form a facade of heroic proportions. The front portico entryway with double doors, fanlight, and sidelights, shrinks into the shadows. In late-Georgian houses the front entryway is the central point of architectural expression. Here it has been subordinated to the mass. The two wings, added in 1831, differ even more in style from the Colonial. The gable roof, of course, has disappeared entirely.

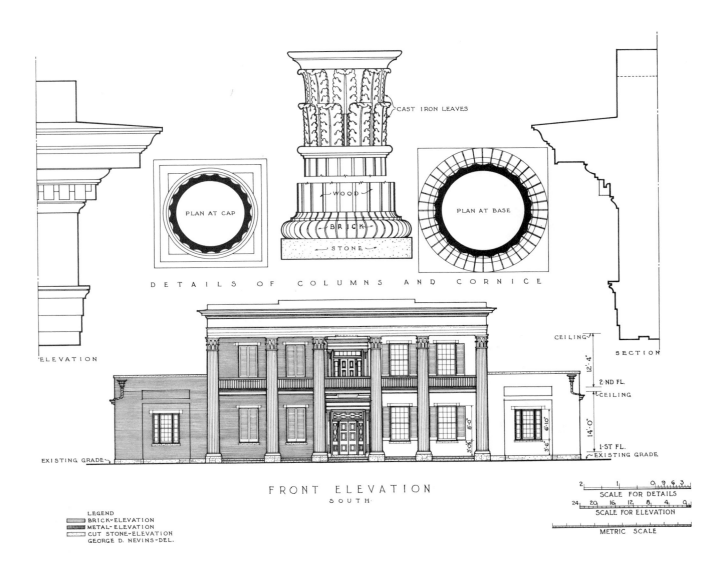

CAST IRON LEAVES

WOOD

BRICK

STONE

PLAN AT CAP

PLAN AT BASE

DETAILS OF COLUMNS AND CORNICE

ELEVATION

SECTION

CEILING

12'-4"

2-ND FL.

CEILING

14'-0"

8'-0"

6'-10"

3'-6"

3'-6"

1-ST FL.

EXISTING GRADE

EXISTING GRADE

FRONT ELEVATION
SOUTH

SCALE FOR DETAILS
SCALE FOR ELEVATION
METRIC SCALE

LEGEND
BRICK-ELEVATION
METAL-ELEVATION
CUT STONE-ELEVATION
GEORGE D. NEVINS-DEL.

19

The interiors of The Hermitage depart even further from eighteenth-century practice. The pictorial wallpaper, ordered by Jackson from France in 1835, is used in the stunning central hall. The spiral staircase is suspended from the rear wall, an interior equivalent in bravura to the imposing exterior colonnade. The doorway mouldings in this hall and in the bedroom illustrated are executed with rosette blocks far removed from the Colonial in style. The bedroom fireplace is surmounted by an Empire-style overmantel mirror. Bed hangings, draperies, wallpaper, and carpeting express a feeling for patterns and textures which would be intensified in years to come.

Credits: measured drawing, HABS; exterior and interior photograph, right, Jack E. Boucher, HABS; interior photographs, left, courtesy of Scalamandré Silks, Inc.

Late Victorian

Colonel Walter Gresham House
Galveston, Texas

built, 1887-1893

architect, Nicholas J. Clayton

The massive, crenelated facade of the Gresham House marks it as an almost perfect example of high-Victorian expression in America. The vast interior is similarly worked in the Romantic Revival style. Greek Revival was a fitting form for the first democratic president, Andrew Jackson; the Romanesque suits the Gilded Age of soldier, lawyer, legislator, and railroad baron Gresham. In 1887, the same year he was first elected to the Texas legislature, he chose Nicholas Clayton, the state's leading architect, to design his mansion. It was six years in the making, and cost anywhere from $250,000 to half a million dollars.

The exterior photograph, taken in 1967, shows how well the building has stood the test of time. The green-glazed tile roof sections are in good condition, as are the chimneys. The main, one-story cast-iron porch extends across the front entrance and wraps around the circular east tower and adjoining facade. The apse-shaped conservatory is visible to the right. The windows on the first two floors are crowned with transoms, some decorated and opaque.

SOUTH ELEVATION

0 5   20 FEET

The measured drawing of the south elevation captures the enormous scale and intricate detailing of the exterior. A three-story masonry block, it is flanked on the east by a round tower and on the west by a polygonal tower. On each side and between these elements are a multitude of architectural details worthy of a European chateau. The overall dimensions of the building are 88 feet by 104 feet at maximum, not including the five highly ornamented chimneys, four of which are visible here. Each aspect of the structure is carefully delineated from the other, but they work together aesthetically to form a most impressive, imaginative whole. Every advance of the Victorian machine age has been employed to architectural advantage.

The interior space is built around a central rotunda which is reached by an entrance hall. In the rotunda is found a high-style open and curved stairway. The dining room opens onto the hall-rotunda area and is magnificently paneled in rich hardwoods. The ceiling has been painted in an angelic fashion. The floor in this room and in others of the ground level are of parquetry.

Credits: measured drawing, Larry D. Johnston, HABS; exterior and interior photographs, Allen Stross, HABS.

Products and suppliers recommended in *The Old House Catalogue* have been chosen from hundred of sources. Every attempt has been made to weigh their merits. Judgments, however, are only finite. We ask the reader, therefore, to pardon us for whatever offenses have been committed in the selection process and, most important, to bring these to our attention. Prices are given when available, and these, of course, are always subject to change. Addresses of suppliers are also listed, and these, too, may become out-of-date quite swiftly.

A number of the products, particularly those in the fabric and flooring sections of the book, are available only through decorators or special supply houses. Unless the reader is using a professional service or has one close at hand, he is urged to contact the manufacturer for information as to how the materials may be secured.

At press time all the products listed in *The Old House Catalogue* were available to the public either directly or indirectly. In time these product lines—like prices—will also change. No manufacturer, however, is likely to suddenly drop from stock those items for which a steady demand has developed. Most of the products recommended are quality reproductions. Each year this market increases in size and sophistication. In all likelihood, the next edition of *The Old House Catalogue* will be an even more complete and necessary guide to the old house market.

Antique supplies and recycled products are given where possible. The antiques market is a highly personal one which defies rational organization and/or explanation. Auction houses and dealers can be extraordinarily good sources for the kind of objects which the old house owner seeks. In many cases, prices for authentic wares may be no more or less than those paid for high quality reproductions. For this reason, the objects offered in the furniture section of this book (Part IX) have been strictly limited to include small pieces, custom-crafted items, and do-it-yourself projects. The purchase of large, mass-produced pieces, except for beds, is not recommended.

There has been no attempt to discuss some of the more technical and complex problems facing the old house owner. Needless to say, excavating, moving of sections or whole houses, the removal of ceilings, walls, and/or entire rooms—these are matters which cannot be covered in a catalogue of this sort. The reader is urged to consult the bibliography for help in this regard and, if there is an architectural preservation society in his area, to seek professional advice. In a similar vein, only a few of the restoration services, contractors, and craftsmen are given space in these pages. These are services usually available only on the local or regional level, and, once again, the reader is advised to consult local preservation experts concerning their recommendations. Attempts to catalogue these services on a national scale by such organizations as The National Trust for Historic Preservation have so far proved inconclusive.

What remains in *The Old House Catalogue* is a wide, varied, and interesting assortment of readily available products and services of an appropriate sort for the period home—*wherever* it is located, in *whatever* state of restoration or preservation it exists. A broad range of prices is offered in almost every category so as to fit the needs of as large an audience as possible. The book's use to interior decorators, both professional and do-it-yourself proponents, should be immediately evident.

There is an integrity to many buildings which have survived for even thirty-five years in North America. Some designed by skilled architects or carpenter-builders are true historic landmarks which contribute a richness to the landscape which is incalculable in terms of dollars and cents. The majority of these buildings, however, are modest dwellings built for simple working people or middle-class merchants and professionals at a time in which building was more than a matter of sheltering individuals as cheaply as possible. Materials were used with respect to their qualities. To say something was stone-*like* or wood-*like* probably never occurred to builders in a day in which there was only *real* stone and *real* wood. Perhaps it is only when we reexamine our past and learn again to build solidly for the future that we recapture our sense of the natural and the beautiful. Hopefully, *The Old House Catalogue* will make a contribution to achieving this goal.

Samuel Page House, Wiscasset, Maine. Historic American Buildings Survey, Cervin Robinson, photographer.

I Structural Products

Of primary concern to every present or prospective old house owner are the basic structural elements with which he must work and live. Windows, doors, ceilings, beams, roofing, flooring, paneling—these are the expensive items as well as those which give an old house its character. Such add-on elements as plumbing, wiring, and heating are designed and accommodated to fit the basic arrangements—within reason. The goal of the restorer is to bring the past alive again in a sensible manner. Costumes are best suited to historical museum mannequins.

Many of these basic architectural elements are covered in this first section of *The Old House Catalogue*. Flooring and floor covering is the subject of another section (Part V), the technicalities of plumbing, wiring, and heating are only suggested throughout the text. Both the Lighting (Part VI) and Fireplaces and Heating (Part IV) sections offer some advice and assistance in meeting the requirements of modern living. Plumbing is one of those mysteries which we cannot begin to fathom. Make sure that you know someone who can explain it. Or, better still, consult a licensed plumber before you come to grief.

The same good principles of design which apply to the selection and use of fabrics, paints, papers, and furnishings are operative in the structural field. However abused or spoiled, an old house is likely to possess a distinct personality, a form, a set of lines and angles which taken all together spell out the right approach to restoration and preservation. Get to know your old house well, both its present shape and its history. Do not be afraid to do a little digging or tearing apart (carefully, carefully). Only in this manner will you be able to discover the position of doors, hardware, even rooms themselves which may have changed over the years. One generation was likely to paint or paper over the work of another. Peeling away the past, documenting

as you go, can be an exciting and satisfying experience.

Study your house. Take pictures of it from many angles. Look at similar structures in the neighborhood. Attempt to construct a chronology of its form-taking. Decide which period suits it best. Just because it was built in the mid-eighteenth century does not mean that a return to this period is mandatory. Perhaps it only assumed its natural form—additions and all—in the early nineteenth century.

And above all, take time. Rushing won't help. Seek advice from professionals. Find out who the craftsmen are in your area, men and women skilled in masonry, carpentry, painting, papering—people who admire good materials and fine workmanship as much as you do.

The structural materials market grows larger each year. Antique and new "antique" brick, paneled fireplace walls of eighteenth-century New England and versions of them crafted today in northern Massachusetts, hand-hewn shakes—these can be found. And *The Old House Catalogue* is designed to help.

Structural Parts and Restoration

Companies specializing in the renewal of old structures are increasing in number each year. New technology has not made this precise and delicate kind of work any easier, but it has enabled the restoration contractor to pursue more ambitious projects. House moving is now commonplace; restoration is a process which can take years if the building is a large one. Most of the contractors work in one general area since much custom work is called for in most cases. Many building contractors are willing to undertake restoration projects, but it would be wise to consult with one of the regional or national preservation groups before committing yourself.

Townhouse Restoration Co., Inc.

An urban area restoration group, Townhouse handles everything from reproduction mouldings, kitchen cabinets, shutters, and doors (all made in their own shop) to the supply of period wallpapers and fabrics. A project can include only the restoration of a facade or it can include all aspects of interior and exterior work.

Townhouse Restoration Company, Inc.
262 Herr Street, Old Mid-Town
Harrisburg, Penn. 17102

A. W. Baker Restorations, Inc.

The members of the Baker team are historians and craftsmen. They understand the necessity of documenting a structure's past—how it was built originally and then added on to or otherwise altered over the years. To accomplish this task, measured drawings, photographs, and archaeological studies are undertaken. Baker's primary interest is in wood buildings of the seventeenth through the nineteenth centuries, and wood analysis plays a part in determining what shape the restoration should take. Reproduction materials are not produced by the group, but are supplied by them when required. The company does keep on hand a supply of antique beams, paneling, flooring, doors, etc.

As with other restoration contractors, work is done only on a regional basis—in this case in the southern New England area, particularly Rhode Island and southern Massachusetts. In the words of Baker: "We feel that by confining our work to a specific area, our knowledge has become specialized relative to these structures and the methods by which they were built. We can also better understand the effects this particular environment has played on them."

After the primary documentation has been completed, many buildings are dismantled, moved, and erected on a new site. The barn pictured here was reassembled on a spot sixty miles from its original location.

In dismantling a structure, every care is taken to see that the basic elements are given extra protection. The placement of these has been recorded in measured drawings and numbered for reassembly. A crane then may be used to lift off the heavy timbers, each one of which is banded with two-by-fours. In the pictures below, banding in foam and lifting of fire boxes is shown. Five such boxes and one oven were saved for use in the reassembled dwelling in this manner.

Eight years have passed now since the restoration of this complex of buildings was begun. The large seventeenth-century house with a later ell addition were first moved and completely restored. All of the other buildings have since been dismantled and reassembled.

A. W. Baker Restorations, Inc.
670 Drift Road
Westport, Mass. 02790

Beams

It has become fashionable to expose the beams of an old house, especially if they are hand-hewn. This is the "rustic" look, and it is not always a suitable one. Plastered ceilings were known in earlier days and may have been the rule rather than the exception. Some ceilings, however, were left open and only later enclosed. Before taking down the ceiling, be sure that you know the general condition of the beams underneath. They may be more "rustic" than you would care for—even unsightly. Replacement antique beams may be purchased from a number of restoration companies; the false, pressed paper variety offered by many home supply firms today are ugly beyond belief. They look phony, are phony, and should be avoided by all but your worst enemies.

Hand-Hewn Beams

Antique Building Supplies is one source of such materials. The beams come in 4 to 25-foot lengths, and in width from 6 to 20 inches. They are available in walnut, oak, poplar, and other woods. The company will send a sample of the type you desire for $2.

Beams are priced at $1.50 to $3.50 a foot; discounts are available on orders of $350 or more. All prices are FOB the company.

Antique Building Supplies
Xenia, Ohio 45385

Diamond K Co., Inc., has available two grades—A and B—of rough cut (3″ x 5″) and hand-hewn beams. These may be used for ceilings or for door frames and mantels.

Brochure and prices available.

Diamond K. Co., Inc.
130 Buckland Road
South Windsor, Conn. 06074

Bricks

As long as the pace of demolition continues to be brisk, the old home owner will have no trouble in finding a supply of used brick. Wrecking companies are glad to get rid of the mess, but don't expect to drive up to the lot as if it were the city dump. Most wreckers will charge you for each piece. Used brick is now being employed as flooring both inside and outside the house—for kitchens and patios. If such a ready source is not available to you, you may have to turn to one of the antique supply houses or to a maker of new "old" bricks.

Antique Bricks

Artifacts, Inc., is paradise for the old home owner—a warehouse full of salvage from demolished buildings just waiting to be adopted. Included among the materials are, of course, bricks. The warehouse is open Mondays, Wednesdays, and Fridays from 10 a.m. to 3 p.m., and will be of special interest to Washington, D.C., area residents.

Artifacts, Inc.
1210 Queen St.
Alexandria, Va. 22314

New "Old" Brick

Old Carolina Brick Co. is the largest producer of handmade brick in the United States. A wide range of styles and colors is available. Illustrated is Park Ridge, shade number 250C, a combination of brown, red, and light purple. Old Carolina will match existing old brick in size, texture, and color, and can duplicate almost any special shape brick that may be needed.

Brochure available.

Old Carolina Brick Co.
Salisbury, N.C. 28144

Ceilings

Ceilings in most homes are simple matters of plaster, perhaps surrounded with a cornice or other type of moulding. Elaborately painted affairs are the rarity in North America, but ornamental plasterwork, wood-paneled, and metal-sheeted ceilings may be encountered. Except for the metal, this is all custom work which may have to be performed anew. Antique ceilings may be moved intact; plaster ornamentation, alas, does not travel so easily.

Ornamental Plaster

Felber Studios offers two ceilings, of which the Haddon Hall Modified is illustrated here. The second is also in the Tudor style and is termed Hopewood Inn. This by no means exhausts their design resources, and, if you have a particular style in mind, this may be the firm for you. When inquiring about work and prices, be sure to send dimensions and shape of the room or space.

Catalogue available.

Felber Studios
110 Ardmore Avenue
Ardmore, Penn. 19003

Steel Ceilings

Metal ceilings of the Victorian period were once regarded with horror by Colonial purists. Thanks to the passage of time, the prejudice against these ornamental, highly decorative ceilings has virtually disappeared. The Barney Brainum-Shanker Steel Co., Inc., is the place to turn for assistance. Just two of their many multiple plate designs are shown here—No. 209 with a small flower design, and No. 307 with bold diamonds.

Each of these plates, as well as the others, measures 24″ x 96″. Shanker also produces the cornices which can be used in conjunction with the plates, as well as the filler plates which fit between the cornice and multiple plates.

Brochure available.

Barney Brainum-Shanker Steel Co., Inc.
70-32 83rd Street
Glendale, N.Y. 11227

Cupolas

Be careful. Cute cupolas are sprouting everywhere. As originally used on farm or public buildings for ventilation purposes, they were an attractive and functional architectural element. They also served as a perfect mount for a weather vane. Today they may make a handsome addition to a barn or other outbuilding if these are of an early or late Colonial style.

Cape Cod specializes in pine cupolas which are hand-painted with two good white coats. Roofs are covered with either aluminum or copper. The cupolas are fully assembled and shipped to the new owner with installation instructions. The manufacturer notes that "A cupola like anything else always looks smaller when high in the air. Do not make the mistake of ordering a cupola too small for your building. A cupola should measure at least one inch for every foot length of a garage, i.e., a garage approximately 22′ x 22′ should have a cupola at least 24″ square." Illustrated is the Paddock Six Sides with copper roof only and ranges in price from $233 to $710 according to size required.

Catalogue available.

Cape Cod Cupola Co.
North Dartmouth, Mass. 02747

Doors

There are collectors of doors, people for whom the entryway to a building is the all-important structural element. Old doors are often beautifully paneled affairs crafted by a master carpenter or cabinetmaker. Interior doors can be about as elaborate in Georgian or late Victorian houses. Because the openings which they enclose vary greatly in size, it is often difficult to replace one door with another. The ready-made doors available today are standard-width affairs which rarely fit and are unsuitably designed for either exterior or interior uses. Fortunately, there are many suppliers of period doors—both antique and reproduction.

French and Ball offers museum-quality reproduction doors for both exterior and interior use. These are made of Maine virgin pine and employ mortise and tenon joints throughout, the end of the tenon being exposed. No glue is used as the use of wooden pins and the tightness of the joint keeps the elements in place. Three different exterior doors are priced at $75 to $85; one exterior door with four panels is priced at $115. All are hand planed on both sides.

Brochure and price list available.

French and Ball
Main Road
Gill, Mass. 01376

Paneled doors for Spanish Colonial homes are produced on the West Coast and throughout the Latin American world. Among the most handsome of the styles available in North America are those made in Spain, in the factory of Estebon y Bartolome in Madrid. They are constructed of samonilla, the tropical monkey pod tree, and are finished in a dark walnut color. The simply styled Lerma is priced at $132 and is available in the United States through Architectural Specialties, Inc.

Brochure available.

Architectural Specialties, Inc.
850 South Van Ness Avenue
San Francisco, Calif. 94110

Decorative doors employing stained glass, etched glass, and carved elements are the specialty of

Gargoyles Ltd. These are particularly suitable for use in mid- to late-Victorian dwellings. All have been removed from doomed dwellings of the period and are available in pine, oak, walnut, mahogany, or satin wood. They have been stripped of paint and can be finished as you wish.

Catalogue available.

Gargoyles Ltd.
512 South Third Street
Philadelphia, Penn. 19147

Elaborately carved doors of rosewood and mahogany can be found at Elegant Entries Inc. These are terribly heavy, solid timber pieces which would enhance any Tudor Gothic interior of the early twentieth century. Prices for mahogany doors start at $88 and run as high as $188; those in rosewood are from $244 to $544.

Brochure and price list available.

Elegant Entries Inc.
45 Water Street
Worcester, Mass. 01604

Fireplace Walls

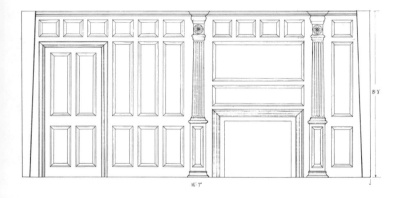

A paneled fireplace wall appeared in many Colonial interiors. It could be a very elaborate affair or a simple composition of beaded boards and moulding. Whole walls of either sort are available from some of the antique materials supply houses; French and Ball are creating new units in traditional styles. An example of their work is illustrated here. Prices for complex work of this sort are approximately $6.50 a square foot; the material is Eastern white pine.

Brochure and price list available.

French and Ball
Main Road
Gill, Mass. 01376

Glass

Old window glass—bubbles included—is in great demand. It is rarely found by most home restorers; purists pursue it to the ends of the earth. It is questionable just how much time you should devote to seeking out what at best is a distorted medium through which to glimpse the outdoors. One experienced preservationist could not bear to remove his wavy panes but disliked the myopic view. He compromised by installing new clear glass in the upper sash and the old in the lower.

Stained glass of many sorts is once again popular. Panels of this colorful medium are regularly saved from the wrecker's ball. In addition, new craftsmen are working in old forms.

The Wrecking Bar is one of those collectors of stained as well as leaded, etched, and beveled glass. These are available as windows or decorative panels.

Brochure available.

The Wrecking Bar
292 Moreland Avenue, N.E.
Atlanta, Ga. 30307

The craftsmen of Virtu specialize in designs from all periods of glassmaking. Their work is done in leaded and copper-foiled stained glass and is of their own inspiration. They do not perform custom work to the specifications of others, but they will listen to suggestions. Sample slides are available for inspection. The design above is one of many original with them.

Virtu
P.O. Box 192
Southfield, Mich. 48075

Paneling

Included in this category are those paneled room ends—with or without a fireplace. Although suppliers of such original paneling usually describe it to be of eighteenth-century origin, such woodwork may have been executed in the early nineteenth century when Colonial styles still held sway, at least in the country far from the centers of high-style craftsmanship. Whatever the century, such materials are a far cry from the knotty pine popular in the 1940s and '50s or the fake wood overlays sold today. Paneling was meant to last and has. Used in a room end, it provided space for storage in the form of cupboards and perhaps a set of tight-winder steps to the floors above and below.

It sometimes seems that the use of paneling became an obsession in the late Victorian period—redwood timbers stretching the length of a foyer, golden oak embracing dining room walls. There was much that was clunky about the Gilded Age. Proportion was often sacrificed to mass; subtlety of line was subordinated to box-like forms. This was no streamline era. Yet there was also considerable craftsmanship displayed in the use of wood—by Gothic Revival stylists in England and America, by the proponents of the Arts and Crafts movement. And this wood was not all dark and gloomy. In the homes of wealthy North Americans, the baronial palaces built until the 1930s, rich woods and veneers were applied to walls with considerable taste and dramatic effect. From the perspective of the 1970s, they positively glow with artistry.

Three eighteenth-century building materials firms dealing in room ends are The 18th Century Company, Kensington Historical Company, and Trump & Co. The two former firms handle restoration and reproduction carpentry and dismantle and relocate old structures. Trump & Co. is primarily a dealer in fine antique objects.

The 18th Century Company
Haddam Quarter Road
Durham, Conn. 06422

Kensington Historical Company
Box 87
East Ingston, N.H. 03827

Trump & Co.
Bethlehem Pike
Flourtown, Penn. 19031

Louis XIV, Louis XV, Louis XVI, and Regency style paneling is offered by Architectural Paneling Inc., of New York and Dallas. Boisserie has a timeless beauty which is appreciated today as much as it was in the eighteenth century, the 1880s, or the 1920s. A great deal of handwork is involved in both carving and finishing the paneled surfaces. Architectural Paneling Inc. does only custom work; that is, it creates a special design for a room. Cabinets, doors, mantels, etc., are often part of the overall scheme. The company will prepare a detailed colored cardboard replica of the new room in 1/2″ scale once they have your requirements and measurements of the space on hand.

Brochure and prices available.

Architectural Paneling Inc.
969 Third Avenue
New York, N.Y. 10022

and

Vivian Watson Assoc.
590 Oak Lawn Plaza
Dallas, Texas

Another firm specializing in fine architectural paneling and cabinet work is Carlo Germana. The photograph above illustrates the high quality of his wood detailing and finishing.

Literature available.

Carlo Germana
318 Hempstead Turnpike
West Hempstead, N.Y. 11552

For simpler tastes, Southern yellow heart pine may be the right wall covering. Also recommended for flooring, this fine-grained wood has been gathered by Period Pine in Georgia from old mills, factories, warehouses, etc. It is cleaned in every respect and re-sawed for new uses. This unique antique lumber is available only from Period.

Brochure and prices available.

Period Pine
P.O. Box 77052
Atlanta, Ga. 30309

Roofing Materials

Slate, shingles, shakes, tiles—all may be used to advantage and in accordance with fire regulations. Only thatch seems to have disappeared from the landscape. Roofs on some homes may be left completely flat as in early adobe structures and later Mission and true ranch homes. The use of solar energy in the future may alter roof lines completely. Until that time most old home owners, however, will turn to common asphalt shingles as a safe and relatively inexpensive investment.

Slate

Fortunate is the man with a slate roof over his head. Although more likely to break when trampled upon than shingling, it resists aging, fire, heat, and cold with tenacity. As a long-range investment, it may be the best of roofing materials. The Structural Slate Co., working through many dealers, is one of the leaders in the industry.

Brochure available.

The Structural Slate Co.
Pen Argyl, Penn. 18072

Tiles

Ceramic roof tiles are found on Spanish Colonial houses throughout the United States. Artifacts Inc. is one of the antique building supply houses carrying these colorful and durable products.

Literature available.

Artifacts, Inc.
1210 Queen St.
Alexandria, Va. 22314

Shingles and Shakes

Anyone can locate asphalt shingles. Fancy butt red cedar shingles, however, are something different. These are produced by Shakertown Corporation in Washington State. Shingling of this sort was used early in this century; it has returned to popularity. There are many colors and textures to choose from and most of them are available in convenient eight-foot panels. They would be suitable for siding on a Queen Anne style house of the late Victorian period.

Brochure and prices available.

Shakertown Corporation
P.O. Box 400
Winlock, Wash. 98596

and

Bestwood Industries, Ltd.
P.O. Box 2042
Vancouver, B.C., Canada

Split cedar shakes are also available today. Dana-Deck of Washington State cuts cedar logs to length and then handsplit and run a band saw through them to produce shakes of uncommon ruggedness. Dana-Deck has two sorts available—regular and extra-long taper split shakes.

Brochure and prices available

Dana-Deck & Laminates, Inc.
Dana McBarron & Sons
Lopez, Wash. 98261

Salvage Yards

Even the most finicky of preservation experts concerned with the integrity of great eighteenth-century structures admit to enjoying a long afternoon in one of the many salvage or wrecking company yards and warehouses. Like the city dump explored in childhood, the junkyard can yield up treasures for almost everyone. For the home restorer pioneering with such recent architectural discoveries as 1930s Depression Modern or Art Deco interiors, the junkyard may be a true happy hunting ground for structural products.

Baltimoreans may visit their own Salvage Depot, a city-run project. City workers remove reusable materials from city-owned buildings before demolition. Mayor William D. Schaefer began the project in April of 1975, and, on sale day (each Saturday), urban homesteaders and renovators sing his praises. Let there be more of these public markets.

Baltimore City Salvage Depot
213 West Pratt St.
Baltimore, Md. 21201

United House Wrecking is the true queen of the junkees. It is known as "The Junkyard With A Personality." Thirty-thousand square feet of buildings are packed with every conceivable kind of object—furniture, doors, windows, lamps, nautical supplies, tools, crocks, hardware, you name it. And if you can get there, go.

United House Wrecking Co.
328 Selleck Street
Stamford, Conn. 06902

Shutters

Handsome appointments to almost any old house, these come in as many different architectural styles as the structures they are meant to fit. Today they are used almost entirely as a decorative accent; their usefulness as insulators from both cold and heat is limited in the storm window/screen age. If properly hung, however, both interior and exterior shutters can serve a functional purpose on a particularly frigid night. Paneled shutters were used on many high style Colonial residences; plain beaded or batten board panels often appeared on simpler country structures.

Two-panel interior shutters of the reproduction variety can be ordered from French and Ball. These are made of kiln-dried Eastern white pine and cost approximately $75 per pair. Both interior and exterior shutters of the original variety are usually found at antique junk shops or yards, if not from such firms as Antique Building Supplies.

French and Ball
Main Road
Gill, Mass. 01376

Antique Building Supplies
Xenia, Ohio 45385

Siding

Good wood siding is not easy to find, especially that which can be used to replace part of a facade which has rotted away. Until recent years, old house owners

made do with new lumber and finished it as best they could to match the antique. It is debatable whether the replacement of old with new is one of those permissible crimes. It is often an essential one. Know well, however, the wood you are seeking and attempt to match its grain, finish, and overall texture. Purists can turn to a number of antique lumber suppliers.

Old clapboards are available from Diamond K. No staining or sealer is required for these weathered gray-brown strips. The boards are 5 inches wide including 1 inch overlap, and are applied over 30 lbs. felt with the use of galvanized nails to plywood and studs.

Brochure available.

Diamond K. Co., Inc.
130 Buckland Road
South Windsor, Conn. 06074

Stone

Anyone who has ever lived in a stone house has come to appreciate its extreme durability and security. Even on the dampest day, one is loathe to trade in this most natural of dwellings for a less earthy home. Stone varies almost as much as wood. Within the stone house territory of the Delaware Valley are nearly twenty different varieties of building material. Colors vary, too, from the whitest of limestones to reddish-brown sandstones. Then, geographically, there are the cobblestone houses of the Hudson Valley, the fieldstone houses of Connecticut and Long Island, and the cut-stone river towns of Illinois, Missouri, and Ohio.

Quarries are the source of almost all stone supplies today. Although a declining business, sufficient demand for fine building stone still exists in many areas to keep the quarryman and the stonemason busy.

Residents of the Delaware Valley are fortunate in having one of America's most attractive and resourceful quarry operations in their midst—the Delaware Quarries of Lumberville, Pennsylvania. Because of strict zoneing requirements, even the largest of boulders are arranged in neat piles. Low grade marble is also available here for plebian use along with the finest of granite slabs.

Delaware Quarries, Inc.
River Road
Lumberville, Penn. 18933

Sealers

Owners of houses utilizing concrete or masonry walls are aware of waterproofing problems. These particularly plague the stone house dweller. Patching up almost any kind of masonry surface, however, can be a difficult and unsatisfying task. Dampness, especially in the subsoil level of the building, seems to creep back with regularity. But help is on its way in the form of new commercial products.

Standard Dry Wall Products has taken the lead in developing compounds, many of which make use of acrylic resin and silicone. These strengthen the solution. They are all part of "The Thoro System" and are marketed under such names as Thoroclear, Thoroglaze, Thorocoat, Thoroseal, etc. An extremely useful brochure is available from the company for the asking.

Standard Dry Wall Products
7800 N.W. 38th St.
Miami, Fla. 33166

Pilasters, Pediments, Cross Heads

These elements come into play in the ornate Colonial entryways which even the most modern of men stop to admire. They handsomely define a doorway. Such components can be found among the stock of the antique building suppliers, are often fabricated by skilled woodworkers, and are now made of polyurethane.

Fypon is a Baltimore firm specializing in such molded assemblies in polyurethane. While not as esthetically satisfactory as finely crafted mill work, the pieces are well-detailed in every respect. The firm claims that these "entrance systems" are virtually maintenance free. The most expensive of the assemblies, Fypon-Eagle, is available in eight door opening sizes and offers a selection of twenty-four pediments and crossheads. Fypon-Cardinal systems are medium priced, do-it-yourself projects. Fypon-Sparrow systems are low cost, one-piece mantel and pediment constructions. It's worth taking a look at them.

Brochure and prices available.

Fypon, Inc.
22 East 24th St.
Baltimore, Md. 21218

Window Sashes, Heads, and Sunbursts

Window sashes are often the shakiest if not the most rotten elements in an old house. Exposed to the elements, such wood frames tend to give way at a relatively early age. Some can be removed and reconstituted; others are more properly junked. Millworkers in the preservation/restoration market can supply you with perfectly good, custom new ones.

One such firm is the Preservation Resource Center. According to their literature, among the most explicit and professional, their "stock sash design is based upon a sash in use during the late 18th and early 19th centuries and is constructed from selected air dried woods, glued with waterproof glue, and assembled with wooden pegs. All sash is constructed square and allowance should be made to fit openings which are no longer square." How many *are* today? You are in good hands here, however. Your specifications are most important and will be followed. If you want the maker to allow for weight attachments, balance assemblies, or other types of window hardware, you must tell him so.

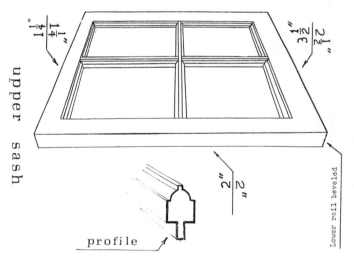

The illustration above is of the stock design. A six-light sash measuring 28" x 32" will cost approximately $27. The Preservation Resource Center will also custom make Victorian sashes as well as other forms of millwork.

Literature available.

Preservation Resource Center
Lake Shore Road
Essex, N.Y.

Window Heads and Sunbursts

Fypon offers polyurethane materials for window use as well. Illustrated are both elements. The window head has a drip cap that can be cut off if necessary. All standard sizes are readily available, and extra-large sizes can be produced. The sunburst is similarly adaptable. Both elements can be affixed to a frame with nails, construction adhesives, or with both. It can be sawed and drilled, and if patching is required, this can be accomplished with wood filler.

Brochure and prices available.

Fypon, Inc.
22 East 24th Street
Baltimore, Md. 21218

Ornamental Metalwork

are beginning to dwindle. Accordingly, prices have risen astronomically. One supplier in New Hope, Pennsylvania, wishes to remain anonymous; he has quite enough dissatisfied customers.

New quality cast-ironwork is being produced today, especially in the South. A leader among these firms is the Tennessee Fabricating Company. It offers a number of traditional designs for use in porches, balconies, gates, etc., in American, French, and Spanish Colonial as well as Victorian styles. Illustrated from left to right are Curly Oak, Spanish, French, and Victorian designs—among several hundred available. Many of these are adapted from wrought-iron motifs.

Catalogue available.

Tennessee Fabricating Co.
2366 Prospect St.
Memphis, Tenn. 38106

Although more properly the subject of Part X (Accessories) and of Part III (Hardware), cast and wrought iron have definite structural uses in many North American homes. Porches, balconies, stairways, gates and screens serve a functional and decorative purpose. Whole cast-iron facades were widely used for commercial purposes throughout the nineteenth century. Handsome structural use of iron is one of the features of the architectural heritage of New Orleans, and Charleston, South Carolina, as well as a number of Northern cities.

Antique ironwork may be found in scrap iron yards across North America. Since World War II, it has attracted the attention of the homeowner, and supplies

Other Suppliers of Structural Materials

Consult the List of Suppliers for addresses.

Restoration Services

American Building Restoration
American Colonies Antiques
Antique Building Supplies
A. Joseph Armstrong
Robert W. Belcher
Bogart Enterprises
Country Salvage and Trading Co.
Dock Street Interiors
The 18th Century Co.
Felicity, Inc.
Gillett Restorations
Howell Construction
John R. Hudspeth, Inc.
Kensington Historical Company
Landmark Restorations Co.
P. B. & Associates
San Francisco Victoriana
George Sarkus Construction
R. Warren Construction Co.
John A. Wigen Restorations

Beams

Architectural Specialties, Inc.
Robert W. Belcher
Dana-Deck & Laminates, Inc.
The 18th Century Co.
Guyon, Inc.
Kensington Historical Co.
Period Pine, Inc.
Tremont Nail Co.

Brick

Antique Building Supplies
Diamond K. Co., Inc.
The 18th Century Co.
Glen-Gery Corp.

Ceilings

A. A. Abbingdon Ceiling Co.
Artifacts, Inc.
Betty Dowd
Kenneth Lynch & Sons

Cupolas

Artifacts, Inc.
The 18th Century Co.

Doors

Antique Building Supplies
Artifacts, Inc.
Driwood Wood Moulding & Millwork Co.
The 18th Century Co.
Fypon, Inc.
International Wood Products, Inc.
Kensington Historical Co.
C. E. Morgan Building Products
E. A. Nord Co., Inc.
The Oval Door
Simpson Timber Co.
United House Wrecking Co.
I. M. Wiese, Antiquarian
The Wrecking Bar

Glass

Alberene Art Glass
Artifacts, Inc.
Blenko Glass Co.
Coran-Sholes Industries
The 18th Century Co.
Gargoyles Ltd.
Glass Masters Guild
J. & R. Lamb Studios, Inc.
Gordon Kemmet
Lumpkin Stained Glass
Rococo Designs
Salamander Glass Works
The Paul Thomas Studio
Unique Art Glass Co.
United House Wrecking Co.
Arthur V. Yariger, Ltd.

Paneling

American SERPE Corp.
Antique Building Supplies
Architectural Specialties, Inc.
Diamond K. Co., Inc.
Driwood Wood Moulding & Millwork Co.
Elegant Entries, Inc.
Felber Studios
French and Ball
Guyon, Inc.
Kensington Historical Co.
Laue Wallcoverings
Old World Moulding & Finishing, Inc.
Simpson Timber Co.
Townsend Paneling

I. M. Wiese, Antiquarian
Wood Art
Wood Mosaic

Roofing

Koppers Co., Forest Products Div.
L. R. Lloyd Co.

Shutters

Antique Building Supplies
Architectural Specialities, Inc.
Artifacts, Inc.
The 18th Century Co.
Mastercraft Industries
C. E. Morgan Building Products
Thomas Moser
E. A. Nord Co.
The Shade & Shutter
Shutter Modes

Siding

Antique Building Supplies
Robert W. Belcher
Guyon, Inc.
Simpson Timber Co.
Vermont Weatherboard, Inc.

Stone

Antique Building Supplies
The 18th Century Co.
Vermont Marble Co.

Sealers

Samuel Cabot, Inc.
Glidden Burkee
Pierce and Stevens Chemical Corp.
Red Devil, Inc.
U. S. Gypsum Co.

Pilasters, Pediments, Cross Heads

Architectural Specialties, Inc.
Driwood Wood Moulding & Millwork Co.
The 18th Century Co.
French and Ball
Gargoyles, Ltd.
International Wood Products, Inc.
Kensington Historical Co.
C. E. Morgan Building Products
United House Wrecking Co.

I. M. Wiese, Antiquarian

Windows

Air Flow Window Systems
Antique Building Supplies
C. E. Morgan Building Products
Window Modes
Window Silhouettes

Ornamental Ironwork

Bailey's Forge
Birmingham Ornamental Iron Co.
Robert Bourdon
Yale R. Burge, Inc.
J. W. Fiske Architectural Metals, Inc.
Georgia Metal Products
House of Iron
Steven Kayne Hand Forged Hardware
Leslie-Locke
Mill Village Blacksmith Shop
Newton Millham, Blacksmith
George W. Mount, Inc.
Robinson Iron Co., Inc.

Two Rivers, Nashville, Tennessee. Historic American Buildings
Survey, Jack Boucher, photographer.

II Woodwork & Other Fittings

These are the architectural elements which help to make a house a home. Mouldings, cornices, brackets, chair rails, inlays, railings, ceiling ornaments, and 1001 other components define space and give it character. While they may perform important structural functions, such fittings are basically decorative additions. It is the absence of these in modern houses today which contributes to an air of sterility.

The woodwork found in most Colonial-style homes is relatively simple in design. Based on classical motifs popular since the Renaissance, casings, mouldings, and rails of various sorts are usually worked in beaded, egg and dart, or relatively flat forms. High-style Georgian interiors may feature additional elements of a neoclassic nature, fluted pilasters and entablatures, inspired by the designs of Andrea Palladio as interpreted by eighteenth-century English architects. Plasterwork also became more complex during this period and involved the use of ceiling ornaments and decorative wall elements such as shells and niches.

Greek Revival styles found their true home in America, both in urban centers and in country areas from Maine to Iowa, in the early nineteenth century. The highly ornate fittings of the Georgian and Federal taste were replaced with simpler forms suitable in a new, democratic nation. They were also more easily shaped by woodworking machinery. Early woodwork was hand carved; by the mid-nineteenth century, however, much of the decorative detailing could be mass-produced. This was true as well of the later Victorian ornaments.

In both Colonial and Victorian styles there was a movement from the simple to the more ornate—from the saltbox to the Georgian manor house, from the Greek Revival to the Tudor Gothic. While the increasing complexity of form was expressed in structural terms (the Italianate villa, the crenellated Renaissance chateau), it was most evident in the use of woodwork and other such fittings. By the end of the nineteenth century, it was difficult for additional decorative elements to be added to exterior and interior surfaces. Houses were stuffed to the gills. Much of it was pure claptrap, but, seen from the perspective of the 1970s, such gingerbread has charm and considerable meaning. Some pieces are truly inspired imaginings of skilled carpenters. Metalworkers, too, contributed handsome finials and crestings. In the baronial homes of the 1920s industrialists are seen perhaps the last expression of the decorative impulse—fine plaster ceilings, intricately carved beams and pillars, garlands, crestings, drapery cornices.

Then came the Federal income tax, and the Depression.

Little extras were thrown out the window. Modern designers urged a return to simpler if not Colonial-style interiors. Square objects were given a curved shape; three horizontal bands replaced concave and convex-carved ornament. It was still a long way from the *Age de Merde*, but the end was in sight.

Mouldings for Multiple Uses

Mouldings form the foundation of decorative wood-work and other similar types of fittings. It is from mouldings that any number of different uses are a-chieved. Woodwork, in particular, is a matter of piec-ing, and mouldings are the units with which one works. Mouldings made of plaster, sheet metal, or urethane are simply one-piece forms which follow those of wood.

Mouldings of all types may be used to create wall panels, fireplace surrounds, chair rails, baseboards, cornices, window frames, and on and on. They can be extremely expensive, elaborate affairs or relatively in-expensive, simple constructions. Almost all are ma-chine-made today. Some are hand-finished.

Redwood Mouldings

A large variety of mouldings appropriate for Victorian dwellings are available from Hallelujah Redwood Prod-ucts. Samples of each are available for 50¢ each.

Catalogue available, 50¢.

Hallelujah Redwood Products
39500 Comptche Road
Mendocino, Calif. 95460

Embossed Mouldings

Relatively simple-shaped mouldings with fancy em-bossed designs can be secured from Minnesota Wood-workers. Some of the designs would suit the interior of a turn-of-the-century or Queen Anne-style dwelling. Others, such as the narrow twisted rope pattern, might be used for wall panels.

Priced catalogue available.

Minnesota Woodworkers Supply Company
Industrial Blvd.
Rogers, Minn. 55374

Urethane Mouldings

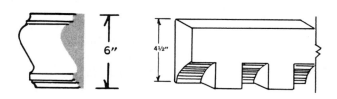

Both a gently-curved surround moulding and a care-fully-etched dentil moulding are to be found in Fy-pon's offerings. These are made of urethane, and eli-minate the assembly of several mouldings. Easy to install and to keep clean, such mouldings are also lower in expense than those of wood, plaster, or metal.

Brochure available.

Fypon, Inc.
22 East 24th Street
Baltimore, Md. 21218

Bright Metal Mouldings

Such shiny metals as chrome and brass are rarely used in old house interiors—at least for mouldings—but they may be found useful, especially in kitchens and bathrooms. Colonial is equipped to supply more than 600 mouldings with wood cores finished in any one of several metals. Among those available are satin and bright lacquer brass; satin brass, lined brass, and bright brass aluminum; bright chrome, lined chrome, and satin chrome aluminum; bright brass or satin chrome zinc; and bright chrome zinc. The mouldings are very simple in form.

Brochure and price list available.

Colonial Moulding & Frame Co., Inc.
37 East 18th St.
New York, N.Y. 10003

Accent Wood Mouldings

These are meant for incidental uses and are packaged in 4' lengths. Their chief use is for frames, but they may be utilized for walls and doors. Some of the designs offered are traditional and fitting.

Literature available.

Klise Manufacturing Co.
601 Maryland Ave., N.E.
Grand Rapids, Mich. 49505

Sheet Metal Mouldings

Lynch can offer a moulding for almost every purpose. They range from the classic to rococo to Art Deco. These are hammered stampings in zinc or copper, the copper being much more expensive.

Catalogue and price list available, $2.50.

Kenneth Lynch & Sons
Wilton, Conn. 06897

Casings

The frame or framework used for doors and windows can be elaborately decorated or, most frequently, simply adorned. Casing is part of carpentry work, and an expert craftsman will be needed for this type of restoration in many old houses. Frames may have badly deteriorated over the years, thus requiring some piece work if not complete replacement. The frame should match the rest of the woodwork in the house and the window or door that it encloses. Like a picture frame, it should be a complementary design element.

Traditional casings, made up of one or more pieces of moulding, are produced by a number of woodworking companies and can be ordered to fit different spaces. These are mass-produced in various woods. Others are handmade by restoration contractors or carpenters specializing in period work. And for purely decorative use, they are now available in urethane.

Driwood Casings

Kiln-dried poplar is used for the casings supplied by Driwood Period Mouldings. These are also available in such woods as mahogany, oak, walnut, and cherry. Twenty-four different designs are offered, including such a moulding assembly as CA-3 illustrated here.

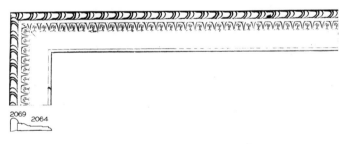

There are six such assembled casings; the remaining are one-piece or unassembled. They are shipped unsanded for painting.

Prices and catalogue available upon request, $1.

Driwood Moulding Company
P.O. Box 1369
Florence, S.C. 29501

Plank Window Frame

French and Ball's window frame with 12 on 12 sashes is of pine with mortise and tenon joints. It is formed in a simple Colonial style appropriate for eighteenth- and early nineteenth-century homes. The frame is finished by hand with a bench plane and is shipped in sanded condition.

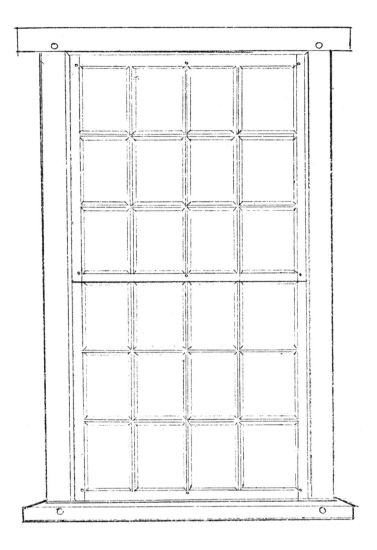

Price, $75.

Brochure available.

French and Ball
Main Road
Gill, Mass. 01376

Bases, Baseboards

Even old houses fitted for baseboard heating can make use of baseboard mouldings. As the top of the wall may be defined by a crown moulding, so the base is detailed by boards of various heights. These serve to conceal the joint between a wall and the floor. Some are only 4" high; others may extend up the wall as much as 9½"

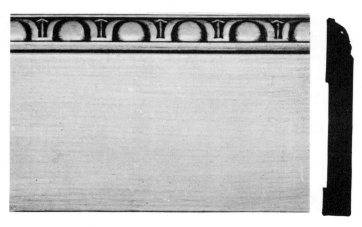

Egg and Dart Pattern Baseboard

Illustrated is Old World Moulding & Finishing's pattern number 1065. Three other baseboard designs are offered in their design stylebook for architects and interior decorators. All are made of hardwood.

Brochure available.

Old World Moulding & Finishing, Inc.
115 Allen Blvd.
Farmingdale, N.Y. 11735

Dentil Pattern Baseboard

Driwood's pattern number B-1 is assembled from three different mouldings, and is much simpler than those offered by Old World. The base projects 1 1/16″ and is 6 5/16″ high.

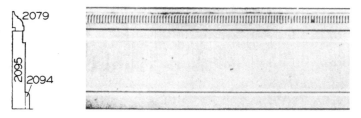

Prices and catalogue available, $1.

Driwood Moulding Company
P.O. Box 1369
Florence, S.C. 29501

Brackets and Corbels

These are used to support cornices and arches as well as shelving. Some are made of stone or metal, but most are formed of wood. Like window frames, these may have rotted with time. Hopefully, some part of the bracket will remain for copying. Any number of woodworking firms will be glad to duplicate old forms. Metalworkers can, of course, perform the same service. In addition, supplies of antique brackets and corbels are available.

Sheet Metal Brackets

Kenneth Lynch & Sons is America's largest supplier of sheet metal ornaments. These are hammered out of zinc and of copper. The brackets are many, some extending as much as 39″. In design they employ scrolls and leaves. Lynch can supply almost any kind of bracket needed for exterior or interior decoration.

Catalogue and price list available, $2.50.

Kenneth Lynch & Sons, Inc.
Wilton, Conn. 06897

Redwood Brackets and Corbels

A California firm, Hallelujah Redwood Products, is imaginatively filling the need for reproduction architectural gingerbread. Owners of mid- to late-Victorian homes can select from a wide variety of traditional designs made of fine-grade California redwood. The brackets, for use on porches or elsewhere, are openwork pieces and curvilinear bars of the Carpenter Gothic variety. The corbels are similar in shape, but are incised rather than open-cut.

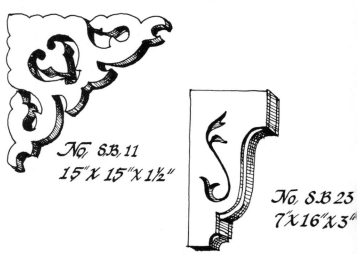

Brackets run in price from $13 to $16; corbels are from $3 to $35.

Catalogue available, 50¢.

Hallelujah Redwood Products
39500 Comptche Road
Mendocino, Calif. 95460

Antique Brackets

Gargoyles Ltd. keeps on hand a supply of this type of woodwork, mainly of English origin. These are of Victorian design.

Catalogue available, $4.

Gargoyles Ltd.
512 South Third St.
Philadelphia, Penn. 19147

Centers and Rosettes

Ceiling ornaments are frequently found in Victorian interiors; these most often take the form of center-pieces or rosettes. While they can be made of wood, they are usually of plaster or sheet metal composition. The ceiling centerpiece serves as a convenient focus for a hanging lamp or chandelier.

Plaster Centers

Felber Studios illustrate forty designs in their catalogue. Many are of deeply-etched flower or acanthus leaf patterns; others are simple sunbursts. There are a few oval and square shapes. Prices range from $40 to $690. Felber also has a fine custom work department that can execute almost any design wanted.

Catalogue available.

Felber Studios
110 Ardmore Ave.
P.O. Box 551
Ardmore, Penn. 19003

Sheet Metal Rosettes

Lynch's rosettes are simpler than those produced in plaster by Felber. A larger selection of square and oval forms is available. These range in size from as small as 2″ square to 15″ square.

Catalogue and price list available, $2.50.

Kenneth Lynch & Sons
Wilton, Conn. 06897

Chair Rails

Rails running along a wall serve to protect the surface from wear and tear. Chairs are usually pushed against the wall, in past or present practice, and mouldings of this sort can provide a useful function. They also serve to ornament the wall in an attractive fashion. Simple houses without elaborate woodwork were often so fitted. A cursory examination of the plastered surfaces will quickly establish whether this was the case.

Both KB Mouldings and the Driwood Moulding Co. offer a number of chair rail designs in ready-assembled form. Some are of one piece; others make use of two mouldings fitted together. A pattern that will match or complement the woodwork of almost any old house is not difficult to find in these offerings.

KB supplies a brochure and price list; Driwood offers a catalogue and price list, $1.

KB Moulding, Inc.
508 A Larkfield Road
East Northport, N.Y. 11731

Driwood Moulding Co.
P.O. Box 1369
Florence, S.C. 29501

Cornices, Crown Mouldings

A cornice may be used on the exterior or interior of a building as the finishing decorative touch. Nothing projects further than this element, whether used above a doorway, as a ceiling ornament, or to ornament and finish off the eaves. It is one of the primary classical devices found in Colonial architecture. Used on the exterior, it may also serve to throw off rain from the wall face.

Cornices are produced in wood, plaster, sheet metal, and in urethane. If they combine three or four different mouldings, they will be an expensive addition. In some old houses cornices have been merely covered over and can be reconstituted. If the cornice work has been destroyed, weigh the advantages of several different types of material.

Urethane Cornices

Focal Point produces cornice mouldings of urethane. In order to reproduce the same design in wood, four different mouldings would have to be used. The highly traditional dentil pattern is reproduced in one piece.

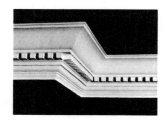

According to the manufacturer, "the material is approximately the density of white pine and can be worked with ordinary tools found on the job site." It is not necessary to add blocking or furring (wood strip lining) to the sections. The synthetic mouldings are produced from molds of original wood or plaster articles. Focal Point provides a mastic or adhesive for affixing the pieces.

Literature and samples of individual patterns available.

Focal Point, Inc.
3760 Lower Roswell Road
Mariette, Ga. 30060

Plaster Cornices

These are also made of one piece, but the cost will be much greater. For those wanting truly authentic mouldings, get into contact with Felber. It is possible that they will be able to supply you with custom- or ready-made cornices which will last for generations. If it is only a section that needs replacing, Felber can do the job. There are over 46 standard designs to choose from. The Old English cornice mouldings are especially recommended for Tudor-style homes.

Catalogue available.

Felber Studios
110 Ardmore Ave.
Ardmore, Penn. 19003

Metal Ceiling Cornices

AA Abbingdon offers molded sheet steel cornices which are used with steel or tin ceilings. Some of the designs are appropriate for Victorian interiors; a few are just right for today's popular Art Deco look.

Literature available.

AA Abbingdon Ceiling Co., Inc.
2149 Utica Ave.
Brooklyn, N.Y. 11234

Wood Cornices

Whether termed ceiling cornices or crown mouldings, these *are* impressive results of the woodworker's skills. Many of the assembled units are comprised of four or five different mouldings. In installation, furring or lining must be added to block out the forms. Illustrated are two of the forty-one ceiling cornice designs offered by Driwood.

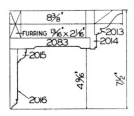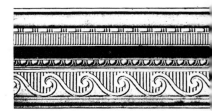

Price list and catalogue available, $1.

Driwood Moulding Co.
P.O. Box 1369
Florence, S.C. 29501

Ornaments

Miscellaneous ornaments—crestings, finials, scrolls, wreaths, appliqué—are frequently encountered in high-style Colonial and Victorian buildings. The exact replacement of such an ornament is likely to involve expensive custom work. Fortunately there are stock ornaments available which may serve the purpose just as well.

Repeating Ornaments, Incised Panels, Appliqué

Hallelujah Redwood Products can supply some highly decorative pieces for gingerbread houses. The incised panels are very handsome squares containing various natural forms such as a tulip and four-pointed star.

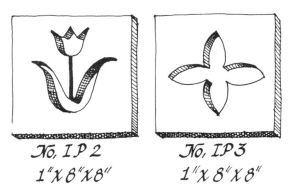

No. IP 2
1"X 8"X 8"

No. IP 3
1"X 8"X 8"

The ornaments range in price from $1.50 to $12.

Catalogue available, 50¢.

Hallelujah Redwood Products
39500 Comptche Road
Mendocino, Calif. 95460

Niche Cap and Casing

As the illustration indicates, the shell form can make a handsome doorway niche decoration. It is formed of urethane, and is approximately 16" deep. The opening width is from 41-42"; the height from 22½-23".

Brochure available.

Focal Point, Inc.
3760 Lower Roswell Road
Marietta, Ga. 30060

Niches and Shells, Cartouches

The experienced plasterer familiar with antique decoration is ideally best equipped to meet your needs— but few can afford him. Felber Studios, consequently, has a number of stock designs in plaster to choose from, and these are reasonably priced.

Literature available.

Felber Studios
110 Ardmore Avenue
Ardmore, Penn. 19003

Leaves, Scrolls, Shields, Wreaths, Crestings, Mitres, Garlands, Festoons, Ribbons, Bows, Capitals, Lion Heads, Gargoyles and Caryatids, Drops and Pinnacles, Crockets, Finials, Eagles, Urns and Balusters

Kenneth Lynch has everyone beat. No one can begin to match his expertise in the area of stamped metal ornamentation. Let us hope that the firm prospers for years to come.

The catalogue is a delight to look through and is available for $2.50.

Kenneth Lynch & Sons, Inc.
Wilton, Conn. 06897

Plate Rails

These are mouldings affixed to the wall for the purpose of holding and displaying china and silver plate. A projection of the top edge of the rail prevents objects from sliding off. This form of decorative, open shelving was used throughout the Colonial and Victorian periods. It seems a somewhat fussy practice, but it might have practical use in the kitchen and dining room.

Both KB Moulding and Driwood Moulding offer the same four plate rail designs. Each are assembled of at least three mouldings. The height is from 2 5/16" to 5 5/8". The rails project from 3 3/8" to 4" from the wall.

Both companies illustrate the rails in their catalogues; Driwood's is available for $1.

KB Moulding, Inc.
508 A Larkfield Road
East Northport, N.Y. 11731

Driwood Moulding Co.
P.O. Box 1369
Florence, S.C. 29501

Railings, Balusters, Spindles, Turnings, Newells

Gargoyles Ltd. has a good supply of Victorian gingerbread—balusters and handrails to match. Turnings and newell posts are also available. These decorative accents, all true antiques, are available in pine, oak, walnut, and cast iron.

Catalogue available, $4.

Gargoyles Ltd.
512 South 3rd St.
Philadelphia, Penn. 19147

Small basic-shaped maple spindles for use on furniture and plate rails, and full-sized hemlock spindles that can be employed for stairways are offered by the Minnesota Woodworkers Supply Co. Six basic designs

—all Colonial in inspiration—are sanded and ready for finishing or painting.

Catalogue available.

Minnesota Woodworkers Supply Co.
Industrial Blvd.
Rogers, Minn. 55374

Carpenter's Gothic porch railings are produced by Hallelujah Redwood Products. A handrail which will fit any one of three designs is also offered. These are whimsical accents. They are priced from $4 to $5.50; the top handrail is $1 per foot. A bottom piece of horizontal railing is 80¢ per foot.

Priced catalogue available.

Hallelujah Redwood Products
39500 Comptche Road
Mendocino, Calif. 95460

Veneers and Inlays

These are minor details which can assume great importance—especially if they are missing. They are most often used in furniture and flooring, but the old house owner may find that they are also necessary for woodwork. The demand for such decorative pieces of wood is great enough to assure an almost constant supply.

Constantine offers a good array of veneers for use in wall panels and doors. Among the woods available are American walnut, English oak, Brazilian rosewood, Indian teak, California redwood, American burl, and African mahogany. For paneling, wood inlay borders are also important. Of the latter, there are eighty-two designs to choose from.

Catalogue available.

Albert Constantine & Son, Inc.
2050 Eastchester Road
Bronx, N.Y. 10461

Minnesota Woodworkers offers fewer inlay designs, but a greater variety of veneers. Birch, cherry, red gum, butternut, curly maple, sycamore, bird's-eye maple, pecan, and ash are some of the woods.

Catalogue available.

Minnesota Woodworkers Supply Co.
Industrial Blvd.
Rogers, Minn. 55374

Wainscoting

Wood paneling applied to the lower area of walls is a stylish feature of fine Colonial homes of English and Continental design derivation. It is often found in lavish Louis XVI interiors as well as in Georgian settings. The tradition of ornately decorating lower walls continued into the Victorian period. Wainscoting, anywhere from 2½' to 3' in height, may unite the mouldings of baseboard, dado, and chair rail. It often includes —in the center dado section—panels formed by pieces of moulding.

Old World Moulding & Finishing has designed the wainscoting for elegant apartments and homes. The trim matches that of doors and cornices. Wainscoting can be used most effectively on stairways to provide esthetic balance for handrail and railings.

Literature available.

Old World Moulding & Finishing, Inc.
115 Allen Blvd.
Farmingdale, N.Y. 11735

Wainscoting is also found on the walls of more modest dwellings. Barn siding may be a suitable choice for a country home interior. Guyon supplies Pennsylvania barn siding cut for this purpose. The boards come in several widths and are without any kind of beading or other moulding.

Brochure available.

Guyon Inc.
65 Oak Street
Lititz, Penn. 17543

Other Sources of Supplies

Consult the List of Suppliers for addresses.

Casings

Focal Point, Inc.
Fypon, Inc.

Brackets & Corbels

Ball & Ball
Decorators Supply Corp.
Focal Point, Inc.
Guyon, Inc.
C. E. Morgan Building Products
Vermont Marble Co.

Centers and Rosettes

Focal Point
Minnesota Woodworkers Supply Corp.

Chair Rails

French and Ball
Hallelujah Redwood Products
Old World Moulding & Finishing, Inc.

Cornices

Architectural Paneling, Inc.
Bendix Mouldings
Decorators Supply Corp.
P. E. Guerin, Inc.
Hellelujah Redwood Products
KB Moulding, Inc.
Jerry Martin Designs, Inc.

Mouldings for Multiple Uses

Architectural Paneling, Inc.
Bendix Mouldings, Inc.
Albert Constantine and Son, Inc.
Decorators Supply Corp.
Driwood Moulding Co.
Elegant Entries
Focal Point
French and Ball
International Wood Products
Old World Moulding & Finishing, Inc.
Orlandini Studios
Preservation Resource Center

Ornaments

Bendix Mouldings, Inc.
Albert Constantine and Son, Inc.
Fypon, Inc.
Gargoyles Ltd.

Railings, Balusters, Turnings, Newells

E. A. Nord Co., Inc.
Preservation Technology Group

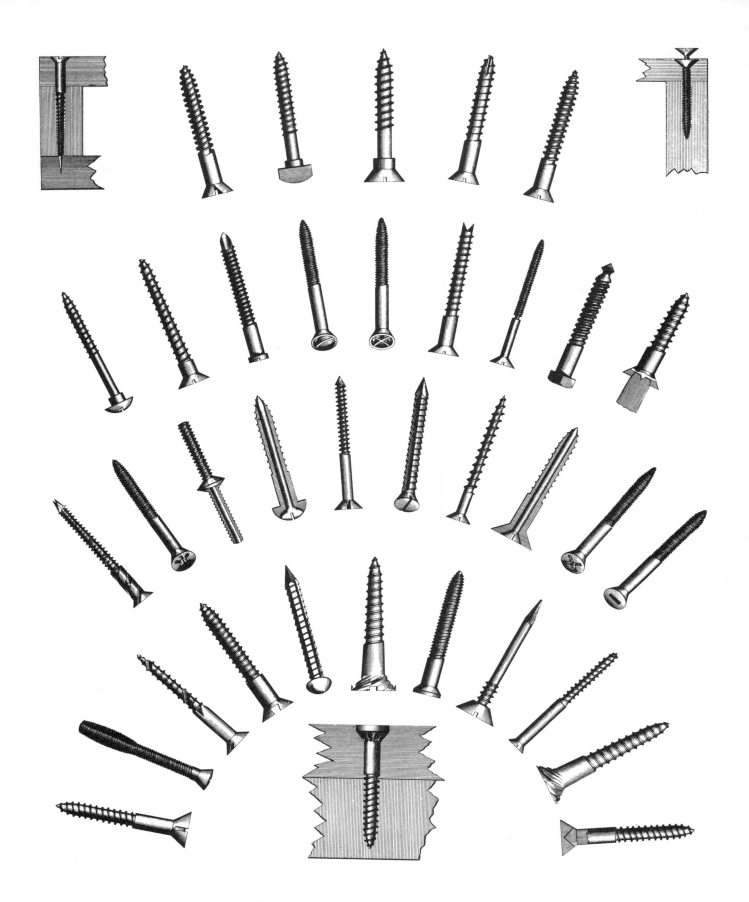

TYPES OF SCREWS.

From *The Growth of Industrial Art*, 1892.

III Hardware

Hardware may be merely decorative accents used on furniture or the most functional of objects found in the home. Used properly, such fittings can greatly enhance the appearance and utility of the old house and its furnishings. Hinges, locks, bolts, brasses, hooks, knobs, pulls—these and sundry other appointments should be chosen with as much care as the selection of upholstery fabrics or floor coverings. Even mass-produced period hardware is expensive these days. And once such fittings are applied, there is little likelihood that they will be changed without considerable additional cost and labor.

Hardware manufacturers have demonstrated considerable ingenuity in appealing to a wide variety of personal taste. There are those reproduction companies such as Ball and Ball and Period Hardware which have conscientiously and profitably offered a fine quality line of traditional styles over the years. If there is any fault to be found in such wares, it is a tendency to overemphasize weight and scale. Hardware need not be massive, clunky, lacking in subtlety. Since castles and chateaux are few and far between in North America, there is little need to emulate the lord of the manor. The "monumental look" in iron and brass, however, still afflicts both supplier and customer.

The use to which hardware is put will determine how faithful a reproduction is necessary. Hand-forged wrought-iron latches and hinges in a 1920s colonial house is as patently absurd as stamped-out hardware used in an eighteenth-century blacksmith shop-cum-home. In the latter case even a reproduction may not be desirable. There are a few firms that handle antique hardware for the purists—or for those who need to be more precise in the use of such fittings. Salvage depots or junk shops can be another source for authentic hardware, especially that of the Victorian and Art Deco periods. Only a few of the larger supply houses are stamping out such later pieces.

Hardware on antique furniture is a special area of interest, and is treated separately in the pages that follow. Chests, tables, high- and lowboys, and other handcrafted treasures from the past are rarely found with their "original" brasses. Beware the salesman who is not prepared to document his claim of authenticity with hard evidence. A simple inspection of the piece itself, including the way in which the fitting has been mounted, will often disclose the truthfulness of the claim. On the other hand, do not regard the absence of such originality as an irredeemable fault. Even some of the greatest museum pieces have been supplied with reproduction escutcheons, pulls, hinges, knobs, etc.

Museum curators have been able to turn to a growing group of custom hardware makers, blacksmiths who have kept the art of forging wrought iron alive in the twentieth century. And you can find several such craftsmen in these pages. Such hand-worked iron is valued for its natural variations and is ideally suited to the old house where the dimensions of handmade doors, windows, and furniture vary. The price is high for such custom work, and the time taken to fabricate these pieces can run into many months. It is an area worth exploring by any serious home restorer.

Aficionados of the "colonial" may be surprised to find glass, wood, and porcelain objects in a "hardware" section. But these, along with bronze, tin, cast iron, and copper, are a proper subject for discussion. In dealing with late Victorian interiors and their furnishings, such non-"hard" materials may be of great importance.

The use of hardware in modern kitchens and bathrooms is a subject fraught with peril. Just plain common sense is called for in the choice of these most functional appointments. The old, comfortable four-legged tub may have a new use; porcelain wash basins with simple designs may be accommodated in modern structures. Beware, however, the "kitsch" market in luxury fittings. A small fortune can be thrown away on French Provincial faucets. It is unlikely that the Gallic peasant or even his seigneur would know what to do with them. Thrones of wicker are fashioned today to obscure that most blessed of modern indoor fixtures, the flush toilet. Blenders and toasters may be hidden behind an elaborate "colonial" facade of veneer and strap hinges. Tart up the john and lazy-susan the kitchen if you wish, but don't look to history for guidance. Time marches on, thank heaven, casting the plumbing, the monstrous fixtures of the pre-electric age into oblivion.

Antique Hardware

The number of firms specializing in this field is slowly growing each year. The supply is regularly replenished thanks to urban renewal and other such destructive pastimes. Iron Horse Antiques, Inc., is one such company offering antique hardware for doors, shutters, etc. In addition, Iron Horse carries one of the most extensive collections of antique tools and books on various crafts fields. Such sidelines as early kitchen implements are also available from the firm.

Literature available.

Iron Horse Antiques, Inc.
R.D. #2
Poultney, Vt. 05764

Awning Hardware

Prior to World War II, awnings of canvas graced the facades of many apartment houses and private homes. Removed in some cities because of their flammability under "enemy" fire, they have never regained the status they enjoyed beginning in the late nineteenth-century. Air pollution has further eroded their use. But what is a 1920s English Tudor house without such softening shades? Or an Eastlake-style villa without the addition of a colorful canopy? Suppliers of such awning material are given in Part X (Accessories); the

hardware needed may be secured below. As an effective way to "air condition" a room in summer, properly installed awnings are almost without rival.

Specialists in window hardware, the Blaine company offers standard wood-awning operators, awning operators, and jalousie operators. Their machine shop and foundry facility will duplicate any obsolete part that is needed. "*Any* part for *any* window" is their motto.

Brochures available.

Blaine Window Hardware, Inc.
1919 Blaine Drive
R.D. #4
Hagertown, Md. 21740

The Blacksmith

Many of today's blacksmiths are young men who take great pride in their honest, hand-forged products. To learn a craft in the second half of the twentieth century is to pursue a most difficult goal, and the new village smithy commands our respect and loyalty.

A note from one blacksmith:

At one time I put out a catalog. However, it put me in the "Ye Olde Hand Crafts" type of atmosphere, and this is what I am not.

What I do is blacksmithing and I forge museum quality reproductions of most anything that can be done by hand. This of course means all kinds of hardware plus difficult "white-smith" wares including pipe tongs, etc.

So, if I may blow my own horn, I forge things of iron for those who accept only the best.

Thanks for inquiring.

Sincerely,

Robert Bourdon

P.S. It should be known that I'm usually working about 1-2 months behind receipt of order.

Robert Bourdon
Wolcott, Vt. 05680

Bolts, Door

To "throw" the bolt on the front door is one of those symbolic domestic acts indulged by the master of the house. It surely is a more satisfying proprietary ritual than putting out the garbage, cat, or the lights. Be sure that the bolt is a secure one, or at least as strong as that used to keep out intruders on the American frontier. Bolts of iron come in 1001 sizes and styles and are used on various size interior and exterior doors.

Hand-forged bolts for interior and exterior doors come in three forms, a light bolt, a heavy-duty bolt, and a fancy version of the heavy-duty bolt. Newton Millham will also reproduce any design.

Brochure and price list available.

Newton Millham, Blacksmith
Bowen's Wharf
Newport, R.I. 02840

Donald Streeter offers four versions of the spring bolt, an offset bolt that latches into a slot in the wood, a nineteenth-century barrel bolt, a nineteenth-century shutter bolt, and a seventeenth- and early eighteenth-century bolt. Floor plates can be supplied when used as foot bolts, and these plates are made in several sizes and are all hand forged. Streeter will also recreate any hardware.

Brochure and price list available.

Donald Streeter
P.O. Box 237
Franklinville, N.J. 08322

Hand-finished bolts in two sizes, 2¼″ and 4″, are offered by the Old Smithy Shop at about one-third the price of the hand-forged type.

Brochure and prices available.

Old Smithy Shop
P.O. Box 226—Powers Street
Milford, N.H. 03055

Brackets

Iron brackets can serve any number of useful purposes in the kitchen, on porches, in fact wherever there are many objects that you want to display or have easily on

hand. They vary in style from the most simple or primitive of forms to the very ornate. Convenience will determine their placement.

An abundance of various sized brackets is offered by G. W. Mount, Inc. They include shelf brackets and decorative brackets suitable for hanging plants, signs, plaques, lanterns, and pots.

Brochure available.

G. W. Mount, Inc.
576 Leyden Road
Greenfield, Massachusetts 01301

Craft House carries fixed and swivel plant holders in iron, plain brackets, scroll hangers, and dish brackets, all in assorted sizes.

Brochure and prices available.

Craft House
1542 Main Road
Tiverton, R.I. 02878

Period offers two kinds of brackets, three shelf brackets with Pennsylvania Dutch motifs and brackets made of wrought iron suitable for hanging plants and utensils.

Catalogue available, $2.00.

Period Furniture Hardware Co., Inc.
123 Charles Street
Boston, Massachusetts 02114

Door Hardware

Used in the front entryway, door hardware can stand out as a sore thumb or as a handsome, functional invitation to the guest. Brass may be appropriate for the Federal town house; iron better suits the country house. Simplicity flatters both. All elements—knobs, plates, handles, pulls, locks, knockers—must work together and belong to the same family.

Door pulls, doorknobs, and push plates in the French style are available from Period. They also carry solid cast-brass doorknobs, letter plates, brass doorbells, brass kickplates, lever door handles, porcelain and brass doorknobs, and engraved solid brass name plaques.

Catalogue available, $2.00.

Period Furniture Hardware Co., Inc.
123 Charles Street
Boston, Massachusetts 02114

Door hardware in French scroll design, English rope design, and rustic iron design is available from Bona. In those various styles are doorknobs, lever door handles, push plates, and door pulls. They also carry leaded clear crystal and brass doorknobs, porcelain and solid brass doorknobs, and plain brass kickplates.

Catalogue available, $2.00.

Bona
2227 Beechmont Avenue
Cincinnati, Ohio 45230

Solid brass-forged doorknobs, door pulls, and lever door handles are made by Baldwin. They offer eleven different styles of solid brass knob as well as a drop ring or stirrup knob. A round porcelain knob is available as well. A letterbox plate is also manufactured.

Brochures available.

Baldwin Hardware Mfg. Corp.
841 Wyomissing Blvd.
Reading, Penn. 19603

Drapery Hardware

The many styles of drapery hanging (see Part VII, Fabrics) call for a considerable variety of mechanisms. Solid brass rods and circular, screw-on holders will suffice for most windows in the house. For more formal use, tiebacks may be an appropriate addition. Heavier curtains or draperies will necessitate the use of tracks if not pulleys or other drawing devices. Certainly, ease of handling is the primary consideration of the home owner concerned with periodic cleaning.

Brass drapery tiebacks are available from Period. They will also adapt any of their knobs—brass, porcelain, and glass—for use as tiebacks.

Catalogue available, $2.00.

Period Furniture Hardware Co., Inc.
123 Charles Street
Boston, Massachusetts 02114

Blaine offers the hardware necessary for the hanging of draperies that open and close. They will also make up parts from samples.

Brochure available.

Blaine Window Hardware, Inc.
1919 Blaine Drive
R.D. #4
Hagerstown, Maryland 21740

Hinges

It is hard to imagine a more important piece of hardware. Thereupon hangs many a tale of woe: hinges that will not carry the weight entrusted to them, hinges that do not move properly without constant oiling, monstrous straps that overwhelm the doors on which they are placed. The varieties made today are almost endless; antique hinges are also widely marketed, but some of these are more properly used on the barn doors from which they were taken.

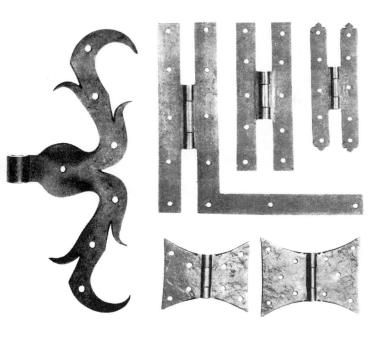

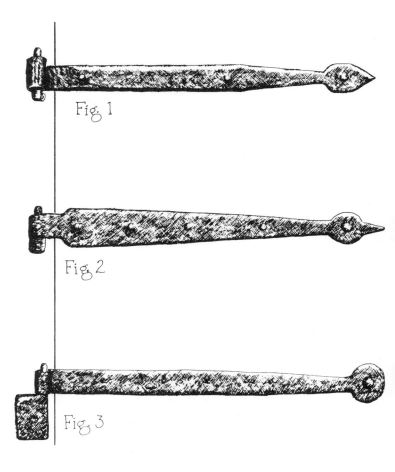

Fig. 1

Fig. 2

Fig. 3

H and HL hinges, surface strap hinges such as the T and butterfly strap hinges, Ram's horn side hinges, Moravian side hinges, Dutch hinges, rat-tail hinges and strap and side hinges in various sizes are offered by Donald Streeter. He notes that since strap and side hinges are "forged to order, length can vary two inches either way without affecting price provided width is the same. This will enable you to end hinge where it best fits." All are hand-forged wrought iron.

Brochure and prices available.

Donald Streeter
P.O. Box 237
Franklinville, N.J. 08322

Newton Millham makes light and heavy strap hinges, butterfly strap hinges, butterfly hinges, cross garnet (T) hinges, and H and HL hinges. All are hand-forged wrought iron.

Brochure and prices available.

Newton Millham
Bowen's Wharf
Newport, R.I. 02840

Strap hinges patterned after seventeenth-century New York and Massachusetts and eighteenth-century Pennsylvania examples are made by Stephen Parker. Also illustrated in his excellent little catalogue (offering historical as well as technical data) are butterfly, Moravian, and serpentine-type barn hinges.

Catalogue and prices available, $1.00.

Stephen Winslow Parker
P.O. Box 40
Craftsbury, Vermont 05826

Colonial hinges in cast bronze, hand-finished, oxidized, and lacquered flat black are sold by Steve Kayne. His catalogue lists various sizes of cabinet strap hinges, Dutch hinges, and H and HL hinges. He also offers forging to order.

Catalogue and price list available.

Steve Kayne, Blacksmith
17 Harmon Place
Smithtown, New York 11787

Ball and Ball offers, by popular demand, hinges in brass, although they warn that only the largest can be used on some light full-size doors. H and HL iron hinges are also available as well as iron "dummy" strap hinges that are for decoration only.

Catalogue and price list available, $1.00.

Ball and Ball
"Whitford"
463 West Lincoln Highway
Exton, Pennsylvania 19341

Hooks

A hook can be the handiest piece of hardware in the house—in the kitchen, an entry hall, on a bedroom wall. The flimsy variety available in many hardware stores will not support much in the way of weight and are ugly as well. Whether it be pots and pans or clothing that is to be hung, invest in well-made hooks. These will stand out as handsome, albeit minor, additions to the overall decor.

Stephen Parker's reproduction in wrought iron of a seventeenth-century Dutch crown pot rack can also be used for drying herbs. It comes in two versions—with cutouts of animals decorating the outside rim or without. The animals double the price from $30.00 to $60.00. Parker also makes single and double hooks for the closet.

Catalogue and price list, $1.

Stephen W. Parker
Box 40
Craftsbury, Vt. 05826

A variety of heavy-duty hooks in various shapes and sizes is offered by G. W. Mount. Herb hooks are available singly or mounted on an iron backing in combinations of two, three, and four. Beam hooks are also available in the same combinations.

Brochure available.

G. W. Mount, Inc.
576 Leyden Road
Greenfield, Mass. 01301

Single and double black iron hatrack hooks in the Victorian style are available from Horton Brasses.

Catalogue available, $1.25.

Horton Brasses
P.O. Box 95
Nooks Hill Road
Cromwell, Conn. 06416

Coat and hat hooks of solid brass and wrought iron are offered by Bona. They range from the simple to the elaborate.

Catalogue available, $2.

Bona
2227 Beechmont Avenue
Cincinnati, Ohio 45230

Knockers

This is the first piece of hardware which is likely to greet the guest. It need not bowl him over or break his arm. A knocker is meant to let you know that someone's at the door, not to impress. While you will want to have a fitting and graceful centerpiece of this sort, it need not be larger than life. Iron knockers are suitable for many simple country houses; brass and bronze are most often used for the main entryway of high style dwellings whether in the city or country. The style of the piece should match that of the other door hardware.

Knockers, of course, were devised ages ago when electric buzzers and electronic chimes were unknown. If possible, it is best to do without the addition of such modern devices.

Brass door knockers from Baldwin's Georgetown line range in style from the Ranch Door Knocker to the Royal Door Knocker. In between are English, Colonial, Dutch, French, Victorian, Anchor, Georgian, Imperial, Penthouse, and four kinds of eagle door knockers. An "S" door knocker is included in the James River line.

Brochure and price list available.

Ball and Ball
"Whitford"
463 West Lincoln Highway
Exton, Penn. 19341

Solid brass and rustic iron knockers are obtainable from Bona. The catalogue illustrates a typical Georgian brass knocker and notes that more designs are in stock. Iron ring knockers of a medieval type are particularly suitable for heavy wooden gates or doors.

Catalogue available, $2.

Bona
2227 Beechmont Avenue
Cincinnati, Ohio 45230

Stephen Parker specializes in Dutch knockers made from hand-forged wrought iron, his brochure illustrating four different styles. He also makes a Dutch knocker latch reproduced from the latch from Washington's headquarters in Newburgh, New York, dated about 1696.

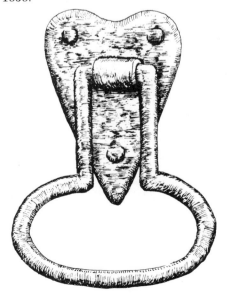

Baldwin Hardware
841 Wyomissing Boulevard
Reading, Penn. 19603

Old Smithy Shop crafts iron door knockers to match all their exterior handles. In addition they stock an iron knocker with a fleur-de-lys backplate. All are finished dead black with hand-hammered beveled edges.

Brochure and price list available, 25¢.

Old Smithy Shop
P.O. Box 226—Powers Street
Milford, N.H. 03055

Horton stocks four black painted iron door knockers that match standard latch designs.

Catalogue and price list available, $1.25.

Horton Brasses
P.O. Box 95
Nooks Hill Road
Cromwell, Conn. 06416

A fine variety of traditional designs as well as some more personally expressive brass door knockers are listed by Ball and Ball. Not lacquered, these knockers will tarnish and attain an "antique finish" naturally. Lacquering is available at $12.00 additional. The average price is $40.00.

Catalogue and price list available, $1.

Catalogue and prices available, $1.

Stephen W. Parker
P.O. Box 40
Craftsbury, Vt. 05826

Bronze knockers are featured by Steve Kayne. Some are also available in brass. Mr. Kayne also does custom forging, using the "ancient" methods.

Catalogue available.

Steve Kayne
17 Harmon Place
Smithtown, N.Y. 11787

Period's catalogue illustrates more than two dozen solid brass knockers of various styles. They range from the classic to representations of fox heads, eagles, and anchors. Some examples come in three sizes.

Catalogue and prices available, $2.

Period Furniture Hardware Co., Inc.
123 Charles Street
Boston, Mass. 02114

Door Latches

Old house devotees are forever inspecting latches for evidence of antiquity. These are important pieces of hardware, but they needn't be old to serve a useful and aesthetic purpose. The number of first-class reproductions increases each year. They vary from early hand-forged wrought-iron latches to those cast in brass for later homes.

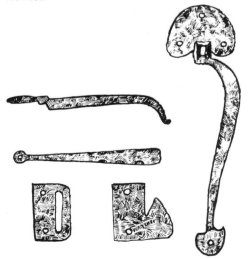

Steve Kayne casts a bronze replica of an early New England "lima bean" thumb latch. A period latch was used as a pattern, and the original hammer marks show. Interior latch sets are manufactured in bronze and brass, and a cast bronze quadrant latch for a Dutch door is also available.

Catalogue and prices available.

Steve Kayne
17 Harmon Place
Smithtown, N.Y. 11787

Stephen Parker hand forges an iron "bean family" latch copied from the one that graces the door of the old Quaker Meetinghouse at Merion, Pennsylvania, dating from 1683. From Washington's headquarters in Newburgh, New York, comes the 1696 prototype of the combination Dutch knocker latch that Parker custom forges.

Catalogue and prices available, $1.

Stephen W. Parker
Box 40
Craftsbury, Vt. 05826

Donald Streeter offers a selection of Norfolk latches historically correct for use in restoration of early nineteenth-century American buildings. Besides the Norfolk latches, he hand forges thumb latches for exterior and interior doors, using for patterns examples from the Hudson Valley, New England, and Pennsylvania.

Streeter also makes exact copies of spring latches of both the eighteenth and nineteenth centuries. For complete information on spring latches see Streeter's article in the August, 1954, issue of *The Magazine* ANTIQUES.

Catalogue and price list available.

Donald Streeter
P.O. Box 237
Franklinville, N.J. 08322

Newton Millham offers four standard Colonial thumb latches with variations in the design of the different elements available at an additional charge. All are hand-forged wrought iron.

Brochure and prices available.

Newton Millham, Blacksmith
Bowen's Wharf
Newport, R.I. 02840

Old Smithy Shop stocks numerous examples of iron exterior and interior Colonial latches. They are hand finished. Old Smithy also hand forges a limited line to order.

Brochure and price list available, 25¢.

Old Smithy Shop
P.O. Box 226—Powers Street
Milford, N.H. 03055

Baldwin makes three latches: keyhole door latches in brass and iron, thumb latches in iron, and square plate latches made of a combination of iron and brass. All are copies of eighteenth-century designs.

Brochures available.

Baldwin
841 Wyomissing Boulevard
Reading, Penn. 19603

Ball and Ball are aware that nothing but iron should be used for Dutch door fittings, but have bowed to popular demand and also make brass quadrants, and strap hinges to match brass locks. Thumb latches are made in traditional iron only.

Brochure and price list available, $1.

Ball and Ball
"Whitford"
463 West Lincoln Highway
Exton, Penn. 19341

Door Locks

Antique or reproduction locks can be extremely good devices to keep out unwanted visitors. Most manufacturers of new locks have combined recent safety features with the old. Although not as complicated or multifaceted as some "anti-theft" mechanisms marketed today, they will provide a reasonable degree of security if properly mounted and maintained. Well-built old houses need not be any easier to enter than today's flimsily constructed split-level.

Baldwin offers heavy colonial rim locks in four basic sizes to fit varying door rail dimensions and lock functions. A beveled edge rim lock is also available. Dutch elbow rim locks and sectional handle lock sets have cases made of wrought iron and of brass with colonial exterior trim in several functions from a basic latch operation to a cylinder key lock for entrance doors.

Brochures available.

Baldwin
841 Wyomissing Boulevard
Reading, Penn. 19603

Period carries two brass rim locks which are sand cast and then hand polished. Large polished reproduction keys are available also.

Catalogue and prices available, $2.

Period Furniture Hardware Co., Inc.
123 Charles Street
Boston, Mass. 02114

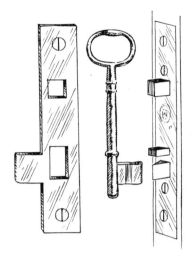

Ball and Ball sells a mortised lock similar to those used in some eighteenth-century houses. It has a key bolt, a turn bolt, and a latch bolt. It and the rim locks in various sizes, also sold by Ball and Ball, are made of solid brass. The firm also makes iron locks with various key mechanisms.

Catalogue and price list available, $1.

Ball and Ball
"Whitford"
463 West Lincoln Highway
Exton, Pennsylvania 19341

Nails

Various forms of head cut nails are attractive solutions to very practical needs. Whether used in the floor, in woodwork, or for hanging pictures and other objects, nails made in old patterns will enhance any surface. Rose and oval-bung head nails are often found in homes built during the eighteenth and early nineteenth centuries. The use of such handmade nails continued in more remote parts of North America for an even longer time. Today they are the specialty of a number of hardware manufacturers. These are machine-made but most acceptable reproductions. Nails made by
machine were common from the early Victorian period on, and some are collector's items.

"For want of a nail" goes the saying. The Tremont company can make sure that nothing is lost. They have been making nails since 1848 in the present factory. Available are decorative wrought head cut nails, masonry nails, common nails, foundry nails, sheathing nails, etc.

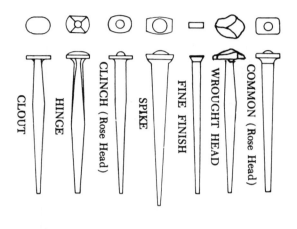

Brochures available.

Tremont Nail Company
P.O. Box 111 21 E1
21 Elm Street
Wareham, Mass. 02571

Donald Streeter sells cut clinch nails with hand-forged rose heads in lengths ranging from 1″ to 4″. Hand-forged points are no longer available but these nails are soft and will easily clinch.

Brochure available.

Donald Streeter
P.O. Box 237
Franklinville, N.J. 08322

Machine-made nails made to look like handmade originals are sold by Horton Brasses. They range in size from ⅞″ to 3½″.

Catalogue and price list available, $1.25.

Horton Brasses
P.O. Box 95
Nooks Hill Road
Cromwell, Conn. 06416

Scrapers

Foot or "boot" scrapers can be usefully employed around any old house whether it be in the city, suburbia, or the country. The simple iron, flared "H" type is the most commonly found in the past. More elegant contraptions of heavy cast iron became popular in the high Victorian period. It doesn't really matter; just so they work effectively and are put outside an entryway in a place where they will not be tripped over. Some old models have iron bases; others are merely sunk into the ground or masonry.

Stephen Parker illustrates two boot scrapers in his catalogue. One is a late eighteenth-century scraper, the original of which is at James Fenimore Cooper's birthplace in Burlington, New Jersey. The other is an early nineteenth-century Yankee scraper from Sharon, Connecticut. All of Parker's products are hand-forged wrought iron.

Brochure and prices available, $1.

Stephen W. Parker
P.O. Box 40
Craftsbury, Vermont 05826

Shutter Hardware

Since the windows of most old houses are now fitted with storm windows and wire-mesh screens, the hanging of shutters is not as easy a matter as it once was. Shutters, of course, served a useful purpose in the Colonial and Victorian periods—they were intended to protect the house from both cold and heat. Today they perform largely a decorative function.

Both screens and storm windows can be altered so that the shutters may be properly hung by hinges. Whether you will be able to close the shutters is another matter altogether. If storms and screens are deep set, then there may be no problem. On many old house facades, however, the shutters are left open, firmly held back by "holdbacks" or shutter dogs. The latter are most often sunk into the wall on each side; holdbacks attach to the sill. In either case, you will want them. The sound of shutters flapping on a winter night becomes only tiresome.

Old Smithy Shop offers sand-cast aluminum shutter dogs finished dead black and a hand-finished steel shutter dog also finished dead black.

Brochure and prices available, 25¢.

Old Smithy Shop
P.O. Box 226—Powers Street
Milford, N.H. 03055

Strap hinges for shutters are available from Ball and Ball. Iron hinges are stocked in 12″ and 18″ lengths. Hand-forged hinges are also available. Strap hinges can be made to the customer's order and will be furnished by quotation only. Ball and Ball carries originals for sale as well as German types made in the last twenty-five years by other makers. Besides hinges, they carry cast-iron holdbacks in different patterns, slide bolts, and shutter rings.

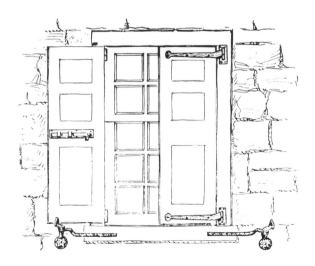

Catalogue and prices available, $1.

Ball and Ball
"Whitford"
463 West Lincoln Highway
Exton, Penn. 19341

Donald Streeter produces handsome forge-welded ring pulls for shutters, typical eighteenth-century shutter bar locks, nineteenth-century shutter bolts, and four different shutter dog designs. Copies can be made of wrought-iron dogs.

Brochure and prices available.

Donald Streeter
P.O. Box 237
Franklinville, N.J. 08322

Stephen Parker notes that shutter dogs or latches have lesser claims to antiquity than other examples of early American wrought iron, yet he produces such later hardware. Five graceful examples of his work in this category are illustrated in a brochure.

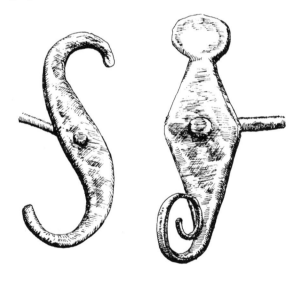

Brochure and price available, $1.

Stephen W. Parker
P.O. Box 40
Craftsbury, Vt. 05826

Special Hardware Castings

If you need exact replacements for small metal hardware items, you may find it worthwhile dropping a letter to the Preservation Resource Center asking them for information. They will provide a detailed explanation of the procedure they follow to make a reproduction.

Send a self-addressed stamped envelope to:

Preservation Resource Center
Lake Shore Road
Essex, New York 12936

Bathroom Fixtures

Owners of late Victorian and early twentieth-century homes may be concerned with appropriate bathroom appointments. Their interest is a legitimate one as indoor plumbing was coming into its own at least in the city. Period fixtures may still be found in junkyards or at flea markets. They are increasingly catching the attention of antique building suppliers.

Gillett Restorations offers this fine set of Victorian fixtures. The solid brass has been coated with chrome, but this can be stripped away.

Lists of supplies.

Gillett Restorations
c/o Suite 420
3550 N. Central Avenue
Phoenix, Ariz. 85012

Furniture Hardware

The search for fine original and reproduction furniture hardware is one of the common pursuits of antiques collectors and dealers. "Are the brasses original?" is one of the most persistently asked questions wherever period furniture is sold. Usually the answer is a polite "no." But as we have stated before, that does not have to be the end of the line for buyer or seller.

Almost all furniture hardware, including such "soft" pieces as those made of wood, are produced by machine. The products which follow are those that have been made with care. Patterns are well etched, materials are solid, and designs are appropriately chosen.

Bed Hardware

Antique beds and those made in imitation of them usually require hardware fittings. In fact, so important are most of the pieces that the bed won't hold up without them. A few pieces such as bolt covers are merely decorative appointments, but they add something to the overall handsome effect.

Horton Brasses can provide cast or stamped bed bolt covers, bed bolts, bed rail clamps, bed irons, and a cast bronze bed wrench that fits three sizes.

Catalogue and prices available, $1.25

Horton Brasses
P.O. Box 95
Nooks Hill Road
Cromwell, Conn. 06416

Ball and Ball offers both plain and fancy brass bed bolt covers. They also carry bed bolts and wrenches.

Catalogue and prices available, $1.

Ball and Ball
"Whitford"
463 West Lincoln Highway
Exton, Penn. 19341

Period carries a whole line of bed hardware, brass bed bolt covers, bed fasteners, bed bolts, wrought angle irons, and a three-way wrench.

Catalogue and prices available, $2.

Period Furniture Hardware Co., Inc.
123 Charles Street
Boston, Mass. 02114

Casters

Casters are rather ugly affairs, but important ones for many pieces of nineteenth-century furniture. It has been fashionable to remove them in recent years, but think it over first. Casters were originally used by furniture makers to make their objects more portable, and even if you are not a purist, it is nice to know that you can roll a piece of furniture away rather easily. There is a demand for reproduction casters, and it is growing with the appreciation of Federal, Empire, and Victorian furniture.

Ball and Ball makes a Duncan Phyfe caster as well as a variety of other styles and sizes.

Catalogue and prices available $1.

Ball and Ball
"Whitford"
463 West Lincoln Highway
Exton, Pennsylvania 19341

Horton Brasses carries a line of brass casters, leg caps, steel furniture glides, and brass ball feet.

Catalogue and prices available, $1.25.

Horton Brasses
P.O. Box 95
Nooks Hill Road
Cromwell, Conn. 06416

Furniture Trim

Trim is sometimes missing from antique furniture, especially that of the ornate Empire period. To supply the need for replacements, hardware manufacturers produce a limited number of designs. Cabinetmakers and refinishers turn to these sources, but they are also available to the home craftsman.

Stamped and cast brass furniture trim suitable for Empire and Federal chairs, tables, mirrors, etc. is carried by Horton Brasses. They also sell a variety of decorative bright brass tacks.

Catalogue and prices available, $1.25.

Horton Brasses
P.O. Box 95
Nooks Hill Road
Cromwell, Conn. 06416

Period notes that they illustrate in their catalogue only a few of the French-style ornaments that are available at the shop for special orders. Those not pictured require at least four weeks for delivery. The ornaments range from top ornaments to sabots. Ornamental tacks are also available.

Catalogue and prices available, $2.

Period Furniture Hardware Co., Inc.
123 Charles Street
Boston, Mass. 02114

Bona offers both wooden and brass ornament, the former suitable for nineteenth-century furniture and the latter in the French style.

Catalogue and prices available, $2.

Bona
2227 Beechmont Avenue
Cincinnati, Ohio 45230

Hinges, Catches, and Turns

These are the most essential fittings to be found on period furniture of all sorts. They are also used on more modern pieces such as kitchen and bathroom cupboards and cabinets. Cheap looking cabinet hardware of the "rustic" sort can ruin the look of a country-style kitchen. Particularly gruesome are the mottled iron hinges and pulls which look as if they have been hammered by a demented ironmonger. Simple wooden or brass turns and steel or brass hinges of the sort offered herewith will be much more attractive and durable.

Brass cupboard turns, brass hinges and latches for doors, screen hinges, dining table catches, card table hinges, tip table catches, butler's tray hinges, desk hinges, and desk locks are a sampling of Period's offering in this category.

Catalogue and prices available, $2.

Period Furniture Hardware Co., Inc.
123 Charles Street
Boston, Mass. 02114

Ball and Ball carries harpsichord hinges, hinges for grandfather clocks, hinges for Terry-style clocks, and knife box hinges, along with the more common varieties. Iron and brass latches are available in several different styles and sizes.

Catalogue and prices available, $1.

Ball and Ball
"Whitford"
463 West Lincoln Highway
Exton, Penn. 19341

Horton Brasses offers cupboard turns in brass and wood, steel and brass hinges and latches, and brass hooks with round head screws. One of their cupboard turns is wooden Victorian, painted black with a brass face.

Catalogue and prices available $1.25

Horton Brasses
P.O. Box 95
Nooks Hill Road
Cromwell, Conn. 06416

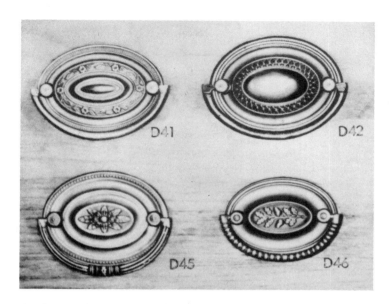

duplicate the originals down to the sand pit marks. Most Ball and Ball brass comes in two finishes, antique and golden-glow. The firm also carries a small line of miniature brasses.

Catalogue and prices available, $1.

Ball and Ball
"Whitford"
463 West Lincoln Highway
Exton, Penn. 19341

Brasses for almost every period and style are carried by Period. They range from the standard Chippendale brasses to esoteric Chinese fittings. Brasses suitable for French-type furniture are also available. Mer-

Pulls, Drops, Knobs, and Escutcheons

These are the finishing touches given to any fine piece of furniture. The supply of period brasses forms the basis for a vigorous reproduction industry. Nearly every style is available from seventeenth-century William and Mary to nineteenth-century early Victorian. In recent years these same suppliers have been meeting the growing need for later Victorian appointments such as porcelain knobs and walnut fruit pulls.

William and Mary, Queen Anne, Chippendale, Hepplewhite, Sheraton, early Victorian, and French-type brasses for furniture drawers and doors are available from Ball and Ball. A great variety is offered in each category. Many items offered are "thincast." These

chandise comes in an antique finish. There is an additional 15% charge for a golden-glow finish. Old style bolt and nut fittings are also furnished for an additional small charge. They also carry a variety of plain and decorated porcelain knobs and campaign chest hardware.

Catalogue and prices available, $2.

Period Furniture Hardware Co., Inc.
123 Charles Street
Boston, Mass. 02114

Horton Brasses lists an extensive line of Victorian pulls, drops, knobs, and escutcheons. They also make chest lifts that match their Chippendale pulls and escutcheons. Hepplewhite embossed oval pulls are authentic copies of old brasses, made in the same manner. Wooden and porcelain knobs come in a variety of shapes and sizes, plain and decorated.

Catalogue and prices available, $1.25.

Horton Brasses
P.O. Box 95
Nooks Hill Road
Cromwell, Conn. 06416

Other Sources of Hardware

Consult the List of Suppliers for addresses.

All Types

Artifacts, Inc.
The 18th Century Company
Kensington Historical Company
United House Wrecking Co.

Awning Hardware

The Astrup Company
Belaire Draperies & Fabrics
Bronx Window Shade & Awning Co., Inc.

Brackets

Acme Hardware Co.
Decorators Wholesale Hardware Co.
P. E. Guerin Inc.
K. B. Moulding, Inc.
Paine and Chriscot, Inc.

Door Hardware

Acme Hardware Co.
Bailey's Forge
Bendix Mouldings, Inc.
Elegant Entries, Inc.
Eriksson's Blacksmith
Folger Adam Co.
Georgia Lighting Supply Co.
Henry Hanger Co.
Wm. Hunrath Co., Inc.
J & R Industries
Mill Village Blacksmith Shop
Old Bennington Woodcrafters
Period Brass, Inc.
San Francisco Victoriana
Sturbridge Yankee Workshop
The Wrecking Bar

Hinges and Latches

I. M. Wiese, Antiquarian

Hooks

Antique Building Supplies

Nails

Antique Building Supplies

Furniture Hardware

Acme Hardware Co.
Bendix Mouldings, Inc.
Cohasset Colonials
Albert Constantine & Son, Inc.
Decorators Wholesale Hardware Co.
E & I Oriental Co., Inc.
Faultless Division, B.L.I.
Gaston Wood Finishes, Inc.
Wm. Hunrath Co., Inc.
Kings Cabinet
Minnesota Woodworker's Supply Co.
Old Bennington Woodcrafters
Period Brass, Inc.
Preservation Resource Center
Sturbridge Yankee Workshop
Tennessee Fabricating Co.

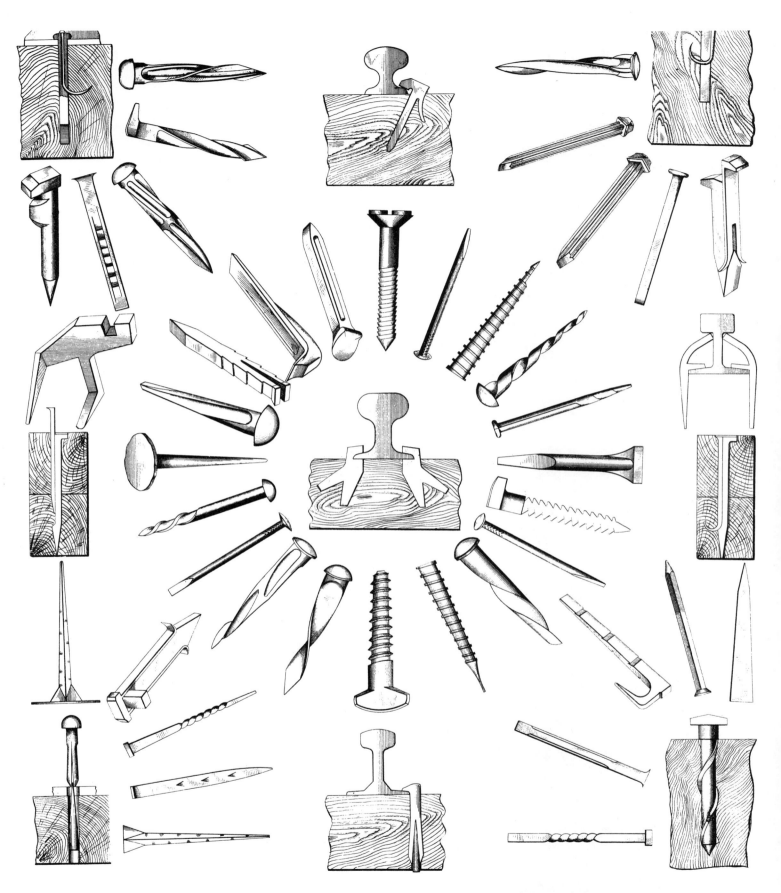

TYPES OF NAILS AND SPIKES.

From *The Growth of Industrial Art*, 1892.

Master bedroom, "Ruthmere," Elkhart, Indiana. Photograph
courtesy Scalamandre Silks, Inc.

IV Fireplaces & Heating

"What Is Home Without A Father?" reads a Victorian wall plaque worked in embroidery. Granting the need for a master of the house, a better motto might be, What Is Home Without A Fireplace? If you follow the real estate ads in *The New York Times* you will notice the cryptic notation "wbf." Appearance of this abbreviation means that the apartment or dwelling is most likely more expensive than the ordinary because it is equipped with a woodburning fireplace. Sitting before the hearth is an all-American tradition, especially on a cold winter's eve. Although electric logs sometimes glow stupidly before our eyes, most of us have not succumbed to the practice of turning the fireplace opening into a center for a display of dried flowers, or, as with the British, hissing gas "coals." If anything we are guilty of inordinate fondness for the homely hearth. President Nixon, it is said, insisted on a roaring fire on sweltering July days.

Fireplaces, of course, were the only source of heat in many early American dwellings. Stoves made of ceramic tiles date from the Roman times, and were greatly improved in Renaissance Germany. While some such early pottery heating devices may have been in use in the Colonies, it was the Franklin stove of cast iron which revolutionized the heating field both here and abroad. In use since the middle of the eighteenth century, it provided a much more efficient vessel in which to burn fuel. While only about twenty percent of the heat developed by a wood fire in a fireplace is delivered to a room, a good stove such as as the Franklin will deliver from seventy to eighty percent. Such a stove could be fitted into the fireplace opening and would make use of the chimney flue.

Franklins were followed in quick succession by a host of other cast-iron devices—parlor stoves with pipes that reached across the ceiling, pot-belly or cannonball stoves, to name just a few. These became more and more elaborate in ornamentation during the Victorian period. An Adam-style Franklin stove was a rather chaste affair with delicate classical motifs; the Victorian pot-belly was a truly bulbous, hulking presence.

By the end of the nineteenth century, stoves were giving way to various central-heating devices. These were first used in public buildings, and with the development of cheap supplies of fuel—first coal and later oil and natural gas—furnaces were installed in domestic basements for warm-air or hot-water systems. Those of us born before the widespread use of oil, that is before World War II, remember with a mixture of fondness and dread stoking the furnace, removing "clinkers," and the clanking of radiators. Oil-fired baseboard heating is a great deal more efficient and involves less labor on the part of the homeowner. It has also become terribly expensive.

A 1930s edition of the *Encyclopaedia Britannica* informs the reader that "The stove is being rapidly discarded in America, where formerly it was widely used, because of the attention and space it needs, its unsightly appearance, and the fact that a separate stove is required in every room for satisfactory results." Now, forty years later, the woodburning stove is making a comeback. We cannot afford to do without them.

Thermostats have been lowered in sensible homes from 72 degrees to 60, and we have survived. Wood fires are kept going on winter nights to supplement the sharply reduced use of the furnace. Reproduction Franklin and parlor stoves have been reinstalled in many homes, and contrary to the encyclopaedia's authority, it is not necessary to have one in every room to gain satisfactory results even if central heating is not used. Newer-model Scandanavian stoves can provide an extraordinary amount of heat from a small amount of wood. By closing off some rooms and opening up others, the warm air will circulate efficiently.

Those who live in old houses may have much to be thankful for. With proper insulation, these structures will be warmer in the winter and cooler in the summer than modern buildings equipped with the latest heating and air-conditioning equipment. Old houses are more likely to have been properly sited away from cold winter blasts and searing summer sun; mature trees and shrubbery provide further protection. Walls are thicker, and both doors and windows are made to open and close securely. Any house with many rooms—old or new—will present problems, and it may be necessary to close some of them off from time to time. High Victorian ceilings are not conducive to efficient heating, but these needn't be lowered or otherwise altered. In such grand surroundings, one lives close to the source of heat, close to the stove or fireplace.

Readers of *The Old House Catalogue* will find in this section on fireplaces and heating almost every kind of appurtenance or device necessary for living comfortably and pleasantly. In the matter of heating, the past has much to recommend it.

Andirons

Standard devices for holding logs, andirons come in all sizes and shapes. Sometimes they are called firedogs or brand dogs or creepers. They may be made of iron, brass, bronze, steel, or silver, and all have a horizontal bar attached to them which supports the logs. The vertical standards or guards, which serve to keep the wood from rolling out onto the hearth, are usually decorated or formed in some attractive shape. Those found in kitchen fireplaces are usually the simplest and are generally made of iron. More elaborate andirons, many featuring classical motifs, have a place in such formal spaces as a dining or living room.

Antique andirons are increasingly difficult to find, and prices go up and up. The bar extensions on such old pieces may have disintegrated or been greatly reduced

by the effect of countless fires, and these will need replacement. If the vertical standards are indeed fine pieces, it may be worth your time and expense to have them fitted with new bars. If not, then turn to one of a number of fine reproduction manufacturers.

English Cast Iron

Something out of the ordinary in cast-iron andirons is offered by Kingsworthy. They manufacture, for example, a set of art nouveau andirons, 11″ high, 9″ deep; Duke of Wellington andirons, 16″ high, 14″ deep; and simple square column andirons, 16″ high, 14″ deep.

Catalogue available.

*Kingsworthy Foundry Co., Ltd.
Kingsworthy,
Winchester, Hants SO23 7QG
England*

Wrought Iron

Steve Kayne, a blacksmith, will hand forge wrought-iron andirons to match designs found on the handles of fireplace tools illustrated in his catalogue—a plain heart, Moravian heart, omega, or volute—or he will follow a design you supply. He also makes small firedogs. The andirons are priced at $35 each.

Pamphlet available.

*Steve Kayne
17 Harmon Place
Smithtown, New York 11787*

A small representative selection of reproductions from early Colonial designs is manufactured by Essex. Among these are the Gooseneck andiron ($62.50) and the simple Forged Loop andiron ($43.50) recommended for an informal hearth. These are of hand-wrought iron.

The Essex Forge
77 Main Street
Essex, Conn. 06426

Polished Steel

Jackson has been selling fireplace mantels and accessories since 1879. Jackson's line of andirons spans a 200-year period and includes cast and wrought iron, brass, and polished steel reproductions of eighteenth and nineteenth-century styles as well as modern andirons of chrome and iron. Illustrated is a pair of polished-steel "knife-blade" andirons with polished-brass finials, 24″ high.

Literature available.

Edwin Jackson, Inc.
306 E. 61st St.
New York, N.Y. 10021

Williamsburg Reproductions

Williamsburg reproduction brass andirons feature steeple tops and Chippendale ball-and-claw, William and Mary ball, and Queen Anne slipper feet. The smallest of these, the Davis andirons, are 17″ high and 15½″ in depth. They are copies of a design signed "J. Davis, Boston," c. 1803-1823. They are available from the Craft House, from department stores featuring Colonial Williamsburg reproductions, or from The Harvin Company, their manufacturer.

Craft House catalogue, $2.95.

Craft House
Williamsburg, Va. 23185

or

The Harvin Co.
Waynesboro, Va. 22980

Bellows

Hand bellows have been used at least since the sixteenth century to increase the combustability of a fire. When the fireplace was the source of heat for a room and the place in which meals were cooked, the pear-shaped bellows were pumped often and with much vigor. The wood on such devices was sometimes ornamented with carving or painting in a style conforming to a particular period. Now that fireplaces are being used again for more than decorative effect, such a simple device for the hearth may be of more than passing interest.

Lemée's bellows are handmade from wood and leather in various colors and finished with large head brass tacks and brass nozzles. Maple or black finishes with handpainted floral decorations or a brass-finish eagle are available. Prices range from $8.50 to $16.50.

Catalogue and price list available, 35¢.

Lemée's Fireplace Equipment
Route 28
Bridgewater, Mass. 02324

Period offers a selection of bellows in a variety of finishes such as walnut, red lacquer, dark oak, and "antique." Two of their most expensive and useful models have long handles that will eliminate the need for kneeling before the fire. The decoration consists of escutcheons, rosettes, eagles, ships, or plain brass straps. The bellows are available from $12 to $36.

Catalogue and price list available, $2.

Period Furniture Hardware Co., Inc.
123 Charles Street
Boston, Mass. 02114

Chimney Breasts

The chimney wall area in many early Colonial interiors was simply finished with carved wood sheathing. The chimney breast combines the functions of mantel and overmantel in a direct, honest manner. It is another reminder that not all early fireplace openings were topped with a shelf for display of a clock, candlesticks, etc.

Kensington carries only pre-nineteenth-century building materials from demolished structures. Chimney breasts are among their specialties—in wood, of course, such as the example illustrated here.

Descriptive literature available.

Kensington Historical Co.
Box 87
East Kingston, N.H. 03827

The 18th Century Co. does restoration work on seventeenth- and eighteenth-century dwellings, using antique building materials. Chimney breasts are among their offerings.

Descriptive literature available.

The 18th Century Co.
Haddam Quarter Road
Durham, Conn. 06422

Ash Dumps/Ash Pit Cleanout Doors

Fireplace walls equipped with pits for the deposit of ashes make maintenance of fireplaces much easier. The floor is fitted with a framed lid which can be opened for "dumping." The pit below is emptied through a cleanout door. Use of some such devices can also improve the flow of oxygen to the fire itself

Washington Stove Works offers four ash dump-cleanout door models. Two of these will provide the additional bonus of better air flow. This may also result in more economical fireplace performance.

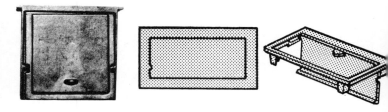

Literature available.

Washington Stove Works
P.O. Box 687
Everett, Wash. 98201

Cranes

Fireplace cranes are used for cooking purposes. Kettles and pots are hung from an iron bar over a fire. The bar, itself hung from two side pins or supports, swings free for easy access. If you wish to restore a kitchen fireplace to its original appearance, a crane is a must.

Hand-forged wrought-iron fireplace cranes are made by Stephen Parker. He must be informed as to whether the crane will be used in a new fireplace or placed in an old one. The pintles used for new fireplaces are set in as the fireplace is built, wrapped around the back of the brick. With old fireplaces, each pintle is nail-shaped so that it can be inserted into a drilled hole. Final height and width depend on the customer's taste and the size of the fireplace. Parker's designs are based on two old Pennsylvania cranes from the Bucks County Historical Society's Mercer Museum in Doylestown, Pennsylvania. The standard crane illustrated here measures approximately 30″ wide and 24″ high. It is priced at $55.

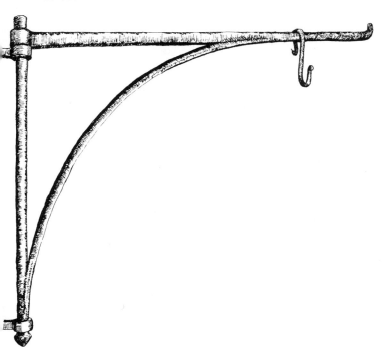

Catalogue and price list available, $1.

Stephen W. Parker
P.O. Box 40
Craftsbury, Vt. 05826

Lemée's fireplace crane is of ornamental wrought iron and comes in four sizes for different-sized fireplaces. The vertical part is made so as to simplify installation. Anchor bars fit into the masonry. In length Lemée cranes vary from 22″ to 41½″, and in price from $14 to $17.

Catalogue and price list available, 35¢.

Lemée's Fireplace Equipment
815 Bedford Street
Bridgewater, Mass. 02324

Dampers

A properly installed damper will provide a good flow of air when your fireplace is being used and will seal it off from the cold at other times. It is hard to imagine a more useful and necessary device. In rebuilding a fireplace, the old house owner will want to make sure that the damper fits snugly and operates easily. Many unrestored dwellings, of course, have never been equipped with such devices.

Washington Stove Works makes dampers of five different sizes to fit your requirements. They are fabricated of quality cast iron and guaranteed for life. You will have to provide information on the width of the fireplace front (in inches) and the size of the flue opening. The damper can be opened to one of three positions by moving an easily reachable, poker-controlled handle.

Literature available.

Washington Stove Works
P.O. Box 687
Everett, Wash. 98201

Fenders

Fenders were introduced during the late seventeenth century as special fireguards. They provide yet another obstacle in the way of falling logs or smaller pieces of burning wood. Most fenders are plain metal railings which enclose the fireplace opening. In the late eighteenth century these fittings became more elaborate, employing pierced fretwork, scroll designs, and finials. Victorian fenders may be truly awesome metal barriers.

Period makes solid brass-rail fenders with a choice of ball or urn posts, and later style rose and tulip perforated fenders in black iron with brass feet. There are three widths available for each style—42″, 48″, and 54″. Other sizes will be made as special orders. Prices range from $40 to $170.

Catalogue and price list available, $2.

Period Furniture Hardware Co., Inc.
123 Charles Street
Boston, Mass. 02114

The Harvin Company makes a very handsome reproduction brass serpentine fender with a simple pierced pattern and a scalloped edge. This is one of the items offered by Colonial Williamsburg and is copied from an English antique, c. 1780. The fender measures 6¼″ high, 49¼″ wide, and 11⅝″ deep. The price is $275.

Craft House catalogue available, $2.95.

Craft House
Williamsburg, Va. 23185
or

The Harvin Co.
Waynesboro, Va. 22980

Firebacks

Many modern devices are now offered to throw more heat from the fireplace into the room; we need this inexpensive source of warmth. Why not add a fireback? It will help to accomplish the same end and will protect the back wall of the fireplace as well. Use of cast-iron fireback slabs started in England in the sixteenth century, and eventually they were produced in America as well. Henry Mercer's The Bible in Iron *is a classic study of fireback designs and is available in a reprint edition for $12.95 from the Mercer Museum, Doylestown, Pennsylvania 18901.*

English Firebacks

Particularly appropriate for grand pre-revolutionary Colonial houses and their hearths are the cast-iron firebacks manufactured by the Kingsworthy foundry in England. Their motifs include the Lion and Unicorn, the Royal Coat of Arms, Knight's Head and Cross, as well as simpler designs such as urns and anchors. One of the designs is illustrated above. These

are rather heavy objects, so be prepared for heavy freight charges.

Catalogues available.

Kingsworthy Foundry Co., Ltd.
Kingsworthy
Winchester, Hants SO23 7QG
England

Reproduction Colonial Firebacks

A fireback copied from one used in the Governor's Palace at Williamsburg and another reproduced from antique fragments excavated there are available from Lemée for $45. These may be the same items manufactured by The Harvin Co. and offered by Williamsburg's Craft House. In any case, they cost $18 less when ordered from Lemée. One design is called Royal Crest; the second is known as the Virginia. The former weighs 68 lbs; the latter, 77 lbs.

Catalogue available, 35¢.

Lemée's Fireplace Equipment
Route 28
Bridgewater, Mass. 02324

Grates

These serve somewhat the same purpose as andirons—providing a bed for a fire that must have air circulating below to burn properly. There is no reason, however, that a pair of andirons can not be used in tandem with a simple iron grate; more elaborate baskets of a nineteenth-century style should stand by themselves.

Simple grates suitable for wood-burning fireplaces are available through G. W. Mount. These are made of steel rods which have been welded at all joints. They may also be used in wood-burning stoves.

Pamphlet available

G. W. Mount, Inc.
576 Leyden Road
Greenfield, Mass. 01301

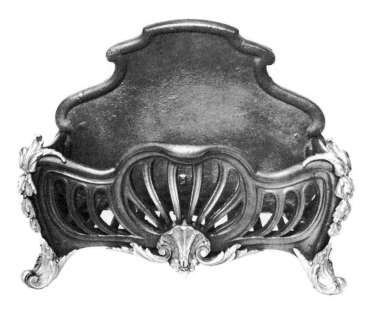

Jackson carries elegant grates to complement elegant fireplaces. No matter what style fireplace you have, one or more of these fancy grates will be suitable for use in burning wood *or* briquets. They come in black iron and brass, polished steel, plain black iron, and black iron with doré mounts. This last grate is illustrated above and measures 19″ wide, 9″ deep, and 16″ high.

Descriptive literature available.

Edwin Jackson
315 East 62nd St.
New York, N.Y. 10021

Mantels

A mantel serves to frame a fireplace opening on three sides, but the term itself may be used only as a designation for the shelf which runs across the top. We are speaking of the complete frame. A mantelpiece is laid over the wall surface or chimney breast. It is a decorative architectural element without much utilitarian purpose but so, also, are the mouldings which accent doorways, cornices, windows, and walls. The fireplace walls of many early and late Colonial-style houses were never blessed with mantels during the seventeenth and eighteenth centuries, but these were added later. Mantels were also moved from fireplace to fireplace when houses were remodeled in the nineteenth century. One that is now in place in a front parlor may have begun its life in an upstairs bedroom, or vice versa. Sometimes in stripping away paint and/or paper, the complicated history of a fireplace wall is exposed to examination.

When fireplaces were closed up in many American houses during the nineteenth and early twentieth centuries, mantels were, of course, removed entirely. A pot-belly stove looks rather absurd with such framing. A goodly supply of antique mantels does remain, and this is added to each year as the toll of old houses climbs. Handsome reproductions are available for those who cannot find an appropriate antique.

Cast Iron

Cast-iron mantels from England are to be found at Gargoyles. These were made in the second half of the nineteenth century and exhibit a truly eclectic aesthetic. "When painted," the distributor writes, "it is virtually impossible to distinguish them from wood." But what is wrong with cast iron?

Catalogue, $4.

Gargoyles Ltd.
512 South Third St.
Philadelphia, Penn. 19147

Faience

A ceramic Louis XV period mantel in an off-white glaze would add grace to a high-style, formal interior, especially one rich in eighteenth-century baroque expression. The mantel contains a shell design as its centerpiece and S-curved scrolls on the sides. These decorations can be rendered in soft blue or coral or left in the off-white shade.

Descriptive literature available.

Edwin Jackson
315 East 62nd St.
New York, N.Y. 10021

Oak and Mahogany

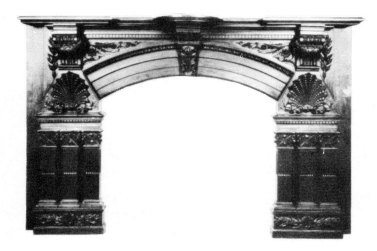

These are Victorian mantels salvaged from fine homes. Illustrated is one mahogany piece removed from Mary Cassatt's Philadelphia townhouse. Almost all of Gargoyles' mantels of oak and mahogany were produced between 1860 and 1905 and are from England. There are some handsome art nouveau designs, as witness the French carved mahogany model illustrated below.

Catalogue, $4.

Gargoyles Ltd.
512 South Third St.
Philadelphia, Penn. 19147

Pine and Walnut

Jackson offers a truly distinguished selection of reproduction mantels in pine and walnut. There are carved English pine, English Regency pine, American Georgian pine, American Chippendale pine, and French Provincial walnut models to choose from— among others.

Literature available.

Edwin Jackson
315 East 62nd Street
New York, N.Y. 10021

Wood and Composition

Wood mantels with compostion carvings are among the specialities of Decorators Supply. Illustrated is one in what is termed "French Design."

Literature available

Decorators Supply Corporation
3610 South Morgan St.
Chicago, Ill. 60609

Jackson offers an Adam-style mantel of pine with composition decoration. It is true in form to the revival of classical motifs which so swept America in the Federal period.

Literature available

Edwin Jackson
315 East 62nd St.
New York, N.Y. 10021

Marble

For real American Victorian elegance, a marble mantel is hard to duplicate. The interiors of the house in which such an imposing piece could stand would have to be similarly monumental. Most Americans of the period turned instead to "marbelized" slate. Gargoyles has true marble mantels in many colors and hues. Slate mantels may be found, too, but you had best search the junk shops first.

Catalogue, $4.

Gargoyles Ltd.
512 South Third St.
Philadelphia, Penn. 19147

Urethane

Focal Point offers two mantels—French Provincial, illustrated here, and Georgian—in this synthetic substance. Each has been hand cast from original wood

models of period excellence. They are ready for shipping, primed beige for stain or white to receive paint.

Brochure available.

Focal Point, Inc.
3760 Lower Roswell Rd.
Marietta, Ga. 30060

Fire Screens

Although these are protective devices, they needn't be unattractive. Fire screens were once very fancy; early forms sometimes contained framed needlework or tapestry. It is unlikely, however, that such decorative panels provided much security from flying sparks; it is better to be prudent than to be authentic. There are fine-mesh screens handsomely framed with bronze or brass which provide sufficient protection. Since old fireplace openings differ in size from one another, most fire screen manufacturers are prepared to handle custom work.

Jackson carries a superb variety of fireplace screens, portable and built-in. One type operates on traverse pulls concealed behind a metal valance; another curtain-screen pulls on a portable frame. Most luxurious is the gossamer mesh of bronze wire that rolls up behind a 2" guard. Also stocked are Boston spark guards, gate screens, and a spark arrestor with cutouts for andirons.

Descriptive literature available.

Edwin Jackson
315 East 62nd Street
New York, N.Y. 10021

Period features screens made with no. 10-gauge heat-resistant black mesh. Several different styles of brass detailing and shapes are available.

Catalogue and price list available, $2.

Period Furniture Hardware Co., Inc.
123 Charles Street
Boston, Mass. 02114

Portland Willamette makes sliding mesh fireplace screens to fit any regular, corner, or three-sided fireplace. The screens themselves come in more than twenty different finishes. They also manufacture spark guards, flat spark arrestors, folding screens and folding tempered-glass doors to fit all fireplaces.

Booklet available.

Portland Willamette Co.
6804 N.E. 59th Place
Portland, Ore. 97218

Scuttles and Wood Baskets

A solid pine box will suffice for the storage of wood in most homes. Fancier devices, however, are appropriate for the hearth as well, and may offer greater flexibility in handling.

Coal Scuttle

This may seem the most plebian of accoutrements, but Washington's cast-iron model is handsome enough for any fireplace. A sculptured top and base frame a gracefully shaped body.

Descriptive literature available.

Washington Stove Works
P.O. Box 687
Everett, Wash. 98201

Iron Baskets

Lemée carries two black iron baskets with brass trim and a solid brass basket, both to be used for carrying and storing wood. They also sell canvas log carriers and a large log hoop that is good for drying out damp wood.

Catalogue and price list available, 35¢.

Lemée's Fireplace Equipment
815 Bedford St.
Bridgeport, Mass. 02324

Stovepipe, Boots

Supplies of this sort are best sought from a good hardware store. Some of the reproduction stove manufacturers, however, are prepared to provide proper fittings for their products.

Heavy-gauge stovepipe which has been spray-painted flat black or Jøtul green for use with Jøtul stoves is available from Thompson and Anderson. Such other pieces of stovepipe used with and made of sheet metal —reducers, thimbles, elbows, wall collars, and adapter collars—are also available.

Thompson and Anderson, Inc.
446 Stroudwater St.
Westbrook, Me. 04092

Jackson offers a special service to its Franklin stove buyers. They will furnish special boots for connecting stoves to flues. In addition, they will also close up the smoke collar in the back of the stove and install one on the top if that is where you wish to connect the pipe for the flue.

Descriptive literature available.

Edwin Jackson
315 E. 62nd St.
New York, N.Y. 10021

Stoves, Antique

Franklin stoves were being thrown away twenty-five years ago; today it is almost impossible to convince an antique dealer to part with them. Heating devices of this sort were in use by the mid-eighteenth century and continued in popularity throughout the nineteenth. With the introduction of central heating and cheap sources of fuel, the stoves were allowed to rust. Many are now in such a state of disrepair that it is worthless to try and resurrect them. If you do find an antique stove in reasonably good working order, hold on to it tightly as it will fetch an exceedingly high price in future years.

Jackson carries an assortment of antique stoves from America and European countries. Many of the European stoves are adaptations of early nineteenth-century American models. The style and decoration generally followed the prevailing mode of the country of manufacture. From central Europe, for example, come ceramic stoves in baroque and Biedermeier styles; the French dressed the Franklin stove up in brass and marble. An inquiry will inform you as to what is available.

Edwin Jackson
315 East 62 Street
New York, N.Y. 10021

Stoves, Heating

Manufacturers of heating stoves popped up everywhere during the years of the fuel crisis, 1973 and 1974, and they have stayed in business since. Doubtless, we again shall be visited by the phenomenon of an oil shortage whether caused by our own wastefulness or the Middle Eastern situation. But who needed the crisis to underline a need for conservation? Sharply rising prices were already forcing cutbacks, and this situation has not improved one bit.

The North American continent is blessed with an abundance of firewood which, if properly cut, can be replenished. Those who live in the country may have learned about the wisdom of the wood lot, an area where firewood is cut and where future supplies can be planted. Burned in a well-built stove, wood can provide an enormous amount of heat which will keep modest-sized rooms quite warm on cold days or nights. Some of these stoves are reproductions of Franklins which have long been known as efficient burners. Others are more modern, contemporary units which have been designed to fit into almost any kind of interior.

Kristia Associates
343 Forest Ave.
P.O. Box 1118
Portland, Me. 04104

Franklin and Atlantic Stoves

Jøtul Stoves

Kristia imports Norwegian Jøtul woodburning stoves that come in two versions, heating and cooking. Both are handsome pieces of craftsmanship with a green enamel finish. They are most appropriate for period-style country homes. To read Kristia's catalogue is to become a believer in the economy and practicality of a woodburning stove. And from experience we can affirm that the Jøtul stoves *do* work very effectively.

Catalogue available, $1.

Portland manufactures a variety of Franklin stoves plus two sizes of the Atlantic box stove and parlor stoves. The Franklins are authentic reproductions of cast-iron models and are based on designs of the eighteenth century. All are suitable for burning wood.

Brochures available.

Portland Franklin Stove Foundry, Inc.
57 Kennebec Street
Portland, Me. 04104

Pot-Belly Stoves

Authentic reproductions of cast-iron Franklin stoves from original molds, parlor stoves, and six Victorian cannonball or "pot-belly" stove models are offered by Washington. There are five parlor stoves to choose from and these differ in use of nickel plated trim and swing tops.

Descriptive literature available.

Washington Stove Works
P.O. Box 687
Everett, Wash. 98201

Shaker Stove

A utilitarian stove that retains the simplicity and straight lines of the original Shaker design is made by

blacksmith Stephen Parker. This was originally made at the Shaker community in New Lebanon, New York.

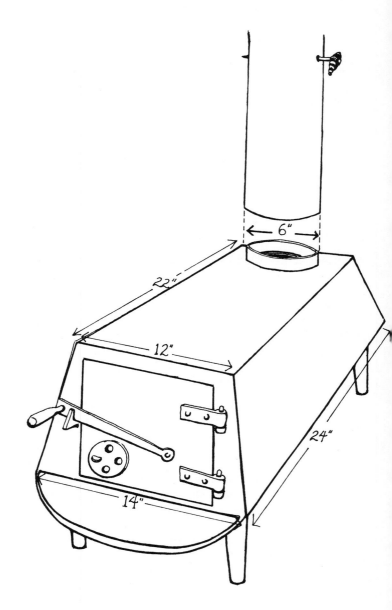

Catalogue and price list available, $1.

Stephen W. Parker
P.O. Box 40
Craftsbury, Vt. 05826

The Trenton

Jackson's Franklin stoves are the most handsome and authentic of all those produced today in cast iron. All models are exact copies of stoves made prior to 1840. Illustrated here is The Trenton, an elegant pattern found near New Jersey's capital city. The stove, of course, need not be used in a fireplace as it is here, but if you are blessed with several fireplaces, why not use one in this manner?

Brochure available.

Edwin Jackson
315 E. 62nd St.
New York, N.Y. 10021

Stoves, Cooking

Cooking stoves using wood, coal, or oil as fuel are rarities today. It is unlikely that they will ever become as popular as stoves for heating purposes only. A good wood cook stove, however, might be used in a summer kitchen if not in the main house as a secondary, back-up appliance. Demand for them is growing each year.

For those who yearn for the good old days, Portland manufactures wood, coal, and oil-burning Queen Atlantic stoves for cooking. Complete with warming ovens and water reservoirs, they're far friendlier than electric and gas stoves. The Queen Atlantic is available with a blacking or porcelain enamel finish. A model for use in small kitchens is also made.

Brochures available.

Portland Franklin Stove Foundry, Inc.
57 Kennebec St.
Portland, Me. 04104

Olympic wood and oil cooking ranges are sold by the Washington Stove Works. The ranges come in porcelain enamel and matte black finishes with optional accessories such as a buffet shelf or copper coils. As the illustration indicates, these are simpler, more "modern" models than those known in the Victorian era.

Descriptive literature available.

Washington Stove Works
P.O. Box 687
Everett, Wash. 98201

Fire Tools

Anyone using a stove or fireplace will need a sturdy set of tools for lifting, poking around, sweeping, etc. Tools of the sort used today were known in the sixteenth century in England and have traditionally been made of iron, steel, or brass.

Lemée's carries a variety of fireplace tools and stands and hanging fire sets. These are traditional designs in black iron with cast brass handles. The company also offers a selection of corn brooms for sweeping the hearth. Maple handles are stained maple, oak, or mahogany.

Catalogue and price list available, 35¢.

Lemée's Fireplace Equipment
815 Bedford St.
Bridgewater, Mass. 02324

Mount's fireplace sets consist of shovel, log roller, and poker; they come in both round and square stock and have handles in four patterns. All pokers come with a "harpoon" tip unless otherwise specified. Mount also sells sets of two tools, fireplace stands, tongs, and single tools.

Brochure available.

G. W. Mount
576 Leyden Road
Greenfield, Mass. 01301

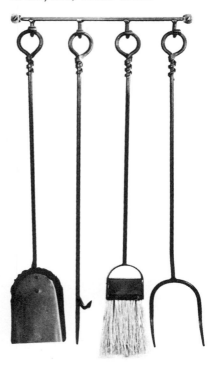

Reproductions of plain and fancy tools from the seventeenth and eighteenth centuries are hand forged by Essex craftsmen. One four-piece set, "The Standish," includes a hearth broom. Hangers for the tools are available.

Catalogues and price list available.

The Essex Forge
77 Main Street
Essex, Conn. 06426

Stephen Parker offers seven versions of the grasp end of fireplace tools and four types of tool to which the handles can be joined. All are hand-forged wrought iron in the length you desire.

Catalogue and price list available, $1.

Stephen W. Parker
P.O. Box 40
Craftsbury, Vt. 05826

If you want to personalize your fireplace tools, Steve Kayne will forge any letter as the tool handle. A male chauvinist pig might use his initial for the poker and the fork and have his wife's initial mounted on the shovel. Besides initials, Kayne illustrates in his "Designs at the Forge" brochure a great variety of handles and tools. He will make left-handed rakes and brushes with natural or white bristles. A hand-forged hook will be provided free with each individual tool purchased, and a rack will be provided with each set.

"Designs at the Forge" available.

Steve Kayne
17 Harmon Place
Smithtown, N.Y. 11787

Hand-forged tools made especially for Jøtul box stoves are the creation of Pete Taggett, blacksmith, and are finished in dead black and available in 24″ or 36″ lengths.

Descriptive literature available.

Pete Taggett
The Blacksmith Shop
P.O. Box 15
Mount Holly, Vt. 05758

Other Sources for Fireplace and Heating Equipment

Consult the List of Suppliers for addresses

Andirons

Ball and Ball
Colonial Shops
Lemée's Fireplace Equipment
G. W. Mount
Old Smithy Shop
E. G. Washburne Co.
Wilshire Fireplace
Ye Olde Mantel Shoppe

Bellows

National Products, Inc.

Cranes

Long Associates
G. W. Mount
Paine and Chriscot, Inc.

Fenders

Ball and Ball
Edwin Jackson
H. Sacks & Sons

Firebacks

Craft House
Period Furniture Hardware Co., Inc.

Grates

Lemée's Fireplace Equipment
Shenandoah Manufacturing Co., Inc.
E. G. Washburne Co.

Mantels

Danny Allesandro, Ltd.
Artifacts, Inc.

Driwood Wood Moulding and Millwork Co.
The 18th Century Co.
Elon, Inc.
European Marble Works
Felber Studios
Georgia Lighting Supply Co.
William H. Jackson Co.
C. E. Morgan Building Products
North Salem Studios
United House Wrecking Co.
Vermont Marble Co.
I. M. Wiese
Wrecking Bar
Ye Olde Mantel Shoppe

Screens

Craft House
Hurley Patentee Lighting
William H. Jackson Co.
Lemée's Fireplace Equipment
G. W. Mount
John P. Smith Co.
Washington Stove Works

Scuttles and Wood Baskets

Period Furniture Hardware Co., Inc.

Stoves, Antique

United House Wrecking Co.

Stoves, Cooking

Kristia Associates
United House Wrecking Co.

Stoves, Heating

Edwin Jackson
Mill Village Blacksmith Shop
The Old Stove Co.
Preway
Shenandoah Manufacturing Co., Inc.
Tremont Nail Co.
Washington Stove Works

Tools

Ball and Ball
Craft House
Edwin Jackson
William H. Jackson
Period Furniture Hardware Co., Inc.
E. G. Washburne Co.

Southern yellow heart pine. Photograph courtesy Period Pine, Inc.

V Floors

Two considerations should be uppermost in the minds of those who tackle the problem of flooring—appearance and maintenance. No element in the make-up of the old house, whatever the style, is so vulnerable to stress and strain. Anyone who has restored a period dwelling has learned that the condition of the floors may tell more about its earlier owners and way of life than the walls. Rare, indeed, is the home with original flooring. Most often one must peel away layers of worn linoleum, if not wall-to-wall carpeting, to discover if there is a virgin surface beneath. More than one home restorer has been surprised to find that the original flooring was the earth itself. Mud-rooms may have been exactly that.

Utility surely must determine the type of flooring to be used in a particular room or area. Gone are the days when servants were available to polish parquet, or, better yet, to follow the advice offered by Hannah Glass in her *Servants Directory* of 1760: "Be sure always to have very clean Feet, that you may not dirty your Rooms as soon as clean'd, nor make any Noise, but learn to walk softly, and not disturb the Family." Although an old house may not be fitted with the most modern central cleaning system available today, there is no reason to spend vast amounts of time maintaining gleaming surfaces. In the eighteenth century in England, in fact, highly polished floors were the exception; they were most often dry scrubbed.

Two of the most popular of twentieth-century surfaces—linoleum and wall-to-wall carpeting—have fallen from favor. Linoleum is no longer made in the United States, in fact, and vinyl sheeting and tiles have taken its place. The hairy shag look of deep pile rugs still appears in bathrooms, but in other areas of the house a more natural appearance is strived for. This is in keeping with the trend toward the use of "real" materials, or better imitations of them, in building. Costs have risen dramatically in recent years, but the old house

patron would rather do with less space than less quality. Even good imitations are not good enough.

The number of attractive materials appropriate for flooring is much greater than that on display at most home centers. Wood, ceramic, brick, and stone products and vinyl substitutes are available throughout North America. Some of these can be put in place by the homeowner; other forms require professional installation. If you are fortunate to own a home with flooring still in usable condition, you will find that there is a wide market of products available for renewing and maintaining them.

As for covering the surfaces, the advice is to go slowly. Oriental carpets are in great demand throughout the Western world. Even mass-produced, North African-made rugs of the late 1800s and early 1900s are bringing high prices. Flat-woven kilims, once scorned as fit only for the feet of peasants, are now the favored decorative floor coverings in the homes of patrons of American folk art. Take your time to search for the right carpet for the living or dining room. A modern form of floor cloth, a covering popular in more modest nineteenth-century homes, might be appropriate for a hall or stairway. A commercially-produced durable oval braided rug could serve well in the kitchen and in bedrooms. Painted or stenciled designs are available now, as they were in the eighteenth and nineteenth centuries, for wood flooring.

Brick Flooring

Bricks can provide the most mellow of surfaces for kitchen and service area floors. It was often used on the ground or basement level in Colonial and Early Victorian homes. Both full-sized and half-bricks are available for this purpose. If properly laid, the floor can present an even and level appearance. Chair and table legs need not get caught between the bricks.

If used brick is not readily available in your area, there are suppliers of the old that can be contacted. In addition, there are also makers of new brick in the old style.

Antique Brick

Antique Building Supplies offers fifty to hundred-year-old bricks at $140 per thousand, and 150-year-old hand-formed bricks at $180 per thousand. These prices are FOB Xenia, Ohio. Samples are available for $3.

Antique Building Supplies
Xenia, Ohio 45385

New "Old" Brick

Old Carolina Brick Co. makes six standard shades of hand-molded brick. These include colors popular in Colonial dwellings of the East and Midwest, as well as later shades such as Alamo White which is found in the West. The company is also capable of producing custom colors and shades as well as shapes.

Literature available.
Old Carolina Brick Co.
Salisbury, N.C. 28144

Ceramic Flooring

Nothing is of more practical use on surfaces exposed to the elements than ceramic tiling. Plain colored squares, imitation and antique Delft, mosaic, reproduction Pennsylvania-German, and terra cotta tiles—all can be obtained today and installed with some ease. The expense of some of these materials will prohibit their use in large areas, but, then, most ceramic work is meant to be exhibited as a decorative accent. It is most appropriately used in entry halls, kitchens, bathrooms, terrace areas, none of which is likely to account for many hundreds of square feet of space. And these are the areas most exposed to water and wear.

Delft Blue Tiles

These are modern tiles made by Peter Van Rossum and his craftsmen. The designs are traditional and hand-painted; the tiles are kiln-fired. Over 120 designs are available on pieces measuring 4¼″ x 4¼″; 6″ x 6″ tiles are also offered. Despite the use of the term "blue," these tiles may be obtained in a sepia brown shade as well.

Price per tile ranges from $3.75 to $8.75.

Catalogue and price list available.
Delft Blue
P.O. Box 103
Ellicott City, Md. 21043

Eighteenth-Century Dutch Floor Bricks

Tiles in the form of bricks, these are true antique masterpieces in a bottle green color. For twenty-five years Helen Williams has dealt in antique Delft tiles and faience, all of which are imported from Holland. The tiles are 8″ square by 1″ thick, and are true faience (tin-glazed) products.

Prices and specifications available.
Helen Williams/Rare Tiles
12643 Hortense Street
North Hollywood, Calif. 91604

Unglazed Terra Cotta Tiles

These ceramic tiles from Mexico are almost as fine as those of eighteenth-century Holland or the Iberian peninsula. Of a natural warmth and elegance, they are handmade with an oil-based sealer finish for easy cleaning. There are a number of designs available, the most appropriate styles being the Square, Lattice, and Hexagon for English Colonial interiors, and the Espana, Venice, and Court for Spanish Colonial. They range in size from 4″ to 15″ and in thickness from approximately ⅜″ to ⅝″. Elon also has available marble

tiles, unglazed chocolate-color tiles for flooring, as well as solid color glazed tiles in squares and rounds.

Catalogue available.
Elon Inc.
150 East 58th Street/964 Third Avenue
New York, N.Y. 10022

Elon Tile of Florida, Inc.
18462 N.E. Second Avenue
Miami, Fla. 33179

Elon Tile Co.
8678 Melrose Ave.
Los Angeles, Calif. 90069

Stone Flooring

When properly finished with a sealer, various stone materials can provide a handsome surface for the same areas most commonly covered with ceramic tiles or brick. Marble is the most distinguished of surfaces; field and cut stone, and slate, however, can be used with dramatic and practical effect inside a home. Materials with the most level surfaces, such as slate, will, of course, be easier to maintain and will better support furniture, fixtures, and appliances.

Structural Slate

Slate, a particularly dense, compact stone, is widely used for industrial purposes and for roofing, walks, and patios. Its compactness recommends it for interior use as well. It is available in two grades—ribbon stock and clear stock, the ribbon being marked by darker bands than the rest of the surface. Lower in price than clear, it is not, however, less suitable for interior use. The natural color is gray to gray-black with blue overtones. There are colored slates or flags available, too, in blue gray, purple, mottled purple and green, green, and red. The latter are offered as The Penn-Mont Pocono and The Penn-Mont Shadow Cleft lines. Prices and sizes are determined on the basis of the particular flooring job.

Brochure available.
The Structural Slate Company
Pen Argyl, Penn. 18072

Vinyl Flooring and Tiles

For convenience, there is no better surface covering than modern vinyl products. Linoleum served many generations since it was introduced in 1863. Now that it is no longer made in America, antique status may not be long in coming. It is hard to imagine, however, a fondness for the tacky sheets of badly-printed floor covering which gradually dissolved under the feet of the housewife, thereby requiring yet another layer. The new vinyl surfaces of the mid-twentieth century are a decided improvement. It is a more resilient and resistant surface making use of sophisticated photographically-printed designs. They are more faithfully rendered and colored. While not authentic in any sense of the word, these products are a possible substitute for the real thing when used conservatively if not sparingly.

Royal Delft Cushioned Vinyl Flooring

Available in 6′ and 12′ widths, this flooring will cost the homeowner infinitely less in labor and overall expense than ceramic tile. The design is part of Armstrong's Castillian line of flooring, incorporating a layer of vinyl foam between the backing and the surface design. The impression given is of a mellow, weathered look, tiles that have "aged" somewhat from use. The blue shade is the most appropriate. There are, however, green, gold, red, and brown colors, too.

Approximate installed price per square foot, $1 to $1.10.

Catalogue available.

Armstrong Information Service
Armstrong Cork Co., Inc.
Lancaster, Penn. 17604

Wood flooring

Because of the abundance of wood in North America, flooring of this very natural of materials is found in most old houses. At one time it was inexpensive enough to replace when necessary. Today lumber is high-priced and varieties are somewhat limited. Fine woods, however, can be found. Salvage and demolition companies have learned to save as many boards and beams as possible. Farmers have discovered a new market for siding and beams from their barns and other out-buildings. Some of the suppliers listed below have recently entered the building materials market to offer just such recycled products.

Wood flooring can have a mellow, inviting look to it. Properly finished and maintained, this type of surface may last for years to come. True hardwoods will give more satisfaction, but even such softer surfaces as pine can hold up well if aged and treated. Imitation wood may be suitable for some walls; it will not support the trample of feet.

Hemlock, Douglas Fir, Red Cedar, White Spruce

Architects and builders may recommend Dana-Deck structural timber for flooring. No two planks of any one of these timbers are alike; only the best of 400-year-old virgin logs, the company claims, are chosen for sawing. If you are attempting to replace or add flooring of any of these woods, it would be worth writing to Dana-Deck.

Brochure available.

Dana-Deck & Laminates
Dana McBarron & Sons
Lopez, Wash. 98261

Herringblok and Prefinished Strip Oak

Oak flooring may provide just the right surface for Victorian interiors. The Herringblok pattern is made up of 3″ x 9″ x ½″ oak strips, and in a warm brown shade that has been baked into the wood. The surface has

been distressed to enhance its antique appearance. The Prefinished Strip Oak planks are offered in random lengths, 2½″ widths, ¾″ thickness, and in three different shades—a light "natural," a golden "bronzetone," and

darker "Gunstock" brown. Bruce also offers its own line of mastics for installation. All finishes and carnauba wax are baked into the wood fibers with infrared heat.

Brochure available.

Bruce Hardwood Floors
E.L. Bruce Co., Inc.
Box 16902
Memphis, Tenn. 38116

Ornamental Borders

Floor surfaces can use a combination of materials and forms. Ornamental borders in teak would add a particularly luxurious touch to a high-style interior. These you surely would not want to cover with any carpet or rug. Bangkok Industries has two such patterns available—Rio and Wall of Troy. The Rio comes in 5/16″ x 7″ x 28″ sections; the Wall of Troy in 5/16″ x 8¾″ x 28″ sections. Corner blocks and divider strips are to

be ordered separately. The company and its distributors offer a special mastic and three finishes appropriate for teak.

Brochure and price list available.

Bangkok Industries, Inc.
1900 S. 20th Street
Philadelphia, Penn. 19145

Redwood

This is a natural choice for areas where moisture is a problem, particularly outside as on porch floors. Be sure, however, that it *is* redwood all-heartwood and not a plywood substitute. Redwood is available in rough sawn or smooth textures, either of which will require finishing. Among the major suppliers of such timber is Simpson.

Literature available.

Simpson Timber Co.
900 Fourth Ave.
Seattle, Wash. 98164

Southern Yellow Heart Pine

Old mills, warehouses, factories, and other buildings throughout the Deep South are yielding up a treasure trove of antique lumber. When these buildings are scheduled for demolition, Period Pine moves in to remove, clean, denail, and ship the wood to their Duluth, Georgia, mill for re-sawing. This fine-grained wood grew only in southern Georgia, Alabama, and Mississippi, and by the early 1900s was timbered-out and never regenerated. Period's supply is generous, and has been left, for the most part, in beam state for custom sawing into boards.

Brochure and prices available.

Period Pine
P.O. Box 77052
Atlanta, Ga. 30309

Wide Plank Flooring

Of composition-hard pine, this is the type of flooring so favored in Colonial-style homes. It is appealing because of the random width strips and the use, not of fake pegs, but of wrought head nails. There are two varieties available—Select Grade A, 12″ to 20″ in width, and Grade A, 6″ to 12″ in width. Thickness is

planed one side to one inch. One side is smooth and the other rough; the former may be stained. According to the supplier, no sanding or waxing is required.

Brochure and prices available.

Diamond K. Co., Inc.
130 Buckland Road
South Windsor, Conn. 06074

Wide-Plank Pine

Antique Building Supplies keeps on hand a stock of this type of traditional flooring recycled for new use. Prices are available on request.

Antique Building Supplies
Xenia, Ohio 45385

Wood Mosaic Monticello

Inspired by a formal floor pattern in Thomas Jefferson's country home, Monticello is of American walnut

and is made to order. This is one of 26 patterns available from Wood Mosaic Architectural Flooring, a company that has survived since 1883. All are offered in two grades: prime and antique. In the words of the supplier, prime "signifies a clear wood, containing only mild variations in color tones, naturally caused"; antique "is much the same as prime, but allows for natural characteristics such as bird pecks, small tight knots and scattered worm holes." Hand-distressing may be requested to enhance the antique appearance even more. The Monticello pattern comes in 10″ x 12″ pieces for on-square or diagonal installation. Wood Mosaic offers its

own mastic or adhesive (#714) for use in installing such flooring. The flooring is shipped unfinished.

Brochure and prices available.

Wood Mosaic
P.O. Box 21159
Louisville, Ky. 40221

Floor Coverings

Few if any old house dwellers will be satisfied to walk on bare surfaces; our desire for creature comfort is too great to be overcome. In the winter we especially desire a soft, warm feeling under foot. During the eighteenth century, however, there was much less in the way of carpeting or rugs. What few rugs were possessed, in fact, were more than likely to be used to cover tables, walls, and/

or beds. The Colonial period was, for the most part, one of hardship in America; carpets were luxuries. Only gradually during the nineteenth century did they assume a permanent place on the floor in the majority of homes.

All of this is not to say that you should shun beautiful and expensive Orientals and other fine floor coverings. Needlepoint rugs, Aubussons, Chinese and Persian carpets—these were found in America at an early date, and can be used most appropriately today. Their absence in the typical North American home of the past was an economic matter: most people could not afford them. But along with these splendid types are most modest coverings which may serve the purpose just as well. Hooked rugs, braided rugs, canvas floor cloths, and Indian rugs, among other types, provide color and comfort. Few examples of an earlier age remain in good enough condition to use again; these were utilitarian pieces, and have served their day. Reproductions are, however, plentiful and well-wrought. New designs from North American and European looms may fit your surroundings just as well. And then there are the carpets made during the late Victorian machine age in Oriental and traditional European designs; such "cabbage rose" weaves may have survived the trampling, the spilled drinks, the cigarette ashes of many years.

Carpeting

If you wish to carpet a nineteenth or early twentieth-century interior, don't stint on quality. It makes no sense to cover a large area with worn-out "antique" fabric or with a cheap reproduction. Rugs are a simpler matter; these can be spotted around in a way that minimizes their wear and emphasizes their good qualities. Carpeting, especially of the wall-to-wall variety, is forever staring you in the face. And once applied to the floor, it can be troublesome to remove. Choose your fabric carefully.

Carpeting is a major financial investment, but one that may be worth making. Used in a Victorian parlor or turn-of-the-century music room, it may enhance both the structural elements of the space and complement its furnishings. Scalamandré is one of the few American firms offering high-quality, reproduction carpeting.

Scotch Ingrain

Ingrain carpeting was popular throughout the nineteenth century. Dry goods firms and such mail order houses as Sears and Montgomery Ward continued to offer it until the 1920s. Carpets of this sort have a ribbed rather than a tufted or looped surface and are made on a 36″ fabric loom rather than on a carpet loom. Ingrains were first produced in Scotland and Northern England and undoubtedly many of the best examples of this type of floor covering were imported to North America.

In several ways the production of ingrain carpeting represents a transitional phase between handwork to full machine manufacture. The fillers of several colors used in weaving are placed by hand, thereby lengthening the time required to produce the fabric but giving to it a more crafted appearance. The first photograph is of a design taken from a Metropolitan Museum document, 1840–1850, and reproduced by Scalamandré in 1970 for use in the museum's American Wing and the "Nineteenth-Century America" exhibition. A loom was built at Scalamandré's Long Island City mill

especially for the museum's needs, and it has continued in operation ever since. The carpet, number 97223, is of 100% wool.

The second illustration is of a simpler and earlier design. Documentation for it was taken from a portrait of John Phillips painted by Joseph Stewart in 1793. Scala-

mandré's reproduction of the floor covering seen in the painting has been used by the National Park Service in some of the Independence National Historical Park buildings in Philadelphia. The carpet number is 97369.

The Smithsonian Institution commissioned Scalamandré to reproduce a mid-nineteenth century Scotch Ingrain carpet used at the 1876 Philadelphia Centennial Exhibition. This has been mounted in the Smithsonian's Art and Industries Building, a structure originally built to show objects returned to the Institution from the Centennial show. The pattern, number 97358, dates from 1870–1875.

Wilton

English-made Wilton carpets are available today through Scalamandré. These are among the best of machine-produced floor coverings. Wiltons have a velvety, luxurious surface that is created by cutting the loops of worsted yarn during the weaving process. All three carpets illustrated are made on the traditional 27″ loom in the same manner pursued during the nineteenth century. Even the same cards are used for separating and combining the wools. The Wiltons were originally of 100% wool, but are now available as well in 80% wool and 20% nylon. The same carpets of 100% wool can also be made with a Brussels-type "loop pile," that is, with a deeper, uncut surface.

In order of appearance, the designs are: "Percier" (French Empire), "French Laurel" (French Empire), and "Brighton" (English mid-Victorian).

For further information regarding all Scalamandre products, available only through interior designers or fine department stores, contact:

Scalamandré Silks, Inc.
950 Third Avenue
New York, N.Y. 10022

Rugs

Rugs, as opposed to carpeting or large-scale floor covering, are made in every variety imaginable. Some styles perfected in recent years which make do with indescribable synthetic components are out of the question for the period house. Floor surfaces which resemble fake fur toilet-seat covers are to be avoided at all costs. Almost as obscene and unnatural are the phony "Orientals" which are mass-produced in Taiwan or the Bronx.

Seek out natural fibers—wool, cotton, linen, canvas, reed, etc. These, if reasonably cared for, will provide pleasing and longer-lasting surfaces. Even such a rough material as hemp may be practically employed on stairs or in exterior areas—on porches or on terraces. Indoor-outdoor carpeting isn't even right for the birds; they prefer grass.

Braided, rag, and hooked rugs are just fine for informal, country-style interiors. There are thousands of domestically-made cotton and wool rug designs to choose from for more formal rooms if true Orientals are out of the question. Flat-woven Indian designs are as suitable for Spanish Colonial homes as they are for contemporary dwellings.

Floorcloths

This most modest type of floor covering has not, fortunately, passed completely out of the picture. Technically, a floorcloth is anything which has a canvas backing and is intended to be walked upon. Linoleum, the most modern of floorcloths, as noted before, is no longer manufactured in the United States. Oil cloth, however, can still be purchased; and hand-painted, stenciled, and silk-screened floor canvases are again available. An early eighteenth-century American inventory speaks of "two old checquered canvases to lay under the table"; another mentions "oyl" cloths. How and where were they used? Certainly in cooking areas and possibly in hallways where traffic was heavy. They may have also been laid down in more formal rooms.

Floorcloths Incorporated offers a number of designs which will certainly suit a modest Colonial-style dwelling. One of these is the historic "checquered"; the other is a livelier "Calico Flower." Each floorcloth

is custom-made by the firm of high quality canvas. It is claimed that the coverings "are light and easy to maintain whether gleaming with a hard-gloss finish or a mellow semi-gloss patina." They should be waxed with a liquid or paste wax that can be removed without use of a solvent-type cleanser.

Prices and brochure available.

Floorcloths Inc.
109 Main Street
Annapolis, Md. 21401

Braided Rugs

These simple floor coverings have found a permanent place in many American homes. They are certainly most suitable for use in country and suburban dwellings—in kitchens, bedrooms, and what was once called the "rumpus" room. Braided rugs are made of narrow bands and are usually worked in an oval form. Unfortunately, many home-owners overdo the "ye olde Colonial" look and use too many of these colorful rugs. Although preferable to the hairy shag textures of the synthetic 1970s, these informal braided affairs should not be given free run of the house.

Extremely high quality braided rugs are available from such reputable dealers as Ernest Treganowan, Inc. The design illustrated is hand-woven and custom-made to the design, size, and color desired. For an informal room with exceptional country antiques, a rug of this sort would be most appropriate.

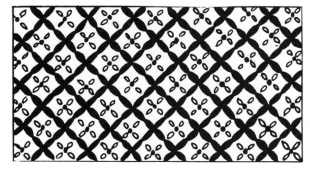

94

Prices and information available.

Ernest Treganowan, Inc.
49 East 53rd Street
New York, N.Y. 10022

If you want a utilitarian floor covering which is also attractive, turn to that American stand-by—Sears, Roebuck. They offer flat braided rugs which are especially useful for use in kitchens, porches, entry-ways—in other words, wherever mud and water is likely to be tracked in. But beware what Sears calls the "braid-look" which is a 100% synthetic variety. They *do* offer some part-wool rugs. These are 25% wool, 25% nylon, 25% rayon, 15% cotton, and 10% "undetermined fiber." It would be best not to speculate too much about the last 10%.

Prices for part-wool braid rugs run from $9.99 (22″ x 44″) to $105 (8½′ x 11′).

Contact your local Sears department or catalog store.

Hooked Rugs

The art of hooking rugs has been highly developed in North America. It is thought that the tradition was first established in French Canada and made its way to the American colonies. It doesn't really matter. Hooked rugs and their makers are here to stay, and everyone wishes them well. Few of those made in the past or in the present are true masterpieces of a fine arts sort, but they are colorful and sometimes inspired floor coverings.

Early American examples often employ primitive animal or floral designs of considerable charm. These are most copied today in wool or cotton. Hookers, pardon the expression, ply their craft almost every-where. If you stop by a needlework shop or visit a country fair, you might just discover a regional artist at work.

And if the craft interests you as a possible avocation, look into some of the excellent design and supply catalogues which service the veritable "industry" of home craftsmen.

Louise Hunter Zeiser's illustrated price list and cata-logue of heirloom rug designs is now into its third printing. Between her designs and those of such other artists as Caroline C. Saunders and Margaret Macken-zie, there are over 500 patterns to choose from. Many of these are illustrated.

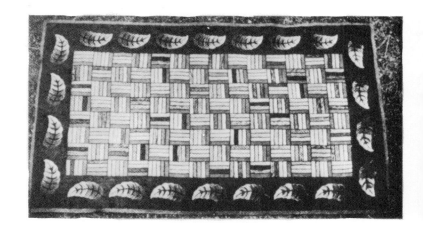

Catalogue and price list available, $1.

Heirloom Rugs
28 Harlem Street
Rumford, R.I. 02916

The Ernest Treganowan firm offers several hand-hooked rugs for those of us who are all fingers. Several of these, as per the illustration, are worked in old patchwork-quilt designs.

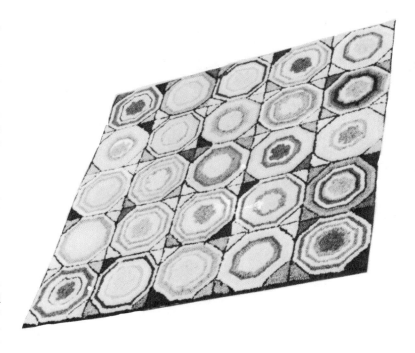

Ernest Treganowan, Inc.
49 East 53rd Street
New York, N.Y. 10022

The Henry Ford Museum has arranged for the reproduction of some of the best American patterns. These are exact reproductions of hooked rugs used in Greenfield Village buildings and stenciled designs originated by Edward Sands Frost. A Maine tin peddler, Frost was a truly inspired craftsman. The stencils he used are now owned by the Henry Ford Museum.

Mountain Rug Mills produces adaptations for the museum. One of the Frost designs is illustrated here. These are made to order.

Prices quoted on request; literature available.

Henry Ford Museum and Greenfield Village
20900 Oakwood Blvd.
Dearborn, Mich. 48121

Indian Rugs

No immigrant American has yet to match a native American in rug making skill. Design, use of color, handling of wool, hand weaving—all elements are almost unconsciously mastered. It is perhaps the use of natural materials—wool cut from family sheep and goats, vegetal dyes made from brush, blackberry, etc.—which accounts for the felicitous results. Among the best are achieved by members of the Navajo tribes of the Southwest.

Chapulin offers a handsome selection of Navajo-woven rugs. Some of these are geometrics of stunning color and composition. Others, such as the Two Grey

Hills weaves, are most subdued works of art. Other particularly beautiful rugs from part of the Storm Patterns series and are made near the Grand Canyon.

The Two Grey Hills series of designs are also available in fine weaves for use as wall hangings. The other heavy woven rugs are also candidates for the art gallery.

Catalogue available, $1.

Chapulin
Route 1, Box 187
Santa Fe, N.M. 87501

Needlepoint Rugs

These are almost as fine a floor covering, if not finer, than the most sumptuous of Chinese carpets. For a grand eighteenth-century residence in the Georgian style, they are virtually indispensable. Antique rugs of this type still appear from time to time, but reproduction designs are also available. It is hard to set a price on a fine original; the reproductions are nearly as priceless.

Ernest Treganowan markets the Tregmaid needlepoint rugs in sizes ranging from 3′ x 5′ to 18′ x 33′. These are produced by hand, of course, and are made in Europe. They are of fine wools and employ traditional eighteenth and early nineteenth-century motifs. Two of the extraordinary designs are the Diana and the Huguenot.

Other Sources of Flooring and Floor Coverings

Consult the List of Suppliers for addresses.

Carpets and Rugs

Decorative Carpets, Inc.
Designer Floors
Dildarian, Inc.
Greeff Fabrics
S. M. Hexter Co.
Charles W. Jacobsen
Marvin Kagan, Inc.
Kenmore Carpet Corp.
Kent-Costikyan, Inc.
Phyllis Morris Originals
Nahigian Bros., Inc.
Oriental Rug Exchange
Persian Carpet Gallery
Reed Wallcovering, Inc.
Rittenhouse Carpet, Inc.
F. Schumacher & Co.

Ceramic Flooring

American Olean Tile Co.
Country Floors
Designer Floors
Parma Tile Mosaic & Marble Co., Inc.

Stone Flooring

Carrara Marble Co. of America, Inc.
Friedman Marble & Slate Works, Inc.
New York Marble Works
Vermont Marble Co.

Vinyl Flooring

Fraser Gold Carpet Corp.
Kentile, Inc.
Signature Floors, Inc.

Wood Flooring

The 18th-Century Co.
William J. Erbe Co., Inc.
Nassau Flooring Corp.
New York Flooring
I. Peiser Floors Inc.
I. J. Peiser's Sons, Inc.
Townsend Paneling

Chandelier, bronze and gold, designed by
Thomas Hope, English, c. 1800.

VI   Lighting

Proper lighting of a period interior is at least as important as suitable furnishing. It is, unfortunately, a factor often left for last—when the electrician wants to know where outlets should be placed. By then, plastering may have been finished. The options left for the homeowner may be few in number, unless he is willing to rip apart extensive structural work. Think about lighting before beginning any sort of redecoration or restoration work. Take an inventory of your present lamps and other fixtures. Where would they be appropriate? How easily can they be accommodated without exposing a horrendous mass of wires?

In planning for the lighting of an interior, remember also that the sun may perform a useful function during the day. The lamp in the picture or bow window may perform glowingly at night, but why block the view during the day? The amount of natural light which enters a room during a typical sunny day will, of course, determine to a large degree the number or intensity of the artificial fixtures which are installed. A good rule is that propounded by many modern designers—less is more. Allow for shadow and the play of light. While you don't want to go stumbling around a room, better that you find the right mixture of soft illumination than be bathed in an unflattering glare.

Ever since the introduction of the incandescent bulb in 1879, the number and variety of electric lighting devices have steadily increased. It is perhaps time to return to basics, time to retire the plastic, "crystal-like" dewdrop chandelier, the butter churn floor lamp. True antique classics of the pre-electric age are hard to find these days and command high prices. Such appropriate fixtures for electric adaptation as brass English candlestands and French tole lamps are beyond the reach of most collectors today. Fortunately, a healthy and imaginative reproduction industry has developed in recent years, producing handsome and fitting lighting fixtures. Working with such traditional and varied forms as the cast-iron chandelier, tin sconce, brass candlestick, cut-glass globe, and Tiffany shade, the craftsmen of the reproduction lighting firms can offer almost any kind of fixture. The recent introduction of dimmers, low wattage bulbs, and thin flexible plastic wiring has made possible a more subtle use of light, a more sophisticated approach to establishing a proper mood or atmosphere.

For the adventuresome and/or romantic, however, there is no more suggestive a lighting form than the old one. Don't forget the candle, the kerosene burner, the gas torch, particularly in these energy-cost-conscious days. These primitive and truly authentic ways of dispelling the dark can be employed most effectively and easily.

Late Gothic candlestick, brass, Flemish 1450-1500.

Antique Lighting Fixtures

Antiques dealers everywhere handle some form of lighting devices, if only candlesticks, sconces, candelabra, and chandeliers. A few specialize in very fine, early open lamps and closed, oil-burning containers. Among the specially recommended antiquarians are:

Axtell Antiques, 1 River Street, Deposit, N.Y. 13754
Jerome W. Blum, Ross Hill Road, Lisbon, Conn. 06351
Florence Maine, 113 W. Lane (Rte. 35), Ridgefield, Conn. 06877
Mrs. Eldred Scott, The Riven Oak, Birmingham, Mich. 48012

Among auction houses offering fine antique lighting fixtures are:

Richard A. Bourne Co., Inc., Corporation Street, Hyannis, Mass. 02601
Robert W. Skinner, Inc., Bolton, Mass. 01740
Richard W. Withington, Inc., Hillsboro, N.H. 03244

Brass Gas Chandelier

The Gilletts have a fine selection of authentic lighting devices appropriate for late nineteenth-century interiors. This gas chandelier has been electrified but re-

tains its antique glass. The brass work is particularly fine. The specialty of Gillett Restorations is Victorian restoration and renovation work. They are in the midst of moving their stock from Massachusetts to Arizona, but can be contacted at the address below through 1977.

Gillett Restorations
c/o Suite 420
3550 N. Central Avenue
Phoenix, Ariz. 85012

Kerosene Hall Lamp

A brass hanging lamp for a front hallway, this Victorian lighting device would suit almost any interior from the 1870s through 1900. It is the real thing with etched hobnail glass. The burner is a Miller, and the device dates from c. 1890. It is available from Gillett Restorations.

For further information and prices on this and other Victorian lamps, in their stock, contact Gillett Restorations.

Gillett Restorations
c/o Suite 420
3550 N. Central Avenue
Phoenix, Ariz. 85012

Late Victorian and Early Twentieth-Century Chandeliers

Gargoyles, Ltd., of Philadelphia, is a good place to contact if you are looking for early electric fixtures, shades and all. They have a number of varieties available in brass of American, French, and English origin.

Catalogue available, $4.

Gargoyles Ltd.
512 S. Third St.
Philadelphia, Penn. 19147

Candelabras

Fine reproduction candelabras are expensive, but not as far out of reach as the brass and silver originals on which they are modeled. A four- or six-branch candelabra can serve as a fine centerpiece for a suitably large dining table; plunked down on the family grand piano, it becomes only a Liberace-style piece of kitsch. Few early or nineteenth-century Americans possessed such sophisticated items. If you are fortunate enough to be able to afford one or more of these most elegant appurtenances, go only to the finest silver dealers or a reputable reproduction manufacturer.

Brass Candelabras

Heavy solid brass two-, four-, six-, and twelve-branch candelabra are available from Baldwin. Bases are circular, and shafts are simply sculpted. Each carries a center holder. These are part of the Georgetown Collection.

Prices—two-branch, $16.50 to $85 for polished brass, $75 to $100 for antiqued brass; four-branch, $55 to $90 for polished brass, $65 to $110 for antiqued brass; twelve-branch, $150 in polished brass and $185 in antiqued brass.

Brochure and price list available.

Baldwin Hardware Manufacturing Corp.
841 Wyomissing Blvd.
Reading, Penn. 19603

Candles

Everyone appreciates candlelight. Blinded in offices and on the streets by high-intensity lighting, we enjoy the welcome relief that candles bring to the home atmosphere. Although the use of such soft, flattering light can be overdone (especially when combined with the less than exotic scents being pushed today in ye olde candle shoppes), candles are both appropriate and comely, in eighteenth and nineteenth-century settings.

Sources for quality tapers are found almost everywhere. Suppliers are not listed here because of the ease of finding the ubiquitous candle in most stores. Be sure, however, that the candles are of the dripless variety. Museum stores and fine gift shops are often well-equipped with beeswax candles and the ever-popular bayberry tapers. If you choose bayberry, be certain that they are real and not merely scented; the latter provide a rather nauseous odor. The type of fixture in which the candle is to be used, of course, determines the size of the taper needed.

In this period of how-to-do-it craftsmanship, candlemaking has become a popular pastime. Kits are available in almost every hobby shop.

A new height in professional candlelighting has been reached with the use of electronic and battery-operated substitutes. In the long run these devices may save you money, and certainly effort.

CIMA Electronic Candle

Imported from Sweden, these extraordinary products of the electronic age fit in well with period interiors. Used in *The Adams Chronicles* on educational television and in Ingmar Bergman's film version of *The Magic Flute*, they have passed many tests of authenticity. Both electronic and battery-operated candles and flames or bulbs are available directly from the Bohemia, New York, warehouse. They vary in size from 3″ to 12″. What makes them particularly unique is that the units simulate a burning wax candle both in appearance

and light by a flame that seems to move. The bulb is replaceable and is of 3 watts. The candle operates on 110V AC. The battery-operated candles are especially good for non-wired fixtures, although electronic candles are available for these, too. The company provides, as well, a recharger for the battery-operated devices.

Flames and candles are ordered separately. The price for each of five electronic candle styles is $17; flames are $2. Battery candles are offered at $10 and $13; flames are $2. The battery rechargers are $95 and $125.

Brochure available.

U.S. Cimaco Corporation
40 Orville Drive
Bohemia, New York 11716

The Starlite, Natural Beeswax Electric Candle

Many of America's major museums, including The Henry Francis du Pont Winterthur Museum, make use of Starlite electric candles in their period rooms. In appearance they can be mistaken for real tapers because they are handdripped to show the true effect of a burning candle of the non-dripless variety. Beeswax is used in the wax coating, and either a pure gold or a creamy white color finish is available. Thin plastic flexible wire leads project from the bottom of the stick for attachment to the main wires through the holder itself. The Starlite candles use Candle Wick bulbs of 3 watts which operate at 6 volts. An adapter is necessary to use the two elements, and this is available from the manufacturer. It is a small unit and can be plugged directly into the nearest outlet or be placed within the wall or ceiling. Any number of candlelights can be used with the one adapter.

Prices and brochure available.

The Electric Candelight Company, Inc.
1 Chelmsford Street
Chelmsford, Mass. 01824

Candlestands

Candlestand with Screen

This device may not produce a brilliant light, but it will be a flattering one. That was the idea in early

nineteenth-century England. The candlestand and screen are hand-painted tin. The stand is decorated in antique black and deep green; the screen, in antique gold. It stands 16¼" high and contains a base for holding small candle matches, a removable candleholder, and removable extinquisher.

This is one of the fine reproductions produced by Sarreid Ltd. for the Henry Ford Museum and Greenfield Village.

Price, $102.

Henry Ford Museum and Greenfield Village
20900 Oakwood Blvd.
Dearborn, Mich. 48121 or

Uniquities
Marketplace
2400 Market St.
Philadelphia, Penn. 19103

Iron Candlestands

The village smith has reappeared in recent years, an individual who thoroughly enjoys and excels at producing hand-forged, custom-made items. Stephen Parker is such a craftsman. He has four different candlestand or candleholder models to choose from and invites customers to submit their own designs and specifications. The iron Hudson Valley candleholder

ker-designed objects, this is a versatile piece. The candle platform which holds one taper can be positioned to rest over the front leg of the stand when in use, thereby adding some extra stability. But if one wishes to remove it from the table when not in use, it can be hung flat against the wall by aid of the hook on the end and by simply moving the platform over the side legs.

Hudson Valley candlestand with finial, $100; without, $90. Shaker table candlestand, $40.

Catalogue available, $1.
Stephen Winslow Parker, Blacksmith
Mill Village
Craftsbury Common, Vt. 05826

has an adjustable platform which holds two tapers. This copy of an early 1700s piece comes with a finial if you wish, and stands 5 feet high. Its width is 20 inches at candle platform. Another unusual stand is the Shaker table candlestand only 1 foot high. As with other Sha-

Candlesticks

The simple candlestick is such a common object that it hardly seems a proper means of illumination. At the dining room table, placed on a candlestand (see furniture, p. 167), poised on the mantel, it can provide a cheerful presence and sufficient light to dispel the gloom of nightfall. It, almost alone among early lighting devices, is still somewhat practical. Few people today are about to fuss with betty lamps, crusies, and other primitive artifacts, however authentic or fitting they may be.

Available in sizes as small as 1½", and as large as a foot and a half, sticks are (and were) made of wood, glass, pewter, silver, iron, brass, porcelain, pottery, and other materials.

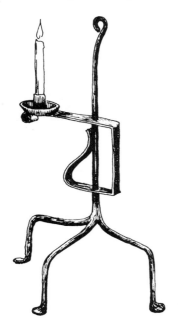

Brass Candlesticks

Seven solid brass candlesticks are available from Period, each expertly cast. Especially handsome is the Newport, 9¾" high with an octagonal base and faceted shaft in the Queen Anne style. Other available forms are the Cathedral, 12"; a spike candlestick, 7"; a middrip candlestick, 8½"; and a beehive candlestick, 7", 10", or 12"—all of these with circular bases. The Governor's Palace stick, 8½" high, is similar to that offered by other suppliers, with an incurved, circular base.

Newport, $34.50 each; other sticks, from $13.50 to $62.50 each.

Catalogue,$2, and price list available.

Period Furniture Hardware Co., Inc.
123 Charles Street
Boston, Mass. 02114

Brass Candlesticks, James River and Georgetown Collections

Brass sticks of almost every variety in the Colonial style form part of these two fine collections from Baldwin. Simple, direct, sturdy, they are among the few "antique" objects made today which could become heirlooms tomorrow. The James River objects, named for brass artifacts found in the stately homes of Virginia, vary in size from 4¼" to 13" in height. Styles are those of the seventeenth and eighteenth centuries with circular, square, and octagonal bases. The Georgetown collection is more extensive and includes a candle cup, chambersticks, and tiny candlesticks no more than 3" high as well as large sticks 18" high appropriate for the banquet table. The same range of styles is available.

Georgetown Collection: Prices range from $3 for the candle cup in polished brass and $4 in antique brass to $125 for a pair of polished brass, 18" sticks or $145 in antique brass.

James River Collection: Prices range from $20 for the Burgess candlestick, 5¾", in polished brass, to $50 for the Old Dominion candlestick, 13", in polished brass.

Baldwin objects may be purchased at gift shops and department stores throughout the United States or may be ordered directly from the manufacturer.

Brochures and price lists available.

Baldwin Hardware Manufacturing Corp.
841 Wyomissing Blvd.
Reading, Penn. 19603

Glass Candlesticks

Glass candlesticks are particularly decorative lighting fixtures. The South Jersey stick, a reproduction of a mid-nineteenth century piece in the Philadelphia Museum of Art, would look striking on a table or set in the window to catch the light. The colors are cobalt blue and the famed South Jersey light green. Free-blown by the Liberty Village craftsmen of Flemington, New Jersey, it measures 5¾" high.

The sticks are $32 each or $64 for the pair.

Catalogue available.

The Museum Shop
Philadelphia Museum of Art

P.O. Box 7646
Philadelphia, Penn. 19101

Pewter Candlesticks

Among the most handsome museum reproduction objects offered today is the Roswell Gleason pewter candlestick. An American pewterer, Gleason worked in Dorchester, Massachusetts, between 1830 and 1840. The shape is extremely simple, featuring a circular base and deep socket with a wide drip pan. The reproduction is 6½″ high.

Price, $40.

Catalogue available.

Museum Shop
Museum of Fine Arts
Boston, Mass. 02115

Pottery, China, and Pewter Candlesticks

A wide variety of handsome candlesticks are available from Colonial Williamsburg's Craft House and stores authorized to carry Williamsburg reproductions (see p. 234). Among the most interesting are the delft sticks of the mid-eighteenth century which have been reproduced by Oud Delft of Nijmegen, Holland. One stands 2½″ high and the other 7″. Each is handpainted. The Stieff Company of Baltimore, Maryland, produces pewter sticks for Williamsburg. A heavy, octagonal stick of seventeenth-century derivation, 9″ high, has all the marks of substance and elegance. The Jamestown pottery candlestick is copied after an original found in the lost colony of the very early seventeenth century. It is almost Scandinavian modern in feeling and comes in yellow glaze with brown decoration; height is 6″.

Delft sticks—2½″, $13.45 each, $25 pair; 7″, $33.45 each, $65 pair.

Pewter sticks, $71.20 each; $140 pair.

Pottery sticks, $5.95 each.

Catalogue available, $2.95, from:

Colonial Williamsburg distributor or

Craft House
Colonial Williamsburg
Williamsburg, Va. 23185

Chandeliers

Among the most graceful of lighting fixtures, suspended from the ceiling or from beams, chandeliers of every type are available today. Nearly all are handmade if not custom-crafted copies of museum originals. Most are electrified. The splatter of hot candle wax in a bowl of soup can discourage even the most dedicated antique buff. Dripless candles, however, have enabled the antiquarian to indulge his enthusiasm for the past with more ease of mind. But the real thing still can be messy and expensive to keep supplied.

Primitive tin, iron, and part wood chandeliers add a pleasant addition to the country kitchen or dining room as well as the hallway. Ceilings, however, must be sufficiently high to allow for their proper display and sufficient clearance for today's taller generations. Well clear of the ceiling and of any looming heads, an appropriate hanging fixture adds another dimension to a room's furnishings. Victorian home owners will find it easier to hang more elaborate brass and cut-glass chandeliers since room heights were generally much greater during the nineteenth century.

A chandelier can be a big investment. Be certain that you know exactly where you want it up before ordering the fixture. And be sure that it can be properly wired in the ceiling or beam, hung without bringing plaster or wood down with it, and that it is supplied with sufficient chain and a canopy.

Charleston Gas Chandelier

If you want a superb reproduction for your Victorian-style residence, learn more about King's six-armed brass chandelier. It is expensive, but the company's customers (whose testimonials are scattered through the catalogue) say that the workmanship is more than equal to the cost. The Charleston has decorative gas cut-offs, tooled middle band, and tooled shade holders. The shades are of frosted glass. The prisms are cut in the Waterford manner and are hung with eighteen strands of graduated crystal buttons. The chandelier measures approximately 34" wide and 36" long.

Price, $825.

Catalogue available, $1.

King's Chandelier Company
P.O. Box 667
Eden, N.C. 27288

Imported Cut-Crystal Chandelier

Crystal chandeliers now adorn the most improbable places—the lobbies of modern apartment buildings, automobile showrooms, the ladies' powder room. They do belong in the home, too, and once lit the rooms of the affluent from San Francisco to Portland, Maine. When not weighted with an excess of gimmickry, they can impart a light, glimmering beauty to either a Colonial or Victorian interior of proper dimensions. This classically designed five-branched chandelier is so executed. It is made of hand-cut crystal throughout and

has imported Swedish-type pendelogues and cut streamers. It has a 22" spread and is completely electrified.
Retail price is $78.50.

Catalogue and price list available.
Luigi Crystal
7332 Frankford Avenue
Philadelphia, Penn. 19136

The New Bedford Whaler

Although better suited to a ship cabin, this reproduction of an eighteenth-century tin chandelier with reflectors suits the needs of informal, period decoration. In a room featuring marine antiques and objects, it would be most suitable. It is available electrified or for candles, and in bright tin or black finishes; the reflectors are available only in bright tin—as is appropriate. The electrified model includes real wax sleeves. It measures 14" high, 24" wide, and is available with a 20" chain. If this length is not sufficient, the customer should specify the total number of inches required.

Price for electrified, $130; for candles, $110.

Catalogue and price list available.
The Essex Forge
77 Main Street
Essex, Conn. 06426

Rosario Wrought Iron Chandelier

Wrought-iron fixtures in the Spanish tradition are the specialty of Mexico House. Now in its 100th year, this

lighting device which was economically feasible in the seventeenth and eighteenth centuries in America. For devotees of naive folk art, of early tinware, this is a most handsome object for the dining room or country kitchen. It is 13″ high and has a spread of 26″. It is also available as a double-cone piece. It is ready for use as an electrical device.

Standard model, $85; double-cone model, $95.

Catalogue available.

The Saltbox
2229 Marietta Pike
Rohrerstown, Penn. 17603

firm prides itself on continuing the handmade traditions brought to the New World starting with the conquest of Mexico by Cortez. The Rosario is a particularly elegant six-branch piece decorated with leaves and curlicues. It measures 25″ in diameter, is 17″ high, and weighs 10 lbs., and is electrified. The maker can also fashion the chandelier in white wrought iron, a finish traditional in the Southeastern United States and in such tropical climes as the Bahamas.

Price, $48.95.

Catalogue available, $1.

Mexico House
Del Mar, Calif. 92014

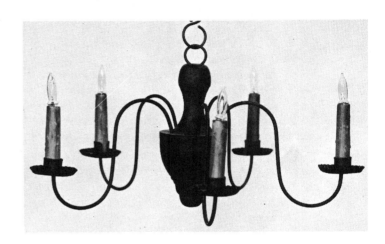

Wood Center Chandelier

Here is a simple, turned wood center chandelier with five arms, each of metal with crimped drip pans and shallow sockets. The "candles," as with other handcrafted chandeliers, are dripped and tapered. The fixture is supplied with a ceiling canopy (painted to match), crossbar, hook, and handmade chain measured to whatever length is desired. Two color finishes are available, old red or green, or this model can be supplied with a stained center and plished brass arms and bobeche. The fixture is 10″ high and 21″ in diameter.

Painted, $95; stained center with brass parts, $135.

Catalogue, $2, with sample finishes and price list.

Gates Moore
River Road, Silvermine
Norwalk, Conn. 06850

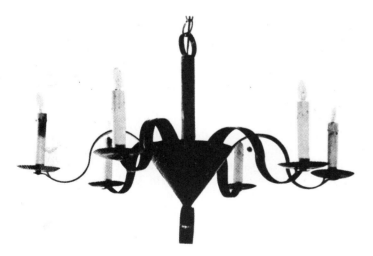

Tin Chandelier

This primitive, six-branch tin chandelier is handcrafted to duplicate in every respect the kind of starkly simple

Lamps

Lamps are a relatively new category in lighting. Thomas Jefferson and other late eighteenth-century tinkerers played with various inventions, but it was not until the 1830s and 40s that such devices with burners were used at all widely in the American home. The introduction of new fuels—whale oil, and later, kerosene—made possible the development of glass, brass, and china lamps. Thousands of different kinds of burners and wick tubes were patented, each offering a different measure of safety and convenience.

Among the most famous and accomplished of lamp manufacturers was the Boston & Sandwich Glass Company. Their pressed and molded lamps have been collector's items for many years. Competition among lamp makers, however, was fierce and healthy. By the time of the Centennial, kerosene had replaced other fuels such as whale oil and lard oil, and simple glass containers were being produced by the hundreds of thousands each year. It is still relatively simple to find these clear glass fixtures in antique and junk shops, for their production lasted well into the electric age. And it is just as easy to adapt them for use as modern lamps with the replacement of the burner (if still attached) by an electric adapter.

The ease in which early lamps are adapted for electrical use has led to some unusual results. Electrified butter churns and spinning wheels are regularly offered by various outlets as "authentic" reproductions of period lighting devices. Coffee pots, milk funnels, coffee mills, candle molds—nothing is too ludicrous for the kitsch purveyor or home craftsman. As Count Rumsford wrote in 1812, "What vast sums are expended in dispelling the obscurity of the night in every house furnished with antiques, and yet in what a deplorable state is the taste which ought to enhance all the details of that important operation." Plus ça change, plus c'est la meme chose.

Brass Desk Lamp

Lamps of this sort can be used for more than study purposes; they are handy for the bedside as well as on the piano. The turned brass is extremely handsome, a mellow tone which blends well with wood appointments. One arm holds a socket which is made to resemble a candle, and which burns a 15-watt bulb. The other arm carries the fittings for an oil betty lamp. The latter touch, however, is merely decorative as the arm does not come with a drip saucer or wick. This lamp is also available with a standard socket fitting

rather than the 15-watt fitting. The base is weighted. Height is 21″ and the width, 15″. Also available non-electrified.

Electrified, $90; non-electrified, $80.

Catalogue available, $1.

Hurley Patentee Manor
R.D. 7, Box 98A
Kingston, N.Y. 12401

Delft Polychrome Lamp

Vases and jars can make superb bases for table lamps. Although there is no way in which the lamp itself can be authentic, such fixtures are fitting and useful. Ginger jars featuring oriental motifs are among the most popular and attractive of such forms; so, too, are the heavy stoneware jugs which were turned out by the hundreds of thousands during the nineteenth century. The base of this Colonial Williamsburg china lamp is hand-painted and is designed after an apothecary jar. It is creamy white with polychrome trim in blues and golds. The wood stand is of dark mahogany and the shade is off-white silk piped in gold. The lamp stands 27½″ high.

Price, $149.

Catalogue available, $2.95, from:

Craft House
Colonial Williamsburg
Williamsburg, Va. 23185

Flower Garden Hanging Lamp

Julia Dent Grant, the General's wife, would surely have approved of this hanging lamp decorated with roses, cornflowers, and daisies. It is meant to be hung from the ceiling in the parlor, and comes with cut glass prisms and a smoke bell. The fixture is electrified. The manufacturer also has two table lamps in the same Flower Garden design. The metal banding is of satin bronze.

Price, $179.95.

Catalogue available.
Magnolia Hall
726 Andover
Atlanta, Ga. 30327

Gas Post Lamps

Welsbach has been an important supplier of street lighting fixtures since the early 1900s. Today it continues as a pioneer in the reproduction field—especially of gas-lit and early electric fixtures. Such designs as

the Victorian are available as a working gas fixture or as an electrified incandescent lamp. An examination

of Welsbach's literature will introduce one to a whole new world of public and private lighting. The company supplies superb pier bases, posts, and post accessories as well.

Literature available.

Welsbach Lighting Products Co., Inc.
3001 E. Madison St.
Baltimore, Md. 21205

Glass-Base Lamps

Glass bases, of the crystal and pressed variety, made their appearance when a burner was perfected for the kerosene lamp. Among the most inexpensive and practical for use today are the kerosene bases found in junk shops. As suggested before, these can be fitted with an adapter. Nothing, however, can match the elegance of a lead crystal base lamp such as those offered by Frederick Cooper. They reflect light with unusual brilliance. Cooper also has one of the finest selections of porcelain-base and wood urn-base table lamps in North America.

For further information, contact:

Frederick Cooper
2545 West Diversey Avenue
Chicago, Ill. 60647

The Spicebush

Available as a hanging lamp or post light, the solid copper Spicebush model is a simple and striking fixture appropriate for Colonial and nineteenth-century interiors and exteriors. The design is an original one with the proprietor of the Washington Copper Works, proof that the art of the craftsman has not disappeared altogether from the American scene. There are four different styles available of this hexagonal, handcrafted lantern, ranging in size from 13″ to 16″ high and 8½″ to 9½″ wide. The model intended for use on a post comes with a glass chimney and post housing, but does not include the post itself; it ranges in size from 17″ high and 9½″ wide to 21″ high and 11½″ wide. The guard bars are entwined in either a horizontal or spiral fashion. The cone top can either be a flat, round one or a pointed, conical shape. The fixtures are completely electrified and available for use with a 75-watt bulb or a 5″ Durolite bulb. There is a choice between three different finishes: shiny copper, dark oxidized copper, and natural-cleaned with normal copper discolorations.

Hanging lanterns, from $74 to $88; post lanterns, $115 and $125.

Brochure and price list available.
The Washington Copper Works
South Street
Washington, Conn. 06793

Gone With the Wind Lamp

Shades of the past, indeed. The lamp made famous by Scarlett O'Hara is almost as popular today as when reintroduced in 1939. Ironically, Scarlett possessed a model that was not available until well after the War Between the States. No trimming of wicks, however, for this model has become completely electrified. Both the upper and lower globes, each hand-painted, will glow with light. The background color is gold with flowers in beige, brown, and greens. The key-switch remains in place but is purely a decorative touch. The metal trimmings are brass finished.

Price, $59.95.

Catalogue available.
Magnolia Hall
726 Andover
Atlanta, Ga. 30327

Turn-of-the-Century Lamp

This lamp is one of many manufactured by Aladdin for use electrically or with kerosene. Many old house devotees will find such a fixture especially practical for use inside and outside—for instance, on a terrace in summer. These are extremely well-made, sturdy lamps with brass or chrome-finished bowls. The glass shades come in a standard form, white, champagne, green, and painted with dogwood, violets, or roses. The metal shade holders are heavy and will not bend out of shape with normal use. The fixture is equipped with an Aladdin kerosene mantle burner which will produce the equivalent of 100 watts of steady light. It will operate for 50 hours on 1 gallon of kerosene.

There are three combination kerosene and electric lamps available in brass finish, solid brass, or silcrom ranging in price from $70 to $90 depending on the type of shade desired. The kerosene-only lamps are priced from $6l to $79.

Brochure and price list available.

Faire Harbour Boats
44 Captain Peirce Road
Scituate, Mass. 02066

Lanterns

What kind of lantern did Paul Revere view in the tower of Old North Church and carry with him on his ride? No one will ever know for sure. Ever since his time, however, the lantern has been a particular American favorite in legend and fact. It appears in 101 different forms. In Norman Rockwell's classic Saturday Evening Post *covers it provided light for such diverse country affairs as the county fair, Halloween shenanigans, and the doctor's emergency midnight visit. Of course there is also the famous kerosene barn-lantern kicked over by Mrs. O'Leary's cow. Today the lantern is most often to be found atop a post, lighting the way from road to front door.*

The lantern is the most versatile of lighting devices. It can be carried, hung, affixed to almost any sort of surface, or simply left standing on a table or stand. Most lanterns are enclosed on all sides as they are designed for use inside and outside, crafted to burn effectively under the most adverse conditions. All, however, are vented in some manner, and most models are built with one panel that can be opened for changing of the light source.

Reproduction lanterns of all sizes, shapes, and forms are available. Look for those which are sturdily built and which provide easy handling. Too many of such devices are designed with handles that heat up as rapidly as the wax or electricity they burn. Others are simply flimsy and weather badly when used outside.

It is made of solid brass, and measures 19″ high by 8¾″ wide. The weight is only 10 lbs. The three candelabra sockets will hold bulbs burning up to 60 watts each. 10-watt bulbs might be quite sufficient. The fixture comes with 10″ of chain.

Price, $98.

Catalogue, $1, available.

Heritage Lanterns
Sea Meadows Lane
Cousins Island
Yarmouth, Me. 04096

Elliptical Lantern

An Empire-style lighting device, this is a reproduction produced by Sarreid Ltd. for the Henry Ford Museum and Greenfield Village. Of French origin, c. 1825, it would be an appropriate fixture for either a late Colonial or early Victorian interior. The lantern is of hand-pierced tin, hand-painted, with handmade

The Beacon Hill

For use indoors in a suitably proportioned entry or hallway, The Beacon Hill would enhance a town house or individual dwelling house. This is a particularly light, sophisticated fixture befitting a high-style setting.

painted with four coats of black lacquer. The overall height of the fixture is 12½"; the body size is 7" high by 5" square.

Price and brochure available upon inquiry.

Village Lantern
598 Union Street
N. Marshfield, Mass. 02059

latches and hinges. It is painted in a very dark blue with an earth-red interior.

Priced at $118.

Further information available from several sources, including:

Henry Ford Museum and Greenfield Village
20900 Oakwood Blvd.
Dearborn, Mich. 48121

Uniquities
Marketplace
2400 Market St.
Philadelphia, Penn. 19103

Orleans Lantern

This is a particularly useful and popular lantern. It is meant for outdoor illumination and comes equipped with a wall bracket and a light bulb in place. The mirrors in the rear are split to diffuse the light. The material used is heavy pewter plate. The lanterns are

Pierced Tin Lantern

This may have been Paul Revere's colonial torch. It can be used with a candle or as an electric lamp. A true eighteenth-century form, it adds a cheerful note to an early American interior. More practically, it can also be used as a hanging fixture. A second model with an open bottom is also available from the maker. This will allow the light to be directed downward. The height of the regular model is 13″, and that of the open, 16″. Each is 5″ wide. If the fixture is to be hung, a chain and canopy will have to be ordered separately from the supplier.

Regular model, electrified, $20; for candle, $18. Open model, electrified, $22; for candle, $20.

Catalogue available, $1.
Hurley Patentee Manor
R.D. 7, Box 98A
Kingston, N.Y. 12401

Victorian Carriage Lantern

Marle Company has been in business since 1925 to satisfy the need for high quality lighting designs in copper and brass. Carriage lanterns made in the traditional Victorian style are available from many manufacturers; few are as well crafted as is this model. It is made of heavy pure brass with punty-cut plate glass, and is 36″ high by 8½″ wide, extending 12½″. Other sizes and styles are available on request.

Price, $300.

Catalogue and price list available.
Marle Company, Inc.
170 Summer Street
Stamford, Conn. 06901

Sconces

These simple fixtures can provide just the right amount of light in a hallway, above a fireplace, in the dining room above a sideboard. They are, of course, devices which attach to the wall. Most common are the flat tin candleholders which do not project very far from the surface. These are most often found with straight or crimped brackets which serve as reflectors of the light and deflect the heat from the wall itself. Sconces can, however, be rather elaborate affairs. The design to be used depends on the basic decor of the room or home in which they appear. Most of the reproduction sconces are fitted as electric fixtures. They can be ordered, however, as plain, candleburning pieces.

Carpenters' Hall Sconce

A large formal room in the Colonial or Federal style would be enhanced with use of this lighting device.

113

The original model is to be found today in Carpenters' Hall, Independence National Historical Park, Philadelphia. The hall is the one in which the First Continental Congress met in 1774 and was the home of one of America's first societies of carpenter-builders or architects. The reproduction is scaled down in size, but is true to the original in every detail. There are five separate mirrors which brilliantly reflect the light of the candle. Essex Forge, commissioned by the Company to reproduce the piece, offers only a non-electric model. It measures 17" high and 7½" wide and has an extension of 5½".

Priced at $45.

Catalogue and price list available.

The Essex Forge
77 Main Street
Essex, Conn. 06426

Pennsylvania Tulip Sconce

Pennsylvania-German designs have become too popular; today they are often rendered in a coy, cloying fashion. But not here. The sconce is unadorned, a pure

rendering of a legitimate and attractive period design. It might suit a "country" interior or a most sophisticated modern setting. This sconce, 7¼" high, 7" wide, and 6¾" deep, is made of solid brass. It is available electrified or

simply as a candle holder. Special finishes, at 15% additional to the regular price, are also supplied. One is antique pewter which ages well, and the other painted. Flat finish, enamel gloss, or antique glaze are available, and if sent a sample chip, fabric, or wallpaper, the manufacturer will do his best to match the shade.

Regular price for electrified fixtures, $30; 15% less for non-electrified.

Catalogue, $1.50, and price list available.
Authentic Designs
330 East 75th Street
New York, N.Y. 10021

Wrought-Iron Candle Sconce

A three-branch sconce in Spanish Colonial style would be a handsome addition in many homes. It is simply shaped and hand-crafted. Fourteen inches high by 17 inches wide, it extends 4 inches from the wall, and weighs four pounds.

Price, $10.95; $18 for two.

Catalogue available, $1.

Mexico House
Del Mar, Calif. 92014

Lighting Supplies

Lamps, both table and hanging, can be do-it-yourself propositions. Unlike many of the standard accessories of the old house, practical, attractive lighting fixtures can be fashioned by the home craftsman. *The simple glass kerosene lamp base, with the addition of an adapter and harp (available at most hardware stores) and a shade is one such, useful inexpensive alternative. There is no reason, however, why a kerosene lamp should not be employed in its original manner—at least outdoors. Burners, wicks, mantels, chimneys, and tripods are available today from a number of sources. In fact, it is possible to fashion your own glass shade in the Tiffany style if piecing together small pieces of stained glass will not fray your nerves.*

Candle Snuffers, Trays, Holders

The scissor-style snuffers offered today by many gift shops were intended originally for the trimming of wicks, a job made unnecessary by the modern wick which burns down with the candle. A simple, conical snuffer with a handle should suffice for extinguishing the flame. It is handy to have a tray on which to rest the snuffer. The Craft House makes and offers both in antique tin with or without a pewter finish, antique copper, or antique brass. The snuffer is 7¼" long, as is the tray. If many candles are used in the house, a holder for them is also a legitimate accessory. The Craft House offers one in the aforementioned materials which is, most sensibly, cylindrical in shape. A hand-pierced star design appears on the top and sides, and two 5" high wall brackets allow the piece to be hung properly. It measures 13" wide and 4½" in diameter.

Snuffer and tray: antique tin or pewter finish, $3.50; antique copper or brass, $6.20. Storage box: antique tin or pewter finish, $15; antique copper or brass, $25.

Brochure available.
Craft House
1542 Main Road
Tiverton, R.I. 02878

Chimneys, Burners, Wicks, Smoke Bells

Supplies for kerosene lighting can be found in many hardware stores. The best in the mail-order market are available from Faire Harbour Boats. Solid brass burners are priced as low as $3. Two different styles of chimneys are offered in base diameters ranging from 1⅛" to 2⅝". Heights vary in size from 3½" to 12". Prices range from 90 cents to $4. Wicks vary in size from ⅜" to 1½" flat or round, and in price from 25 cents to $1.25.

The smoke bell can be used with any kerosene-burning lamp placed overhead or against a wall. It is of solid brass and will fit any lamp, as the bell adjusts out to 7½" from the mounting surface.

Parts for Aladdin Mantle kerosene lamps distributed by such outlets as Faire Harbour Boats are listed and priced differently from the above.

Illustrated price list available.
Faire Harbour Boats
44 Captain Peirce Road
Scituate, Mass. 02066

Duro-Lite Bulbs

These are relatively inexpensive, effective ways in which to impart a soft glow to electric lighting fixtures, especially wall sconces and chandeliers. Among Duro-Lite's best products are the Candle Flame bulbs which are flame-shaped with a curved tip. They are 9-watt size and come in candelabra or medium bases. Another bulb, the Tini-Brite, is recommended for use in heavy crystal chandeliers. These are avilable in 15-, 25-, or 40-watt candelabra-size bases. Almost all Duro-Lite bulbs are available in electrical supply and hardware stores.

For further information, contact:
Duro-Lite Lamps, Inc.
17-10 Willow Street
Fair Lawn, N.J. 07410

Hurricane Shades

These simple glass cylinders are used most often in a decorative fashion. They are, however, rather practical devices to shield a candle flame from drafts or, when used outside, to ward away unwelcome breezes. A 1001 varieties are available in such lowly establishments as Woolworth's and Sears; they are five and dime period pieces. Tiffany carries crystal shades, but you needn't go that far. The Williamsburg shops feature a fine line of handsome pieces ranging in size from 9" to 17¾". They are available in clear, amethyst, amber, sapphire, and emerald colors.

Prices—9", $16.70; 14", $40; 17¾", $47.25.

Catalogue available, $2.95, from:
Colonial Williamsburg distributor, or

Craft House
Colonial Williamsburg
Williamsburg, Va. 23185

Tiffany-Style Shades and Bases

Scorned by the aristocrats of the antiques trade until recently, the original, striking creations of Louis Tiffany and his craftsmen are now priceless. Most appropriate for the turn-of-the-century interiors, they should be prized as gas-lit and electric lighting fixtures. Several manufacturers of reproduction shades and bases are now supplying attractive copies. Coran-Sholes Industries offers a Tiffany-style lamp base of antique brass, the shaft casted in a layered manner reminiscent of art nouveau design. They supply the harp, finial, and an 8-foot cord. The base with harp measures 23"; without harp, 14½". The base weighs 4 lbs. and is 9¼" wide.

Price, $30 plus shipping.

Brochure and price list available.

Coran-Sholes Industries
509 E. 2nd Street
South Boston, Mass. 02127

Many types of shades are available from Rainbow Art Glass, either in do-it-yourself kits or ready assembled. One attractive floor lamp carries a 22" diameter dome in amber or green background with red or dark green cathedral accents. If you are into soldering, you may want to buy the kit, available for $110, which includes glass pieces, copper foil, lead, brass, solder, illustrated instructions, and electrical parts with 3-foot chain, soldering flux, and antiquing solution. The ready-made dome retails for $298.

Brochure available.

Rainbow Art Glass Corp.
49 Shark River Road
Neptune, N.J. 07753

Tin Tinder Box

A tinder box was once a necessity; it can serve today as a suitable candleholder. Before matches were available, a fire steel was used to strike a flintstone, thereby creating a spark. The tinder, usually a charred piece of homespun, caught the spark and ignited a chip of wood. The candle, strategically placed in the center of the box, was then lit and used to light others. The metal disk is a "douter," a device used to extinquish

the tinder, and was kept inside the box. This black tin reproduction is modeled after an English device of the early eighteenth century and has a walnut handle. Henry Ford Museum and Greenfield Village have licensed Sarreid Ltd. to produce it.

Priced at $34.

Further information available from:

Henry Ford Museum and Greenfield Village
20900 Oakwood Blvd.
Dearborn, Mich. 48121 or

Uniquities
Marketplace
2400 Market St.
Philadelphia, Penn. 19103

Other Sources of Lighting Fixtures

Consult the List of Suppliers for addresses

Antique Lighting Fixtures

Nesle, Inc.
Joseph Richter, Inc.
Stansfield's Antique Lamp Shop
Charles J. Winston

Betty Lamps

Hurley Patentee Manor

Candelabra

Lester Berry
King's Chandelier Co.
Kenneth Lynch & Sons
Phyllis Morris Originals

Candleholders

Mexico House
G. W. Mount, Inc.
Stephen Winslow Parker, Blacksmith
The Saltbox
Sarreid, Ltd.
The Village Forge
The Washington Copper Works

Candlesticks

Cohasset Colonials
Gates Moore
Hurley Patentee Manor

116

Liberty Village
Wilson's Country House

Ceiling Fixtures

Farmington Craftsmen
Gargoyles Ltd.
Newstamp Lantern Co.

Chandeliers

Authentic Designs, Inc.
Baldwin Hardware Mfg. Corp.
Ball & Ball
Chapman Mfg. Co.
Cohasset Colonials
Colonial Tin Craft
Colonial Williamsburg
Frederick Cooper
Empress Chandeliers
Farmington Craftsmen
Heritage Lanterns
Hurley Patentee Manor
Newstamp Lantern Co.
The Village Forge
The Washington Copper Works
Wilson's Country House
World Imports

Floor Lamps

The Lamp Shop
Magnolia Hall
Phyllis Morris Originals
Rainbow Art Glass Corp.
The Village Forge

Gas Lamps

City Knickerbocker, Inc.
Georgia Lighting Supply Co.
Phyllis Morris Originals
Nesle, Inc.
Pilgrim Glass Corp.

Hall Lights

Ball & Ball
Frederick Cooper
Gates Moore
Newstamp Lantern Co.
The Saltbox
World Imports

Lanterns

Casella Lighting Co.
Colonial Williamsburg
Farmington Craftsmen

Gates Moore
Luigi Crystal
Marle Co.
The Saltbox
Village Lantern
The Washington Copper Works

Post Lanterns/Lights

American Lantern
The Essex Forge
Farmington Craftsmen
Gates Moore
Heritage Lanterns
Kenneth Lynch & Sons.
Marle Co.
Mexico House
Newstamp Lantern Co.
The Saltbox
Welsbach Lighting Products Co.

Sconces

Baldwin Hardware Mfg. Corp.
Ball & Ball
Cohasset Colonials
Colonial Williamsburg
Frederick Cooper
Farmington Craftsmen
Gates Moore
Heritage Lanterns
Hurley Patentee Manor
King's Chandelier Co.
Luigi Crystal
Mexico House
Phyllis Morris Originals
G. W. Mount, Inc.
Newstamp Lantern Co.
Wilson's Country House
World Imports

Shades/Domes

Farmington Craftsmen
J. & R. Lamb
Whittemore-Durgin Glass Co.

Table Lamps

Cleveland Lamp Co.
Cohasset Colonials
Georgia Lighting Supply, Inc.
Kieffer's Pacific
L & S Lighting Fixtures Co.
Magnolia Hall
Phyllis Morris Originals
Norman Perry, Inc.
Rainbow Art Glass Corp.
Sarreid, Ltd.
Virginia Metalcrafters

Drapery and tie back, family dining room, Bauer House, Austin,
Texas, now the home of the Chancellor, University of Texas.

VII Fabrics

Interior decoration is often considered to consist only of the selection of fabrics. At a time when furniture was not only upholstered but also slipcovered, this may have seemed to have been the case. Undoubtedly small fortunes were spent and made on plump pillows and overstuffed chairs and sofas. In the more sober 1970s, fabrics are being used with greater restraint and utility. They are viewed in light of their contribution to an overall decorative statement. In terms of period furnishings and old house styles, this approach makes a great deal of sense.

Many high-quality fabrics made from natural fibers are very expensive. You may find that the reupholstery of antique furniture, for instance, will have to be stretched out over a lengthy period of time. Certainly this economic scheme is preferable to one that substitutes appearance for long-lasting quality. This is not to say that synthetic fabrics are *verboten*, but rather that they should be used sparingly. This is a rule just as applicable to informal, country-style interiors as it is to formal, high-style surroundings.

Silk and cotton are the two materials used most frequently in highly-decorative Colonial and Victorian interiors. These may be employed in curtains or draperies, on furniture, in bed hangings and coverings, and for walls. Few old houses in North America were or are fitted out with fabric wall coverings, but these were used long before papers were available. Watered silk and velvet are not the only materials appropriate for this purpose; various printed cottons can be used in a limited way to good effect.

Homespun, muslin, and plain cottons are most often found in modest urban or country dwellings of the Colonial and Victorian periods. Many ye olde fabric shoppes do a land-office business in supplying curtains, spreads, and cloths which are merely cute and not in the least handsome. These should be avoided like the plague. Hours spent clipping a ridiculous ball fringe off pillow ticking curtains taught this writer one lesson in consumer protection. The fringe was not visible in the package.

Anyone even moderately skilled with a needle will find that making one's own curtains, other kinds of hangings, and seat and back covers for chairs can be an economical, if not pleasurable, task. Unpholstery, too, can be a skill worth developing on at least a modest scale. If needlework is not your forte, try to find an experienced needleworker who can do the work for you. Custom-made commercial products purchased from stores or shops are unduly expensive.

Most quality fabric manufacturers sell only to interior decorators and special retail outlets. This does not mean, however, that you cannot obtain their fabrics without struggling. Most of these are widely available in fine department stores, and the manufacturer can supply you with a list of such sources. A good decorator, of course, can be your best friend and should be consulted if the project in question requires an expertise that you do not possess.

Velvet draperies, great hall, Stan Hywet, Akron, Ohio.

Awnings

These are among the only fabrics used on the exterior of a house. They add a note of grace and perform a useful function during hot weather. The Canvas Awning Institute claims that awnings keep homes from eight to fifteen degrees cooler. The Astrup Co. is one of the quality manufacturers left in America, and they can produce almost any shape, color, or pattern of awning to fit your needs.

Literature available.

The Astrup Co.
2937 W. 25th St.
Cleveland, Ohio 44113

For the names of other manufacturers and of dealers, contact:

The Canvas Awning Institute, Inc.
1918 N. Parkway
Memphis, Tenn. 38112

Bed Coverings, Hangings, and Other Fabric Supplies

A true Colonial four-poster can be fitted with as many as four or five different fabric hangings. These are canopies, valances, side and back hangings, and dust ruffles. All are available ready-made today if the use of such fabrics is desired. Even the simplest antique or reproduction bed, however, is likely to make use of at least a quilt, coverlet, or spread. Antique coverings are to be preferred over reproductions, but considering the current craze for quilts and coverlets, they may be hard to come by. And having purchased such an expensive object, one is loath to use it as an everyday covering.

Patchwork Quilts

Appalachian Fireside Crafts makes a number of handsome patterns. Among the full-sized quilts are a Lone Star and a Log Cabin. A crib quilt is available in the traditional Nine-Patch pattern. A more modern design is the Barnyard quilt, illustrated here. All the quilts are

made of cotton and are Dacron filled. Several color combinations are available for each. The crib Nine-Patch is priced at $35; the Barnyard is $85. The many-pieced large Log Cabin is offered at $175; the Lone Star is $150.

Literature available.

Appalachian Fireside Crafts
Box 276
Booneville, Ky. 41314

Simpler patchwork quilts made of 4″ squares are available from two New England firms—The Pumpkin Patch and Country Curtains. Both offer them in sizes ranging from crib to king. Prices are similar, too—from $50 to $125.

Brochures are available from both sources.

The Pumpkin Patch
R. D. 1, Pumpkin Hollow Road
Great Barrington, Mass. 01230

and

Country Curtains
Stockbridge, Mass. 01262

Blankets and Spreads

Fine woolens used to come from New England. That industry is being revived by such firms as Harrisville Designs. A limited edition reproduction of an antique blanket will be issued each Fall. That offered in 1975 and illustrated here is a copy of one from the Merrimack Valley Textile Museum in North Andover,

Massachusetts. It measures 72″ x 60″ and is made of 100%-pure virgin wool. The yarn was spun at Harrisville Designs and the blankets woven at Homestead Woolen Mills in West Swanzey, New Hampshire. The basic color is a natural white against which indigo blue yarn has been woven. Price, $80 postpaid.

Literature available.

New Hampshire Blanket
Main Street
Harrisville, N.H. 03450

Bedspreads and blankets are among the specialties of Carol Brown. All of her fabrics are of the natural fiber variety. The spreads are made as prints, cords, and stripes in various colors and natural whites. Single cotton bedspreads start in price at $7.50

Brochure available.

Carol Brown
Putney, Vt. 05346

Hand-embroidered crewel bedspreads are included in Gurian's line of crewel products. Ranging from single to king size, they are priced from $70 to $100.

Brochure available with prices.

Gurian's
276 Fifth Ave.
New York, N.Y. 10001

Williamsburg bedspreads are made by Bates. There are three basic patterns available, the most handsome of which is the William and Mary. This is a copy of a late-seventeenth-century quilted coverlet and is made in snow white or antique white. Motifs worked in the border are of birds, animals, leaves, and plants. An over-all diamond pattern fills the center portion. Twin and double sizes are available. Twin, $96.75; double, $111.90.

Color samples available along with further information.

Craft House
Williamsburg, Va. 23185

Canopies, Ruffles, and Hangings

Covers for standard twin, double, and queen-size four-poster canopy beds are made by Country Curtains. These are made of unbleached muslin or perma-press fabric and are priced at $18 for twin or double and $20 for queen size. Dust ruffles in the same materials are also available.

Brochure available.

Country Curtains
Stockbridge, Mass. 01262

Fabrics particularly appropriate for use in bed hangings are supplied by Brunschwig & Fils. Illustrated is a reproduction eighteenth-century India chintz that is found in the nursery bedroom of the Stenton Mansion, Philadelphia, Pennsylvania. The original colors are indigo and white; there are four other combinations available. A related wallpaper may also be ordered.

For further information, contact:

Brunschwig & Fils, Inc.
979 Third Ave.
New York, N.Y. 10022

Two handsome shades of blue appear in the fine cotton valance, cover, dust ruffle, and window and

bed hangings used in a bedroom of the George Wythe House, Williamsburg. This is a resist-dyed fabric made by F. Schumacher & Co.

For further information, contact:

The Craft House
Williamsburg, Va. 23185

Curtains, Draperies, and Other Fabric Uses

The term "yard goods" is an old-fashioned way of referring to rolls of fabric, sold by the measure and used for sundry purposes around the house. A primary use of such printed and/or woven textiles is in window hangings. Few homes, new or old, are without some sort of curtains or draperies, for not only are they decorative accessories, but they provide protection from both the sun and the cold. It was once the practice to alternate summer and winter-weight curtains. Most home owners now feel fortunate to possess one set of handsome draperies for each room which will suit both purposes.

The hanging of curtains or draperies is an art in itself. Styles have changed dramatically over the years. Fabric-covered valances over the windows, for instance, were used in many late-Colonial interiors; they became popular again during the Colonial revival of the 1920s. Today they are considered much too fussy. In addition to valances there are also such extras as jabots and festoons, but these are appropriate to only very formal, high-style interiors. Even the average Victorian old house is an unlikely place to hang such decorative contrivances.

Many of the fabrics listed below, supplier by supplier, are, of course, suitable for other purposes. Some are appropriate for use as upholstery or for slipcovers. Others may even be applied as a wall covering in very elegant surroundings of the Colonial period. Still others are suitable for use as bed hangings, table coverings, and on small household objects.

Brunschwig & Fils

Chinoiserie Tree

From the Winterthur Collection comes this cotton print which is suitable for curtains and upholstery. It is seen

used on a wing chair and as window curtains in the Readbourne Stairhall at the Winterthur Museum. It has been reproduced from an English block-printed cotton, c. 1770-90, and is available in four color combinations.

Wickham Floral Stripe

A stenciled and painted "Indienne" border document, c. 1770, from the Valentine Museum, Richmond, Virginia, forms the basis for this handsome cotton-and-linen print. It has been reproduced in its original colors of madder red and indigo and is offered, as well, in green and gold, orange and blue, and brown and red. It is also available on chintz.

Chelsea

This is a glazed chintz printed in different colors. The design is an English one of considerable charm. It is an

appropriate fabric for early- and mid-Victorian interiors.

Homage of America

A cotton toile, this pattern was first printed in France in 1786 and is still made there by Brunschwig. It de-

123

picts a figure of the young American republic being congratulated on her new-found independence by friendly France.

Philadelphia Stripe

One of the oldest documented American printed textiles, c. 1775-1776, is available in a linen print copy by Brunschwig. It is available in four color combinations.

Bargello

This pattern makes use of the popular flame or Hun-

garian stitch in parallel zigzag patterns. It is available in a linen cloth. Among the color combinations are a very handsome plum and blue on cream.

For further information regarding these and other fabrics, contact:

Brunschwig & Fils, Inc.
979 Third Ave.
New York, N.Y. 10022

Historic Charleston Reproductions

Rainbow Row Taffeta, Charleston Pillement, and Santee Floral

Three Greeff fabrics are illustrated here. The first is a strie taffeta, 100% cotton available in twelve colors. In the middle is an Oriental design taken from the work of the French painter, Jean Pillement. It, too, is 100% cotton, and is offered in four color combinations. Santee Floral to the right features a design adapted from an eighteenth-century English hand embroidery. It is made of 73% spun rayon and 27% cotton.

Russell House Quilt

A patchwork quilt on a bed found in Charleston's historic Russell House contains a pattern that became the basis for this adaptation. Wallpaper in the same pattern is also available.

Plantation Bridges

A linen panel in the Charleston Museum's historic textiles collection contains this charming motif. It has been reproduced in faithful detail by Greeff. The fretwork railings of the bridge suggest that it is a pattern made popular in the second half of the eighteenth century in England.

For further information regarding Charleston fabrics by Greeff, contact:

Historic Charleston Reproductions
105 Broad Street
Charleston, S.C. 29401

Cohasset Colonials

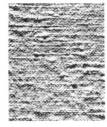

Plimouth Cloth

This is a soft homespun woven from 100% flax. It is available in natural or white shades. Cuttings may be ordered for 25¢. Price, $6.50 a yard.

Carver Cloth

A much coarser cloth than most homespuns, Carver features an open weave with uneven yarns. It is priced at only $3.95 a yard.

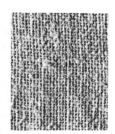

Colonial Check

This is a reproduction of old bed ticking and can be used for slip covers as well as for curtains for small windows. It is 50% cotton, 50% polyester, and is Scotch-

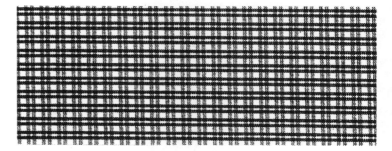

garded and machine washable. It should be line dried. The fabric is available in five colors—cherry, lemon yellow, evergreen, delft, and indigo. Price, $5.25 per yard.

Pine Tree Stripe

A stenciled liner from an old hat box contains this pattern. Three color combinations are available: antique gold and olive on white; federal blue and parchment on white; and light and dark brown with parchment on white. This is a 100% cotton fabric with Scotchgard protective finish. It is machine washable but should be line dried. Price, $5.50 per yard.

For further information regarding these and other fabrics, contact:

Cohasset Colonials
Cohasset, Mass. 02025

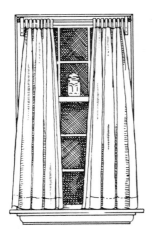 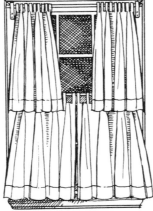

Country Curtains

Unbleached Muslin

These are ready-made curtains available in several different lengths. There is probably nothing simpler than unbleached, unprocessed muslin or anything more appropriate for simple Colonial-style interiors. The muslin will shrink, so it is recommended that one allow for about 1″ loss per yard. The curtains are 80″ wide per pair and are fitted with 1″ wide by 3″ long loops of muslin at the top for hanging. The lengths available are 30″, 36″, 40″ ($10 a pair); 54″, 63″, 72″ ($15 a pair); 81″, 90″ ($20 a pair).

Country Curtains
Stockbridge, Mass. 01262

Henry Ford Museum

The American Classics series of reproduction textiles is produced by S. M. Hexter for the Henry Ford Museum.

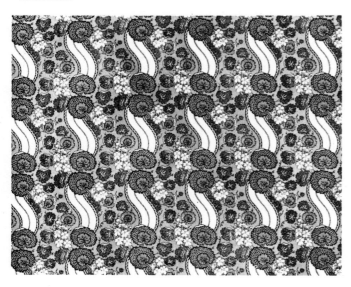

Abigail

A 100% cotton fabric, this dates in pattern from the 1790s. It is available in five color combinations. Price, $13.50 a yard.

Chrysanthemums

This very handsome floral design in the Japanese manner dates from the mid-1800s. It is reminiscent of those fabrics designed by William Morris and other Gothic-Revival stylists in England and America. The fabric is 100% cotton and is available in six color combinations. Prices quoted on request.

For further information regarding these and other fabrics, contact:

Henry Ford Museum and Greenfield Village
20900 Oakwood Blvd.
Dearborn, Mich. 48121

Lee/Jofa

Capucine

Capucine is one of four designs offered in Lee/Jofa's Toulouse collection of historic fabric reproductions.

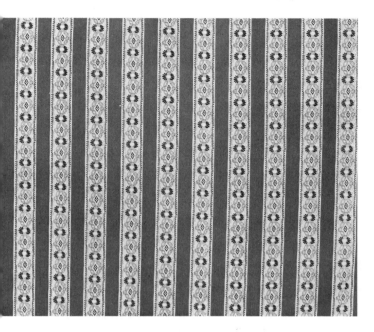

Derived from a French pattern, it is made of cotton and is water repellent. There are five color combinations available.

Eagle Fitzhugh

Designs appearing on China-trade porcelains brought to America in the 1820s are the inspiration for this

fabric. It is made of 100% glazed cotton and is given a Zepel finish. Six color combinations are offered.

For further information regarding these fabrics and others, contact:

Lee/Jofa, Inc.
979 Third Ave.
New York, N.Y. 10022

Scalamandré

Floral Design

This stunning fabric is based on a French wood-block floral print, c. 1785. Scalamandré has printed it on semi-glazed chintz. Printed cottons of this sort were widely produced in Europe in the mid- to late-eighteenth century to compete with the painted and dyed cottons imported by the various East India companies. Ten screens are involved in the silk-screen printing of this fabric at Scalamandré's plant.

Pompilio Texture

A high quality 100% *wool* homespun made by Scalamandré has a wonderful texture and appearance. Such material can be used for upholstery, of course, but is also suggested for curtains in simple American interiors. There are a number of different homespun cloths in many colors available from Scalamandré.

Branche de Vigne

Originally handmade as a brocade in mid-eighteenth-century France, this is now available as a chintz. It is of 100% cotton and is, of course, a great deal less expensive than a hand brocade. A coordinated wallpaper design is available for use with the material.

The Hermitage

A pattern from the eighteenth century was chosen by Andrew Jackson as one of the fabrics to be used in

The Hermitage. The background color is brown, over which are laid red and signs of yellow and blue which combine to make the green of the leaves. Scalamandré reproduced the design from a section of The Hermitage fabric. It is made of 100% cotton.

Madame de Montespan Damask

This French design reflects the movement from the curvilinear Louis XV period style to the more straightforward Louis XVI. Both elements are present here in this 100% cotton reproduction.

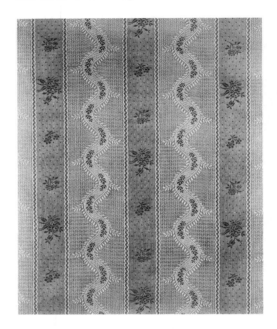

Elsie De Wolfe

Franco Scalamandré, founder of the firm bearing his name, was presented with this early eighteenth-century textile by the famed interior designer Elsie De Wolfe. It displays a very graphic interest in botanical forms and details. The reproduction is made of 100% linen and would enhance any piece of furniture or window that it covered.

Around the World

Scalamandré has reproduced a printed cotton originally inspired by a French eighteenth-century print. The reproduction is a hand-printed glazed-chintz adaptation from a document in the Textile Collection of the Metropolitan Museum. A coordinated wallpaper is also available.

Unicorn

This unique and charming design is taken from an early English print in the collection of Franco

Scalamandré. It is a particularly primitive rendering of folk motifs. The material of the reproduction is 100% cotton. Also offered is a coordinated wallpaper.

Flower Basket

This is a reproduction of an eighteenth-century American fabric known as a "blue resist." Such fabrics were

used in the Hudson River Valley, in Connecticut, and on Long Island. Just how and where they were produced is not known. In "resist" dyeing, the areas that were not to be covered by the printed design were painted so that they would "resist" the color. The reproduction is made of 100% linen.

Summer Flora

Cottons featuring floral sprigs of this sort were very popular in the eighteenth century. This is a copy of a French textile, c. 1775, that was intended for use in

clothing such as aprons, petticoats, and night clothes. It was originally printed on cotton sheeting. Scalamandre produces it on heavier cotton duck. It is adapted from a fabric in the Textile Collection of the Metropolitan Museum. A coordinated wallpaper is also available.

Bourgogne

A very exuberant, colorful pattern, Bourgogne is based on an early document in Scalamandré's Museum of Textiles. It is produced on a chintz which is hand screened and highly glazed. There is a wallpaper available in the same pattern.

Library Window Study

Scalamandre is one of several reproduction fabric companies aiding in the restoration of historic homes and other buildings. A current project is that of the restoration of the Missouri Executive Mansion in Jefferson City. Illustrated is the blueprint which has been prepared of a window in the study and a sketch showing the use of carpeting, wall covering, and window hangings. The mansion is a particularly fine mid-Victorian structure.

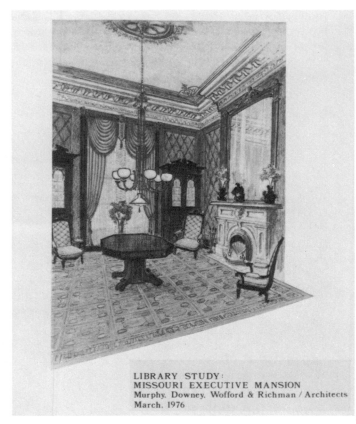

LIBRARY STUDY:
MISSOURI EXECUTIVE MANSION
Murphy, Downey, Wofford & Richman / Architects
March, 1976

For further information about these fabrics and others made by Scalamandré, contact:

Scalamandré Silks, Inc.
950 Third Avenue
New York, N.Y. 10022

Williamsburg Craft House

Williamsburg Stripe

F. Schumacher manufactures some very handsome fabrics for Williamsburg's Craft House. Among the most popular of these is the Williamsburg Stripe. It is a

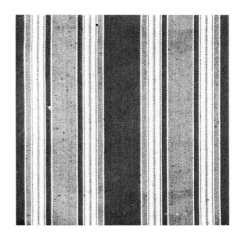

copy of an eighteenth-century Italian textile and is made of silk and cotton. A related wallpaper is offered.

Floral Stripe

A cotton fabric, this is a reproduction of an eighteenth-century French textile. It alternates ribbon-looped bou-

quets with wide stripes of flowers. A wallpaper of the same pattern is available.

For information regarding Williamsburg fabrics, contact:

Craft House
Williamsburg, Va. 23185

Needlework Kits

The old house owner is not completely at the mercy of manufacturers or suppliers when it comes to fabrics or textiles. While few of us can spend time making our own yarn or in weaving it, there is a great deal to the finishing of fabrics that can be performed at home. In addition to the more obvious chores of hemming and stitching curtains, bed hangings, and various cloths, there is the pleasure of decorating such pieces. The passion for needlework can be satisfied in many different ways. There are a great variety of kits on the market which will serve and instruct a beginner. Those which are listed below are for more experienced needleworkers.

Boston Museum of Fine Arts

The Museum Shop offers some very handsome projects of a useful sort. Illustrated is a crewel flower motif for a chair seat. It is embroidered on a 36″ linen

square. The kit includes the square, hot iron transfer, needle and wools which are matched to the original

131

design, adapted from a petticoat border said to have been made in the mid-eighteenth century in New England. Price, $20.

The Shop also offers other kits and an intriguing "Pattern Book," containing fifteen pages of patterns for an appliqué quilt. This was written by Mrs. Harriet Powers, an Athens, Georgia, Negro between 1895 and 1898. Price, $1.75.

Priced catalogue available.

Museum Shop
Museum of Fine Arts
Boston, Mass. 02115

Cantitoe Corners

Illustrated is the Bird of Paradise appliqué quilt which is available in kit form. It includes fifteen yards of

cotton fabric, embroidery thread, full-scale drawings, and step-by-step instructions. Both the original—worked in 1854—and the reproduction measure 88″ x 72½″.

Literature available.

Cantitoe Corners
36 West 20th St.
New York, N.Y. 10011

Philadelphia Museum of Art

Needlework kits for crewel embroidery, needlepoint, and bargello designs have been adapted by the Museum Shop. The designs are adapted from works in the museum. Among the most handsome of these is a crewel wall hanging, 32″ square, on Irish linen twill.

The kit includes the material, English crewel yarn, needle, and complete instructions. The design is based on a block-printed calico fabric by John Hewson, an English printer who worked in the Philadelphia area from 1774 to 1810. Price, $65.

Catalogue available.

The Museum Shop
Philadelphia Museum of Art
P.O. Box 7646
Philadelphia, Penn. 19101

Williamsburg Craft House

Flamestitch patterns are among the most beautiful of those worked by Colonial women. This is a zigzag pattern formed by a bargello or florentine embroidery stitch on canvas. Williamsburg's Craft House has eight different kits available which supply you with canvas and yarn and instructions. These are offered in different color combinations and sizes. Some are large enough to use for the upholstery of chairs or large benches. They range in price from $18.95 to $49.95.

Literature available.

Craft House
Williamsburg, Va. 23185

Tablecloths

Fabrics for tables have generally been better preserved than those used for curtains, beds, or upholstered furniture. Antique cloths in lace, fine cotton, damask, etc., were brought out for special occasions only. These may be found today for similar use in the home. If you are seeking attractive coverings and place settings for everyday purposes, you can turn to several suppliers of period-style fabrics.

Homespun Weavers

Despite the trade name, these are *not* wool fabrics but 100% cotton weaves. Two simple patterns—check and diamond—are available in ready-made cloths, placemats, and napkins. The material can also be purchased by the yard. From long experience we can state that the fabric is, as the manufacturer claims, "easy to care for." It is color fast, machine washable, reversible for double wear, and it never needs ironing. The cloths, in seven custom-made sizes, are priced from $8.95 to $17.95. Placemats cost $1.50 each; napkins, $1.

Brochure available.

Homespun Weavers
Ridge and Keystone Sts.
Emmaus, Penn. 18049

Quaker Lace

Eleven different lace cloths are offered by the Quaker Lace Co. These are made of cotton and dacron polyester. If used with various colored underliners, such a cloth can take on different dimensions. These are all inexpensive (averaging under $20 in price) machine-made fabrics which are permanent-press and machine washable.

Literature available.

Quaker Lace Co.
Fourth St. and Lehigh Ave.
Philadelphia, Penn. 19133

Trimmings

Such elements as fringes, tassels, tiebacks, braids, and gimp may be necessary additions when using period-style fabrics. Finding such high-quality products is no easy matter. Fortunately, a number of the reproduction fabric manufacturers include them in their general offerings.

Historic Charleston

This collection includes materials made by Greeff and Conso Products Co. There are 100% wool and pure silk cut fringes for use on curtains as well as French-style tiebacks, tassels, and fringe of 100% rayon. Charleston also offers a wide-woven braid and a chain-weave French gimp, both of which can be used for upholstery or other fabrics.

Catalogue available.

Historic Charleston Reproductions Shop
105 Broad Street
Charleston, S.C. 29401

Brunschwig & Fils

A selection of Brunschwig & Fils' trimmings is illustrated here. The complete collection has been color-

coordinated for use with their fabrics. Pictured are those trimmings selected for use in the Valentine Museum, Richmond, Virginia.

For further information, contact:

Brunschwig & Fils, Inc.
979 Third Ave.
New York, N.Y. 10022

Scalamandre

Scalamandré's collection of trimmings is very extensive. Braids in Directoire, Louis XV, and Empire styles

are especially attractive and useful for both upholstery and other purposes. There are over forty fringes and thirty tassels and tiebacks to choose from.

For further information, contact:

Scalamandré Silks, Inc.
950 Third Avenue
New York, N.Y. 10022

Upholstery Fabrics and Supplies

Fabrics suitable for use on furniture are generally heavier and more durable than those chosen for hangings. There is an obvious need for more strength when it comes to fitting out a chair, sofa, or loveseat. The range of fabrics and their textures is also wider than that usually offered for curtains or draperies. In addition to various synthetics, cottons, and silks, there are wools and horsehair, as well as flax and linsey-woolsey.

Even the most obscure of materials such as horsehair is available today from one of several leading fabric manufacturers. Because of this great assortment, these fabrics and other supplies are broken down according to supplier rather than by type of material in the listings that follow. Few of the materials can be called inexpensive. A high-quality fabric that is also fitting for a particular interior is a must. There is no sense in paying for expensive upholstery work which will be performed with second-rate materials. The simpler the house style, the simpler the fabric which should be used in it. Damasks and brocades have no place in a modest country interior. Similarly, homespun and pillow ticking have no place in the elegant town house.

Brunschwig & Fils

Embossed Wool Moreen

For the Winterthur Collection Brunschwig has reproduced the Vermicelli embossed wool moreen fabric shown on the chair. An eighteenth-century embossed

wool in the museum's collection provided the inspiration. The Vermicelli pattern simulates the look of damask and was popular in the 1700s and 1800s. A moreen is a sturdy ribbed fabric, particularly suited for upholstery. Brunschwig will also emboss the Vermicelli pattern on other fabrics by special order.

Victoria Damask

The Victoria damask illustrated here is a pattern worked in wool and based on draperies from the mid-

nineteenth century which were used in a Virginia plantation house. The chair is one of a set that appears in the Victorian parlor of the Valentine Museum, Richmond, Virginia.

Davout Snowflake Damask

A handsome Empire design has been woven in the cotton-and-silk fabric illustrated here. It is one most

appropriate for early-nineteenth-century high-style interiors. Brunschwig has used it in the Chillman Empire parlor in the Bayou Bend Collection, Houston. The design is available in four period colors and may be matched with seats, backs, borders, and plain background material in coordinating fabrics.

Horsehair

A scroll-back chair from the Bayou Bend Collection is covered in horsehair texture material. The material

usually has a linen or cotton warp and may be found in plain, striped, or checkered patterns. Although it is identified with Victorian furniture, horsehair was used for such items as dining room chairs as early as the late 1700s.

For information regarding these and other Brunschwig fabrics suitable for upholstery, contact:

Brunschwig & Fils, Inc.
979 Third Ave.
New York, N.Y. 10022

Cohasset Colonials

Franklin Cloth

A 100% cotton material, this is a heavy check similar in some respects to a half-inch fabric found in the Old Sturbridge Village collection. The background color is beige. It is available in the following second colors: blue, red, mustard, or green. Price, $6.95 a yard.

Essex Cloth

This is a weave of 52% linen, 27% cotton, and 21% rayon. Without pattern, it comes in brick, gold, blue, or green. The maker recommends it for slip covers and provides the material with a Scotchgard finish. Price, $6 per yard.

Catalogue and samples available. For further information, contact:

Cohasset Colonials
Cohasset, Mass. 02025

Constantine

Muslin

In addition to various tools needed for upholstery work, the Constantine Co. supplies such materials as burlap, cotton felt batting, and white unbleached muslin. This light cotton material is often used as a backing or undercover for upholstery and may need replacement from time to time.

Catalogue available.

Albert Constantine and Son, Inc.
2050 Eastchester Rd.
Bronx, N.Y. 10461

Guild of Shaker Crafts

Chair Tapes

Tapes in authentic Shaker colors may be used on almost any chair with a seat supported on rungs. Instructions for taping seats can be ordered from the Guild along with ten different colored tapes. The

shades are dark olive; red with light and dark olive stripes; black; light olive; red; dark brown; dark brown with light and dark olive stripes; light olive; dark olive with black and brown stripes; and dark blue. The tapes measure from ⅝″ to 1″.

Catalogue available.

Guild of Shaker Crafts
401 W. Savidge
Spring Lake, Mich. 49456

Gurian's

Crewel

There are nine different crewel patterns available from Gurian's in an off-white cotton ground. These are offered in a number of color combinations. Gurian's also features a hand-embroidered, ready-made chair seat or back in a 24″ square. It is priced at $10.

Brochure available.

Gurian's
276 Fifth Ave.
New York, N.Y. 10001

Minnesota Woodworkers Supply

Black Cambric, Cotton Batting, Webbing, Cord

The upholstery supplies available from Minnesota are those used in quality work—natural cotton batting for stuffing, black cambric for the underside of a furniture piece, jute webbing and cord.

Catalogue available.

Minnesota Woodworkers Supply Co.
Industrial Blvd.
Rogers, Minn. 55374

Scalamandré

Nan Chang Damask

Chinese designs have been as popular in textiles as they have been in porcelains. Silk from China was used in eighteenth-century France, England, and Italy for the production of such upholstery fabrics as Nan Chang. This particular pattern was developed in France, 1730 to 1770. Scalamandré's reproduction is made of 26% silk (imported from China in the raw stage) and 74% cotton.

Damas de Toulouse Damask

An Italian fabric made for Scalamandré, this is a classical eighteenth-century pattern which was revived in the 1800s. Originally woven in 100% silk, it is now

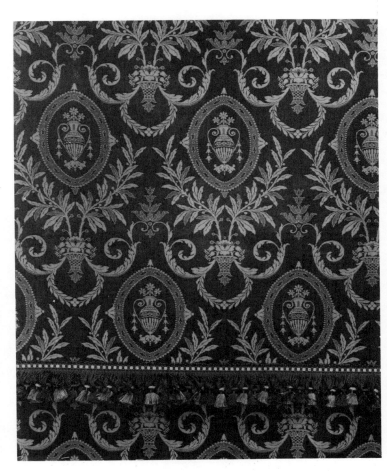

available in 21% silk and 79% cotton. A related fabric for hangings is also available.

Brocade

A polychrome brocade of the Louis XV period, this is hand woven today in Italy for Scalamandré of 28% silk and 72% rayon. A pattern of free flowing ribbons and floral sprays expresses the mid-eighteenth-century Baroque love for natural curves and other forms.

Ferronerie Velvet

One of the earliest patterns in the Scalamandré collection, this is handmade today in Italy. The design is Gothic in feeling, with tightly enclosed geometric forms. Originally made in Genoa, it is also known as a Genovese velvet.

Chinese Chippendale Lampas

A 100% silk weave, this fine fabric is most appropriately used for mid- to late-eighteenth-century Chip-

pendale-style furniture. Thomas Chippendale was one of the first English cabinetmakers to introduce the kind of patterns seen here in furniture.

Medallion Chair Seat

The seat displays a pattern that became popular in the United States in the Federal or late-Colonial period. Made by Scalamandré of 100% silk, the material has been used in the Blue Room of the White House. It

reflects the intense American interest in French Directoire design and in that of Adam in England.

Gardner Museum Chair Backs

Both of these weaves are made of 77% silk and 23% cotton, and Scalamandré can supply coordinated fabrics to be used with them. These are known as lampas weaves. The designs are those used during the Empire period.

Natchez

A lavish pattern, this is one which originated in Italy during the late-seventeenth century. It is woven as a brocatelle, but with cotton filler rather than linen. The overall effect is much flatter than that achieved in the usual brocatelles. The reproduction was first used in the dining room of Stanton Hall, Natchez, Mississippi.

Love Bird Damask

This is one of Scalamandré's most beautiful and popular reproduction fabrics. It is based on an early Italian

pattern, and is made of 100% silk. A wallpaper of the same design is also available.

For further information regarding these and other fabrics, contact:

Scalamandré Silks, Inc.
950 Third Ave.
New York, N.Y. 10022

Other Sources of Fabric Supplies

Consult List of Suppliers for addresses.

Awnings

American Abalene Decorating Service
Norton Blumenthal, Inc.
Brunschwig & Fils, Inc.
Scalamandré Silks, Inc.
Weblon, Inc.

Bed Coverings

Artmark Fabrics Co., Inc.
Auffray & Co.
Norton Blumenthal, Inc.
Domino Patchworks
Phyllis Morris Originals
Nettle Creek Industries
Norman's of Salisbury
Scalamandré Silks, Inc.
F. Schumacher & Co.
Stahl & Stahl
Sunshine Lane

Vermont Quilts

Needlework Kits

B & B Needlecrafts
J. P. Enterprises

Tablecloths

American Needlecrafts, Inc.
Mary Michael
Mottahedeh & Sons
Nettle Creek Industries

Trimmings

Barclay Fabrics Co., Inc.
Bergamo Fabrics, Inc.
Clarence House
Connaissance Fabrics & Wallcoverings, Inc.
Leonardo Looms, Inc.
Old World Weavers, Inc.
F. Schumacher & Co.
Tolland Fabrics, Inc.
West Coast Trimmings Co.

Curtains & Upholstery

Robert Allen Fabrics
Barclay Fabrics Co., Inc.
Bassett McNab Co.
Bergamo Fabrics, Inc.
Doris Leslie Blau Gallery, Inc.
Boussac of France, Inc.
Henry Calvin Fabrics
Constance Carol
China Seas, Inc.
David & Dash, Inc.
A. L. Diament
Ferguson Fabrics, Inc.
Maurice Franks
Gabriel Fabrics, Inc.
S. Harris Co., Inc.
Heritage Patterns
House of Verde
Leonardo Looms, Inc.
Mather's
Phyllis Morris Originals
Norman's of Salisbury
Old Colony Curtains
Old Stone Mill Corp.
Old World Weavers, Inc.
Reed Wallcoverings
Stroheim & Romann
Robert Tait Fabrics
Richard E. Thibaut, Inc.
Trend of the Times Fabrics, Inc.
Norman Trigg, Inc.
Waverly Fabrics

Drawing Room, Powel House, Philadelphia, Pennsylvania. Courtesy Scalamandre Silks, Inc.

Stair hall, Ruthmere, Elkhart, Indiana. Courtesy Scalamandré Silks, Inc.

VIII Paints & Papers

The choosing of materials and colors for walls and other surfaces requiring covering can be a pleasurable event. It should be one of the old house tasks which is most easily accomplished. The range and quality of products available are both wide and high. No one expects to find truly inexpensive items, but there is more choice in price than in such other decorating areas as, for instance, furniture.

The style of the house will determine to a large degree the extent of its decoration. While almost all interior walls need some sort of paint, if only for protection, they needn't be all gussied up. A mid-nineteenth-century farmhouse was unlikely to have contained scenic or documentary papers. The walls of many simple Colonial-style dwellings were more likely originally to have been white-washed than to have been given a heavy coat of paint. You may find, consequently, that one of the contemporary "whitewash" paints will do the job very nicely or that even a milk paint, still produced by several firms, will work. It may be that only the woodwork will need a coat of color.

As for the colors chosen for exteriors, that is a personal matter. North Americans in general have been extremely conservative in their use of bright tones. While it may be advisable to play it safe (most of our ancestors did), there is no reason why one should have to follow the white-house syndrome. Architectural critics from Europe and North America often wrote during the nineteenth century in despair over the dull, monochromatic aesthetic of the public. They urged the use of such natural shades as brown, green, and red —colors that would blend more naturally with the landscape than does stark white.

A much livelier sense of color did emerge in the mid- to late-Victorian period. Sometimes up to five different kinds of wallpaper would be used in one room. If this seems a bit excessive today, think of spending your life in a twentieth-century International-style glass box without any hint of decoration or color. The antithesis is no more pleasing a prospect.

Wall coverings have almost always been luxury items. The first papers were very expensive; they became less dear in price when machine production was perfected in the mid-nineteenth century. Quality papers, however, are not simple to manufacture and are limited in production even today. Most home owners find that their use of such decorative materials has to be similarly limited. This is probably just as well.

There are alternatives to the use of both interior paint and paper. Wood paneling is the most obvious. This is a more expensive proposition if properly executed. Stenciling has captured the interest of many home craftsmen in recent years. This *can* be an economical alternative to papering and was so considered in the nineteenth century. Stencil designs, of course, must be applied to some sort of finished surface and require a skilled if not imaginative hand.

Paints

Paints for exterior and interior uses have been available in ready-mixed form for many years. Historical or period colors have become increasingly popular, and now these, too, may be found in the paint and hardware stores accross the country. Unfortunately, it is impossible to include paint chips or samples in this book; we can only list the colors available and suggest those which seem most suitable for various uses. Most old house owners will find that they can meet most of their exterior and interior paint needs from these commercial lines of oil-based and latex products.

Paints which are mixed to your specifications will be considerably more expensive. There may be no alternative, however, to such custom mixing, particularly if you are attempting to match an unusual shade or tint. In the restoration of old houses, paint analysis is one very important step to be followed. Samples are gathered from many areas to determine just how the past owners decorated their walls and woodwork. This may involve the removal of at least a dozen layers of paint.

The argument between use of oil-based or latex paints continues to rage on unabated. If time allows, it is best to try out samples of both in order to determine their respective durability. Surfaces should be painted as infrequently as possible not only to save money but to cut down on the build-up of layers. In general an oil-based paint is to be preferred for exterior purposes because of its greater adhesive quality and glossy appearance. Most of these are lead free.

Cohasset Colonial

Known primarily as a manufacturer of quality period furniture kits, Cohasset is also a good source for oil-base paints. These are based on traditional milk-paint colors found in the trim, furniture, and other cabinetwork of eighteenth- and early nineteenth-century New England homes. With the exception of one color —Parchment—all are suitable for interior or exterior use. As Cohasset notes in its literature, "Since many of the same dyes were used in the coloring of cottons and linens as in paints there is a natural harmonious effect achieved in a true Colonial setting."

The nine colors, in addition to white, are: Wayside Green, a very dark, almost black shade based on a color found at the Wayside Inn, Sudbury, Massachusetts; Indian Red, a brown-red used at the Wayside Inn; Parchment, a dark ivory; Pewter; Mustard; Bayberry; Brown, Federal Blue, a dark blue; and Boston Blue, a gray shade.

All except Parchment are available in pint, quart, and gallon containers. Parchment can be had in quarts and gallons only. A pint is priced at $2.75; a quart, $4.50; and a gallon, $16.

Catalogue available, 50¢.

Cohasset Colonials
Cohasset, Mass. 02025

Devoe, Historic Charleston Colors

Devoe's colors for the Charleston collection are subtle and elegant. These are documented shades from many of the city's fine homes and public buildings. Most of the Devoe products are latex or acrylic paints, but the company also offers alkyd enamels and house paints. The interior latex enamel, known as Regency House, is particularly recommended for walls and trims of Colonial houses. Many of the Charleston colors, however, are also suitable for Victorian structures. The palette is more delicate and at the same time livelier than that found in New England buildings. It is in keeping with Charleston's graceful Southern exposure.

Among the paints especially recommended for interior use are Russell House Stairhall, a pewter shade; Meeting Room Green, a light gray-green; Edmondston-Alston Hall Walls, faint pink; and Battery Blue, warm gray-blue.

Suggested for interior *and* exterior use are Russell Library Panelling, beige; Blake House, a gray-brown; Chalmers Street Pumpkin; Edmondston-Alston Hall Woodwork, gray; and Radcliffeborough Columns, cream.

Paints suitable for exterior use only are Thomas Rose Shutters, dark gray-green; Harleston Village, peach; Ansonborough, light lilac, Huguenot Brown; Tradd Street, mauve; Primerose House, yellow; Rainbow Row Pink; Charleston Shutter Green, a forest green; Edmondston-Alston House, a very light pink; Arch House Trim, indigo; Broad Street Red; and The French Coffee House, dark pumpkin.

Color card and information available.

Devoe Paint Division
Celanese Coatings
#1 Riverfront Plaza
Louisville, Ky. 40402

or

Historic Charleston Reproductions Shop
105 Broad Street
Charleston, S.C. 29401

Finnaren & Haley, Authentic Colors of Historic Philadelphia

The National Park Service has authenticated a number of shades used during the Revolutionary period in Philadelphia. Through Finnaren & Haley these are now available to the general public. The company offers twenty-six colors in all, eleven of which are historically documented. These are available in both oil and water base and in matte, semi-gloss, and high-gloss finishes.

Four of the colors are drawn from Independence Hall: Ash, Quill (medium gray), White, and Long Gallery Blue. Four others are copied from the Todd House or Congress Hall in Independence National Historical Park: Bronze, Yellow, Red, and Tan. The remaining colors, Liberty Gray, Tower Stairhall Blue, and Supreme Court Yellow, are found in other buildings documented by the experts from the National Park Service.

Although they are not historically documented, two other Finnaren & Haley colors deserve special mention. These are Germantown Green, a warm gray-green; and Penn Red, a rusty shade found up and down the Delaware Valley.

Brochure available.

Finnaren & Haley, Inc.
1300 N. 60th St.
Philadelphia, Penn. 19151

Glidden-Durkee

This company has no recognized line of authentic or historical colors, but does offer some exterior paints which will serve the need of the old house owner. These, of course, are much more readily available than some of the specialty lines. If you are not trying to match a particular color, Glidden's paints may be suitable. They are available in latex and alkyd base. Their interior colors, however, do not begin to match those needed for period rooms.

Suitable for both exterior walls and trim are Colonial or Cape Cod Red, a rich red-brown; Revere Green, a soft gray-green; Old Salem, a mustard shade; Stratford Brown, a rich cocoa brown; and Country Blue, a warm Wedgwood color.

Literature available.

Glidden-Durkee
900 Union Commerce Bldg.
Cleveland, Ohio 44115

Benjamin Moore

One of the largest paint manufacturers in America has now joined the field of historical colors. Their collections of interior and exterior paints are handsome and well-conceived. The colors are not as carefully authenticated as those of smaller firms, but no one can argue over their suitability for a vast majority of old buildings. They are widely available through paint and hardware dealers.

The exterior paints are available as alkyd or latex; the interior are made as latex paints only.

Moore offers more than 1,400 colors in its total line, of which seventy-six are part of their historical collections. It is thus impossible to mention more than a few of the most interesting shades.

For interior needs these are: Lancaster Whitewash, a light ivory color; Monticello Rose, a dusty shade; Sussex Green, a gun-metal shade; New London Burgundy, a rich maroon; and Tyler Taupe, a yellow-brown.

The exterior colors especially recommended are Lynchburg Green, a light gray-green; Morristown Red, a rusty shade known as Penn Red in other paint lines; Tudor Brown, a very rich chocolate; and Hamilton Blue, a warm gray-blue.

Literature is available from your Moore paint dealer or by writing to:

Benjamin Moore & Co.
Chestnut Ridge Road
Montvale, N.J. 07645

Janovic/Plaza

Residents of the New York Area are fortunate in having in their midst a superb retailer of paints and papers—Janovic/Plaza. Among the historical paint lines they handle are those of Martin Senour, Pittsburgh, and Benjamin Moore. The stores, however, are prepared to mix special colors appropriate for Colonial, Victorian, and early twentieth-century buildings.

Literature available.

1292 1st Avenue
New York, N.Y. 10021

or

159 W. 72nd St.
New York, N.Y. 10023

Pittsburgh Paints

These paints are suitable for a wide variety of buildings, and not just the Colonial-style structure. In fact, if you are looking for truly authentic Colonial colors, don't turn to Pittsburgh. Their palette is much more modern. The names of the colors reflect an interest in nineteenth-century Western interiors and exteriors—Santa Fe Sunset, Cherokee Rose, Arizona Clay, Canyon Coral, Mission Gray, Dodge City Tan, Alamo Stone. These are not the bright pigments that once were made from berries or grasses, but earth colors reflecting the mineral wealth of the West. Such shades as Oregon Rose and Colorado Sandstone, both light pinks, would suit many late-Victorian houses; Hammered Iron, a dark gray, and Gold Dust, a mustard, could also be used with dramatic effect on ornate trim or gingerbread. Most Pittsburgh paints are of the latex variety, but some "oil type" or alkyd paints are available.

A brochure on Pittsburgh's "Historic Colors" is available from most paint and/or hardware stores, or from:

Pittsburgh Paints
1 Gateway Center
Pittsburgh, Penn. 15222

Martin-Senour, Williamsburg Paint Colors

Williamsburg's colors were authenticated many years ago and are based on those found in the buildings which make up the historical village complex. Today these shades are about as familiar to the public as the hot, vibrant colors of the mid- and late-twentieth century. There are forty-three interior and forty-nine exterior colors to choose from, each of which is in use somewhere in Williamsburg. All are of flat, satin, or satin-gloss latex.

Anyone determining the color scheme for a Colonial-style house should consult the Martin-Senour literature. There are subleties in shade and hue here which are not to be found elsewhere in ready-mixed paints. The interior blues such as Brafferton, Brush-Everard, and James Southall are particularly rich combinations. The greens available for exterior use—Levingston Kitchen, Palmer House, Archibald Blair, Barraud House—are extraordinarily deep, natural shades.

Literature available from most paint and/or hardware stores, or contact one of the following:

The Martin-Senour Co.
1370 Ontario Ave., N.W.
Cleveland, Ohio 44113

or

The Craft House
Williamsburg, Va. 23185

Old Colonial Paint Colours

Turco's paints are well known in the Northeast. The exclusive licensee of Old Sturbridge Village, Sturbridge, Massachusetts, the company has produced quality paints since 1816. Particularly handsome are their Bayberry Green and Penn Red paints. Turco is one of the few remaining manufacturers of milk paints, and these, in addition to regular oil-based or acrylic paints, may be secured from them.

Literature available.

Turco Coatings, Inc.
Wheatland & Mellon Sts.
Phoenixville, Penn. 19460

Shaker Colors

The Guild of Shaker Crafts produces six basic colors which were commonly used by members of Shaker communities in the eighteenth and nineteenth centuries. These were used with restraint against almost overpoweringly white backgrounds. Those available in oil base with a semi-gloss are Heavenly Blue, Ministry Green, Meeting House Blue, Burnt Orange, Saffron, and Shaker Red. They are offered in quart size only for $5.

Samples sent on request.

Guild of Shaker Crafts
401 W. Savidge
Spring Lake, Mich. 49456

Victorian Paint Guide

The Athenaeum of Philadelphia in association with The Victorian Society in America has issued a most important guide for the painting of Victorian-style houses. This is a republication of *Exterior Decoration*, originally published in 1885 by the Devoe Paint Company as a display book of their ready-mixed paints. The volume contains twenty chromolithograph plates illustrating the use of various colors on Victorian houses. More important, fifty large paint chips have been tipped in and keyed to the plates. To duplicate the 1885 chips meant the blending of modern paints. In addition to historical background and a bibliography on color use, the volume contains detailed information on color combinations and schemes which can be implemented today with the proper mix of modern paints. The volume is priced at $35.

Brochure available.

Athenaeum of Philadelphia
East Washington Square
Philadelphia, Penn. 19106

Stenciling

Stencils were widely used during the nineteenth century to decorate furniture, other small objects, and such structural elements as walls, floors, and ceilings. It has become almost as popular a decorative technique in the do-it-yourself '70s. Today there is a great appreciation for the handcrafted folk-art look of country Americana. Unfortunately, the naïveté which marked so much of that work is no longer with us. Many of the commercial designs purveyed today are neither fresh nor inspired, but are rather insipid.

Stenciling was an art and can still be. Designs should be chosen with care and even more concentration devoted to their proper application. There are any number of step-by-step books and booklets available today (see the bibliography at the back of this book for assistance) which will aid the home artist. There are also imaginative patterns which can be purchased in stencil form.

Two of Megan Parry's handsome designs are illustrated here. She executes wall stencil and mural designs and works primarily in the Boulder, Colorado, area. The

stencils, made of the finest board and precisely cut, are available to those who wish to execute the work themselves. In addition, Ms. Parry will create original designs for use in borders, friezes, stripes, medallions, etc., of any period or style. Stencils range in price from $15 to $25.

Ms. Megan Parry
1727 Spruce
Boulder, Colorado 80302

Wallpapers

Printed papers for the walls are among those "extras" which help to define a period interior. Depending on the space, they may be used lavishly or merely as border accents. High-quality papers are expensive and have always been beyond the reach of a majority of home owners. The French visitor Brissot de Warville reported in 1795 that use of wallpaper was "universal in the United States. No other decoration is known there; almost all houses are neat and decent." The gentleman was either blind or traveling only among the urban elite. Although wallpaper was being made in America as early as 1739, it was considered a luxury item, and most supplies were imported from France or England, thereby adding immeasurably to their cost.

The manufacture of such papers was perfected in France during the eighteenth century. Scenic papers featuring classical motifs were among the most popular, and these were used to decorate household objects as well as walls, but only grand homes such as the Hermitage would make extensive use of panoramic views. By the mid-nineteenth century the first color-printing machine had been brought to America from

England, and thousands of geometric and floral patterns were introduced. The art of papermaking was brought to an all-time height in the mid- and late-Victorian period under the impetus of such Gothic-Revival stylists as William Morris and Charles Eastlake in England and their followers in North America.

A need for fine reproduction papers in the great historic buildings of America and Canada has given birth to a revival of the art of wallpaper making. Scalamandré Silks, Inc., and Brunschwig & Fils, Inc., have led the way in providing quality papers of authentic detail. These firms have been joined by others such as Schumacher, Reed, Hexter, Katzenbach & Warren, and Greeff. They, in turn, have influenced the selection of papers now being offered by more general manufacturers. Authentic designs from almost every period of architectural history can be found in almost every collection. For purposes of *The Old House Catalogue*, however, we are focusing only on the medium- and high-quality papers which either have been documented or are recognized to be historically correct. These are presented, company by company, with a minimum of commentary. Each is illustrated, and these pictures tell most of the story. Prices are generally not available, but may be secured from the firms themselves. The firms will also supply you with the names of retail stores and interior designers carrying their papers.

Allumé

Papers from Allumé Handprints are especially suitable for early twentieth-century, high-style interiors. These are by no means documented patterns, but highly imaginative designs of contemporary artists with a feel for past styles. Illustrated are two such papers: top, Quintan Dinha, and, below, The Ritz.

For further information, contact:

Allumé Handprints, Inc.
D & D Building
979 Third Ave.
New York, N.Y. 10022

Brunschwig & Fils

Produced in France, the Brunschwig documentary wall coverings and fabrics have been used in countless museums, historical homes, and private residences. Included in their collections of papers are reproductions for the Henry Francis du Pont Winterthur Museum; the Valentine Museum, Richmond, Virginia; the Metropolitan Museum of Art; The Museum of Early Southern Decorative Arts, Winston-Salem, North Carolina; Liberty Hall, Kenansville, North Carolina; Gallier House, New Orleans, Louisiana; and the Bayou Bend Collection of The Museum of Fine Arts, Houston.

All papers are reproduced in their original colors as well as in three or four alternative "colorways" or combinations. Most are also duplicated in fabrics suitable for curtains, upholstery, etc.

Rosebud

From the Bybee-Howell House, Sauvie Island, Portland, Oregon, this paper was originally used in a child's bedroom, c. 1856.

Mary-Anna

A solid, one-color hand print, this paper is also copied from one found in the Bybee-Howell House, and dates from c. 1856. It was used in a bedroom.

Little Bird

A charming, one-color hand print on vinyl, Little Bird is not an authenticated paper. It is, however, one that could be used effectively for decorative accent in areas of the kitchen, if not in a child's room.

Penelope

This is a very handsome formal stripe. The original, c. 1810, was found in Liberty Hall, Kenansville, North Carolina. It was used in a bedroom, but certainly could be employed elsewhere.

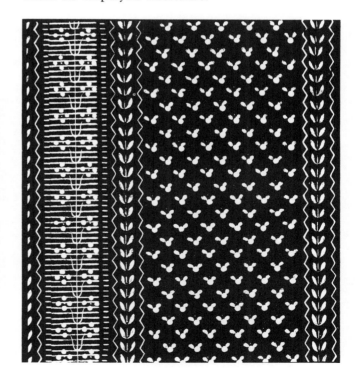

Powhatan Toile

The design here is based on a fabric used in the Wickham-Valentine House, Richmond, Virginia, c. 1785. Eight colors are used to reproduce the idyllic Indian scene from early Virginia.

Elvire

This is a second pattern available in wall and border papers. The border, not illustrated here, employs exuberant swags and bows. The wallpaper, despite its regularity, is a lively, if not busy, pattern.

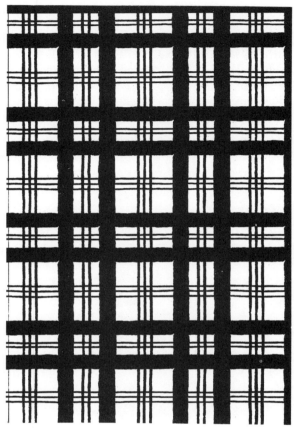

Cloud Dot

This illustrates papers for walls and borders that might be used just below a ceiling cornice. They are lavish, rich hand prints.

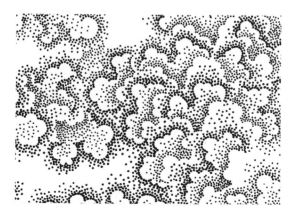

China Fancy

This paper is from the Winterthur Collection and is based on an English document, 1750-1780. It is shown here in the Blackwell Vestibule of the Winterthur Museum. Four colorways or combinations are available.

150

Parrot

As the name implies, Parrot is exotic in feeling. The paper is in the main entrance hall at Liberty Hall, Kenansville, North Carolina and is based on an early nineteenth-century French paper document. It is available in five colorways.

Maytime

A fanciful feminine paper, Maytime was reproduced from fragments of a French Directoire paper, c. 1815. It is used in a bedroom in the Wickham-Valentine House, Richmond. The original colors are grey and orange on blue; four other colorways are available.

Gallier Diamond

An early nineteenth-century French paper was used to reproduce this Directoire design. It is hung in the Gallier House (1857), New Orleans. Five colorways are offered.

For further information on all the Brunschwig papers, contact:

Brunschwig & Fils, Inc.
D & D Building
979 Third Ave.
New York, N.Y. 10022

Historic Charleston

Greeff produces wall coverings and related fabrics for Historic Charleston. There are ten designs available, each one of which reflects the elegance which was and still is Charleston. These have been drawn from fabric and paper fragments, family documents and records, etc. Among the ten are three which are especially handsome for use in many kinds of homes. These are available in one colorway or combination only.

Kiawah Gardens

This design is based on a fragment found in a plantation house located on one of Charleston's nearby sea islands. It is a particularly fanciful, colorful paper.

Low Country Indigo

Illustrated is a very handsome stripe in a typical eighteenth-century blue resist pattern. Indigo was one of eighteenth-century Charleston's most important crops, and the blue used here is faithful to that tradition.

White Point Garden

Here is an Oriental design of birds and flowers which will delight any viewer. Although it is adapted from an English wallpaper of the early nineteenth century, it is also appropriate for later interiors.

Catalogue and price list available.

Historic Charleston Reproductions Shop
105 Broad Street
Charleston, S.C. 29401

The Greenfield Village Collection

S. M. Hexter Company has been licensed to produce papers and related fabrics for the Michigan historical museum complex. As with other historical or documentary papers, the sources are wide and varied—paper fragments, printed and woven textiles, engravings, chinaware, quilts and coverlets, etc. These reproduction papers are available in various color combinations.

Clover Hill and Clover Hill Stripe

Two related papers derive their pattern from a small clover design found on an antique coverlet. The simpler contains the stripe pattern as a border which

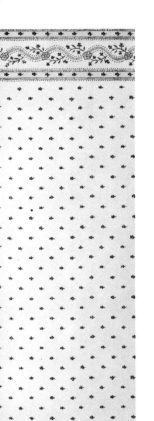

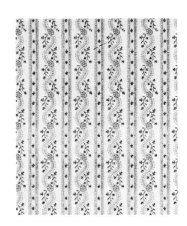

can be removed for use around windows, doors, or to frame the ceiling.

Rose Cottage

A very colorful floral stripe, this pattern was adapted from an English chintz similar to those shipped to America by English manufacturers during the late-eighteenth century. A related fabric is also available.

Dearborn Inn Damask

As the name implies, this is an adaptation of a textile pattern used in the Dearborn Inn. It is a rich, well-detailed paper which suggests much of the texture of the fabric.

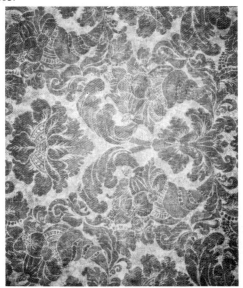

For further information about these and other Greenfield Village papers, contact:

*Henry Ford Museum and Greenfield Village
20900 Oakwood Blvd.
Dearborn, Mich. 48121*

Old Stone Mill

This firm produces some very handsome moderately-priced papers well-suited to period interiors. As is the practice almost throughout the trade, these are vinyl coated and pre-trimmed. Some are handcrafted, but most are machine-printed.

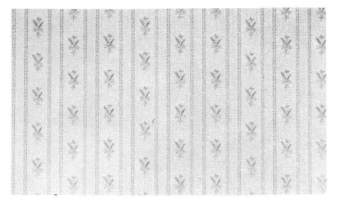

Wheat Stripe

A very simple, neutral pattern suitable for a fairly formal room, this is one of the most popular of Old Mill papers.

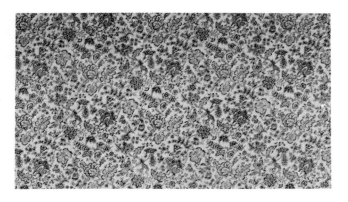

Indian Tracery

A very intricate design, this is one that would probably be used in a sparing way. It is appropriate for Colonial and Victorian interiors.

For further information about these and other papers, contact:

Old Stone Mill
Adams, Mass. 01220

Reed "Early American Homes"

Reed, Ltd., is one of the latest wallpaper manufacturers to introduce a line of hand-printed period papers. These are extraordinarily well-documented and produced and are available in only the original colors. The papers are known solely by the name of the house or structure and room in which they are used.

Morris-Jumel Mansion Tea Room or Parlor

Here strips of paper and borders are used to splendid effect. The basic color is a mint or Georgian green.

Morning glories surrounded by daisies and dark-green leaves provide the basic motif. The borders also contain doves and vases. Stephen Jumel, a New York wine merchant, brought the original of this paper from Paris, c. 1810.

The Joseph Priestley House Hallway

A simple lacy-ribbon design paper in blue and white has been recreated for the hallway and stairwell of the home of the famed eighteenth-century philosopher and scientist. The paper is based accurately on a sample found in the building in Northumberland, Pennsylvania, which is now administered by the Pennsylvania Historical and Museum Commission.

Graeme Park Study

Fragments of the original wallpaper were found under plaster when this Montgomery County, Pennsylvania, Georgian mansion was restored. The reproduction matches its details: small gold stars and borders of bright orange, cream, and brown. The room was first used as the family dining room.

Ford's Theatre

Following the assassination of Abraham Lincoln, the owner of the theater, John T. Ford, was forced by the public to close it down. Before this, however, small pieces of the wallpaper and fabrics used in the Presidential box were taken as souvenirs. Such a fragment provided the documentation for Reed's reproduction. A ruby-red paper, it surely is most suitable for mid-Victorian interiors.

Burwick House Hallway

A 1780s wallpaper found in a Philadelphia parlor has

now been used most effectively in reproduction form in a Canadian merchant's home of the 1840's. The building, moved from its original site, is now located at Black Creek Pioneer Village near Toronto. The paper is in the harlequin pattern in ivory, black, and Regency cream on a Roman-gold ground.

Glanmore House Master Bedroom

Reed supplies a perfect paper for such late-Victorian interiors as that in this Belleville, Ontario, mansion. It is a design which combines swags, flowers, and grapes on a ginger-brown ground. The copy has been made from a paper in a Philadelphia merchant's home. It is remarkably similar to that used originally in Glanmore House.

For further information and copies of Early American Homes, 1707–1880, *Reed's illustrated color catalogue of period papers, $4.50, contact:*

Reed, Ltd.
P.O. Box 52899
Atlanta, Ga. 30305

Scalamandré

One of the true pioneers in authenticated historical papers, Scalamandré can produce almost any kind of work at their Long Island City, New York, manufacturing plant. The list of restorations successfully completed by the firm is too extensive to duplicate here; it includes Monticello, San Simeon, Sturbridge Village, and Old Deerfield. Scalamandré's prints are produced by the hand-screened method, and the firm is well supplied with silk screens. The range of colors they can supply, therefore, is almost without limit.

Borders

The borders available are many, and most date in pattern from the mid-nineteenth century. Shown here are, top to bottom, a classical Lancaster grill border from Old Economy village, Ambridge, Pennsylvania; a Cataldo mission border from Idaho, c. 1851, available as a special order; a carnation border from Old Economy; and a drapery swag with roses from the Shelburn Museum, Shelburn, Vermont.

Regency House

This pattern was found on a bandbox exhibited at the Shelburn Museum in Vermont. It is of the mid-nineteenth century.

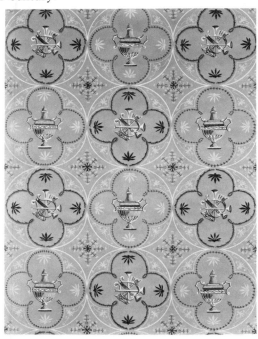

Tulip Hill

A Georgian or late-Colonial house of the same name (near Annapolis, Maryland) contained the original of this fanciful paper. It dates from the late-eighteenth or early-nineteenth century.

156

E Pluribus Unum

The eagle was frequently used with other patriotic insignia in both folk and high-style interiors. This paper is obviously of the latter form. It is a reproduction of a mid-nineteenth century paper in the Shelburn Museum.

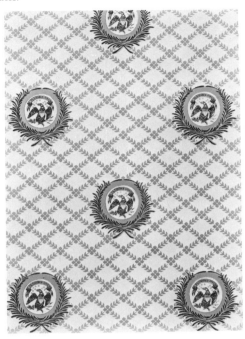

Kensington

This is a copy of one of the oldest pieces of wallpaper known, printed c. 1516 in England. The effect simulated is of what was then known as Spanish embroi-

dery. The original piece is a black print on white paper. Scalamandre has greatly enlarged the design for their paper and a related fabric.

Abercrombie House

Among the papers found in the restoration of Old Deerfield, in Massachusetts, was this pattern. It dates from the late-eighteenth century.

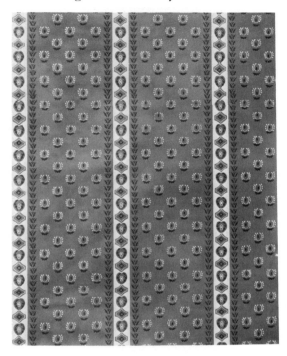

Abner Young's Pastoral

A large scaled paper from Old Deerfield is available by special order and is one of the prizes of Scalamandre's line. This is a very charming American-inspired pattern from the early nineteenth century.

Durham

The inspiration for this paper was a woodblock-printed fabric of the nineteenth century. It would be most suitable for limited decorative use in both early- and mid-Victorian dwellings.

Washington-Franklin Toile

A true documentary design, this is one used in the West Sitting Room of the White House during the Truman Administration. It is based, of course, on a fabric made in the Revolutionary period. The Stamp Act sign has been placed upside-down to indicate the bitter resentment the legislation caused at the time. There is a related fabric available.

Barry

A late-Victorian paper dating from c. 1870, Barry was found in the archives of the Grand Rapids (Michigan) Museum. A coordinated fabric can be obtained as well.

Blakeslee House

This is a handsome mid-Victorian design originating

from a paper found at Old Economy Village in Pennsylvania. Like other ornate Victorian papers, it should be used with some restraint as decorative elaboration.

Isaac Royal House

This is certainly one of the most beautiful of papers known to have been used in eighteenth-century America. Royal, a very wealthy Boston merchant, had this pattern in his bedroom of the Medford, Massachusetts, house. A related fabric is also available.

For further information regarding availability and prices of Scalamandré papers, contact:

Scalamandré Silks, Inc.
950 Third Avenue
New York, N.Y. 10022

Williamsburg Wallpaper Reproductions

Katzenbach and Warren have been making Williamsburg's popular patterns for many years. These are based on documentary material unearthed at the Williamsburg restoration—wallpaper fragments, fabrics, and other paper ephemera—and at other restoration sites. Each pattern is reproduced in its original colors, but is available in other combinations as well.

Charles II

The design for this copy may date from as early as the mid-seventeenth century. It features the four seasons and a medallion which contains a lion, unicorn, and the crowns of England, Scotland, and Ireland. Such a paper as this would be best used in a limited manner.

Potpourri

This is the kind of pattern which is suitable for eighteenth- and nineteenth-century interiors. It is an adaptation of a cotton fabric and features birds, flowers, and fruits.

Edenton

The original of this copy was found in the Joseph Hewes House, Edenton, North Carolina. Dating from the first quarter of the nineteenth century, the pattern is typical of those which so captivated the public at that time. The motifs, of course, are neoclassical.

Palace Garden Damask

Damask fabrics were used to cover the walls in many grand eighteenth-century homes in North America and abroad; Palace Garden captures the look, if not the feel, of that material. It is based on a fabric document of the second quarter of the 1700s.

Williamsburg Tavern Check

Checks were popularly used in fabrics during both the eighteenth and nineteenth centuries. As wall coverings they have been less familiar, but there is no reason why they should not be used in this manner in informal areas of the house.

Winterberry

This is a particularly neat and proper pattern. It is copied from a late-eighteenth-century house in Melrose, Massachusetts. The stripe is dotted, and the bands contain a simple leaf motif.

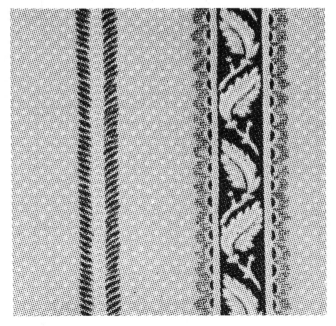

A special catalogue of wallpapers is available. For additional information regarding these papers as well as others offered by Williamsburg, contact:

Craft House
Williamsburg, Va. 23185

Other Suppliers of Paints & Papers

Consult List of Suppliers for addresses.

Paints

Samuel Cabot, Inc.
Maine Line Paints
Miss Kitty's Keeping Room Kolors
Munsell Color Products
Old-Fashioned Milk Paint Co.
Sherwin-Williams Co.

Wallpapers

Artform Designs, Inc.
Artmark Fabrics Co., Inc.
Ash Saul Co.
Charles Barone, Inc.
Bassett & Vollum
The Birge Co., Inc.
Norton Blumenthal, Inc.
Louis W. Bowen, Inc.
Charterhouse Designs, Inc.
Clarence House
Continental Felt Co.
Robert Crowder Associates
Crown Wallcovering Corp.
A. L. Diament
Fine Art Wallcoverings & Fabrics, Inc.
Charles R. Gracie & Sons, Inc.
Philip Graf Wallpapers, Inc.
House of Verde
Janovic/Plaza
Jones & Erwin, Inc.
Laverne International
Lawrence Wallcovering Co.
Manuscreens, Inc.
Martha M. House
Nancy McClelland, Inc.
F. Schumacher & Co., Inc.
Shriber's Wall Papers
Stamford Wallpaper Co.
Thomas Strahan Co.
Richard E. Thibaut, Inc.
Winfield Design Associates, Inc.

Plate 50.

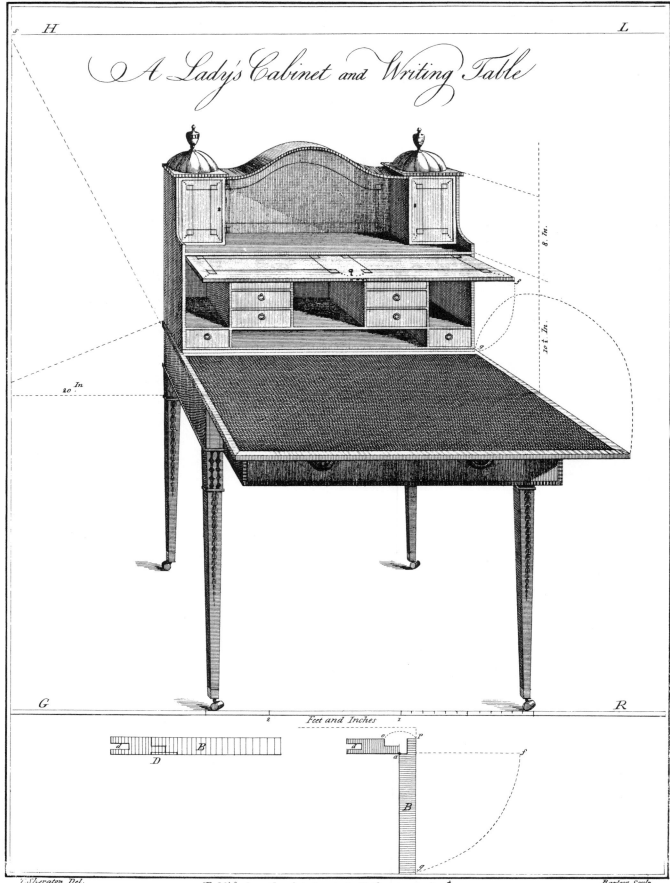

A Lady's Cabinet and Writing Table

Feet and Inches

T. Sheraton Del.   Published as the Act directs by T. Sheraton April 10.ᵗʰ 1792.   Barlow Sculp.

IX Furniture

The furnishings of any interesting period home reflect the taste of several generations —at least. We are speaking of the domestic dwelling and not the historic museum in which time may have stopped in 1740, 1828, or 1890. No one really cares to live as a curator. The "don't touch" way of life under glass is suitable only for mannequins or prematurely stuffed antiquarians. Students of history may no longer believe in the idea of progress, but they do understand that history is something that happened yesterday as well as one hundred years ago, and will continue tomorrow.

What has this to do with furniture? Actually, a great deal. American furniture manufacturers spend millions of dollars each year telling the public that they can live again in a Colonial manner or in a Gay-Nineties style, to mention just two of the popular themes. And in this Bicentennial year of our Lord the message is more strident than ever. Even the Castro Convertible girl has been seen sporting a dust cap and hoop skirt. The next development will be CB radios in curly-maple cases. It would all be rather funny if it weren't so sad.

While the basic structural elements of a house may have taken shape at one particular time, the interior appointments have shifted with the styles. Back in 1740 they were probably mixing Queen Anne with Pilgrim Century in Boston; one hundred years later the Philadelphia housewife was more than likely to be introducing heavier Gothic cabinetwork to her Empire-style front parlor. While some extremely wealthy Americans may have been able to transform their mansions or townhouses from one style to another in an instant, the vast majority made changes slowly. Grandfather's Windsor rocker was kept in the same room with the new Victorian love seat. Furniture from the past that was useful and well-made was saved for the future.

This approach is valid today. Anyone approaching the furnishing of an old house should remain flexible. While it would be foolish to mix wildly disparate elements, as, for instance, Chinese Chippendale and art nouveau, there is no need to ban the nineteenth century from an eighteenth-century house or vice versa. Rather, there should be a core of similarly styled pieces which make a general decorative statement. Around these can be grouped the honest pieces by craftsmen of other periods.

In considering furniture, the old house owner should first study the antiques market. It is very possible that there may be no need to depend on makers of reproductions. Certainly there is no reason to Ethan Allen a house up with modern historical kitsch. Nostalgia lasts no longer in wood than it does in plastic. For large pieces of furniture such as cabinets, chests, sofas, dining tables, and desks, it is likely that antique objects will be no more expensive than reproductions. If you have to have a rocker like Abraham Lincoln's or one of Duncan Phyfe's masterpieces, then you may have to settle for a copy. But something more personal, something which has the true veneer of age, will bring more pleasure in the long run and will certainly leave you and your descendants richer men. It is, of course, very difficult to say just what is available out there in the vast field of antique furniture. The market is changing constantly. Dealers are often delightful, but somewhat mercurial, creatures with shops open at odd hours. Their "products" cannot be logically catalogued.

The reproduction furniture market is a more formal business, although it, too, has its individualists. Thank God for them. They are the persons making the most handsome quality pieces, true new antiques in the old manner. It is to them that we look for special items such as beds, chairs, copies to fill out a set, authentic appointments not to be found in the antiques market at any decent price. Colonial Williamsburg was one of the first major institutions to encourage the manufacture of such reproductions, and, although the look they made famous is now considered a bit too studied, one can only admit that the effort was an important and pioneering one. It continues at a relatively high level of quality.

This section is devoted almost entirely to reproduction furniture suitable for various kinds of period homes. Except for beds, that most staple of functional objects, almost all the pieces are small ones. There is very little in a style later than Victorian. Anyone seeking twentieth-century pieces should look no further than the auction barn or salvage depot.

All the objects presented here, we hope, are well-made, honest copies that can be used about as they were intended.

Beds

One-third of our lives, bed manufacturers are quick to remind us, is spent in bed. But does this mean that period style has to be sacrificed to practicality? Not by any means. Almost any antique bed can be fitted for modern use, and every reproduction made today is intended to be used with the latest improvements in mattresses and box springs. One can rest comfortably and securely with a canopy overhead or any other kind of period appurtenance which strikes the fancy.

If it is economical to convert an antique bed for present-day use, then by all means choose this alternative. There is something reassuring about climbing into a handsome Colonial curly-maple or Victorian oak bedstead. If it is a family heirloom, the feeling of "belonging" is intensified. Of all antique furniture, beds are surely the most personal.

A reproduction will not be quite as familiar an object, but it is surprising how quickly such an object is made

one's own. A copy, of course, can be manufactured to almost any size, and since twentieth-century people are longer if not heavier than their ancestors, the extra space afforded by a reproduction can be a definite plus. Resist, however, the temptation to go all the way to "king" size. A poster bed, for instance, will appear to resemble a football field, complete with goal posts, or, if canopied, an astrodome. Period styles should be rendered as faithfully as possible; proportions should be kept within a reasonable approximation.

Brass

Brass beds are unqualifiedly Victorian. In disfavor during most of the twentieth century, they are now the favorites of young married couples everywhere in the Western world. Relatively light in weight, the brass form can also be quite delicately worked. The comparatively simple tubular forms, however, are those which are most authentic and, interestingly, contemporary in feeling.

President 101

This is a straightforward design—vertical brass rails enclosed by horizontal tubing curved at the corners.

The material is hard-drawn solid brass tubing which has been backed with an enamel coating to protect the luster. The complete frame, including head and footboards, is available in king, queen, double, twin, and day bed sizes, and is priced from $550 to $840.

Catalogue and price list available.

Brass Bed Company of America
1933 S. Broadway
Los Angeles, Calif. 90007

Design 134

Straight lines are found everywhere in this brass bed by Bedlam. Both headboard and footboard, as illustrated, are topped with brass finials. The bed is shown queen size, but is available also in single, double, and king size, and with a straight footboard rather than a curved one. Prices are similar to those of The Brass Bed Company of America. The brass can be given a lacquered finish or one of chrome or nickel.

Catalogue and price list available.

Bedlam Brass Beds
19-21 Fair Lawn Ave.
Fair Lawn, N.J. 07410

Canopy

Beds with canopies or testers, as they were termed in England from the sixteenth century on, are those which most people find most "Colonial." A covering such as this could be suspended over many different kinds of beds, but it is most often found on the four-poster. The canopy was only one of the elements hung from a frame; head, foot, and side curtains or hangings were also sometimes used to enclose the bedstead, as well as valances and flounces or dust ruffles. It is unlikely, however, that a very large proportion of the public ever enjoyed the luxury of such a private, luxurious bed. The bed has always been an indicator of one's financial if not social station, and a canopied bed was long the property of the relatively well-to-do.

Canopy Frame Bed

The craftsmen of Berea College offer a handsome four-poster with delicately-turned woodwork. The bed

with canopy frame is 78″ high. Each bed is made to order of walnut, cherry, or mahogany. King, queen, full, and twin sizes are available in prices from $900 to $1,200.

Catalogue and price list available.

Berea College
Student Craft Industries
Berea, Ky. 40403

Chippendale Four-Poster Canopy

Kittinger has copied for Williamsburg's Craft House a four-poster made in New England during the second half of the eighteenth century. The original is found in the Brush-Everard House. It has a flat canopy and

posts at the foot which end in cabriole legs with claw-and-ball feet. It is available as both a double or a single bed; both are 87¾″ high and are reproduced in solid mahogany. According to the Craft House, these will take standard springs and mattresses. The Craft House is also a good source for bed hangings (see section VII, Fabrics). Prices, according to finish, run from $1,785 to $1,930.

Catalogue and price lists available from Craft House, $2.95.

Craft House
Williamsburg, Va. 23185

Chippendale-style four-posters are, of course, produced by other craftsmen—among them is Ernest Lo Nano. His finely-crafted reproductions are copied from authentic pieces. The four-poster, No. 209 in Lo Nano's listings, is 7′9″ high, 56″ wide, and has a depth of 6′8″—more than enough room for most people. It is made of mahogany. The firm also will design period bed hangings for the piece.

Brochure available.

Ernest Lo Nano
South Main St.
Sheffield, Mass. 01257

Hired Man's Bed

The man who did all the dirty work around the house during the day was fortunate enough to sleep at night in such a handsomely-worked bedstead—at least that

is the story. More than likely, he had to put up with a lumpy mattress and broken springs. This comparatively simple bed, however, is suitable for hired men and women today—that is, those of us who have to work for a living. It is made by the Berea craftsmen, and is available in walnut, cherry, or mahogany by special order. The head posts are 37¼″ high and the foot posts, 32½″. It is available in king, queen, twin, and full sizes, and is priced from $375 to $765.

Catalogue and price list available.

Berea College
Student Craft Industries
Berea, Ky. 40403

Low-Post Bed

The Williamsburg mahogany low-post bed is adapted from an original made in Newport, Rhode Island, in the mid-1700s. The headboard is simply curved and the posts deeply fluted. It is made by Kittinger and is available in double and single sizes. Priced from $445 to $505, depending on finish desired.

Catalogue and price lists available from Craft House, $2.95.

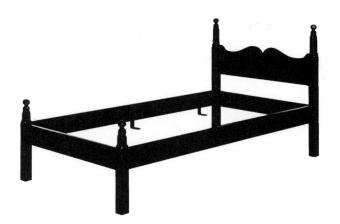

Craft House
Williamsburg, Va. 23185

Spool Bed

This is a medium-height, fancy bed deriving its name from the threaded, turned posts and rails. It is made at Berea College and is available in all sizes. The head posts are 61½″ high; the foot posts, 53½″. As with other Berea furniture pieces, this is made by special order in walnut, cherry, or mahogany. Prices for this sort of intricate workmanship range from $1,025 to $1,485, depending on size and kind of wood used.

Catalogue and price list available.

Berea College
Student Craft Industries
Berea, Ky. 40403

Benches

Benches first came into regular use during the Middle Ages. They are brought out when there are not enough chairs to go around. For years they served the one-room schoolhouse, church, and public halls, as well as the home. One wonders if body posture was not better in the "old days" when such straight-forward forms were used.

Brace Bench, Utility Bench

It is fitting that two of the most handsome benches should derive their form from Shaker designs. The Guild of Shaker Crafts has reproduced two such pieces of furniture. The utility bench is made of pine or cherry and is based on an early piece from the Hancock, Massachusetts, community. It is 48″ long,

9½″ wide, and 15½″ high. The butterfly brace bench is an especially handsome form which is thought to come from the Sisters' workroom at New Lebanon, New York. It, too, is made of pine or cherry, and measures 9″ wide by 35½″ long by 16½″ high. Both are priced at $60.

Catalogue and price list available.

Guild of Shaker Crafts
401 W. Savidge
Spring Lake, Mich. 49456

School House Bench

The original piece on which this reproduction is based is found today at the Farmer's Museum, Cooperstown, New York. It is also known as a deacon's bench as the form was used in churches as well as in schools. This example is made of pine and measures 42″ long, 16″ deep, and 36″ high. Many benches used by blacksmiths, cobblers, sailmakers, woodworkers, etc. are now offered as coffee tables, plant stands, and knick-knack centers; they are not suitable. To so distort the original use of a piece is to render it kitsch. Fortunately, neither Lennox nor other distributors of similar seats have found an adaptive use for this simple piece.

Literature available.

The Lennox Shop
1127 Broadway
Hewlett, N.Y. 11557

or

Route 179
Lambertville, N.J. 08530

Candlestands

Stands of this sort are suitable for at least late-Colonial interiors. They can be used, of course, to support candlesticks, but there is no reason why they should not be employed to hold other lighting fixtures if small in stature. Candlestands were first introduced in Europe during the Renaissance and came into widespread use in England and the Colonies by the mid-eighteenth century. Most candlestands have a tripod base, turned shaft, and a small, circular top.

Independence Candlestand

This is a copy of one found in the Bishop White

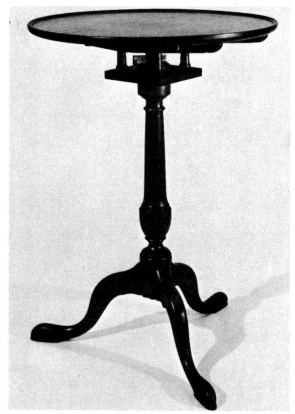

House, Independence National Historical Park, Philadelphia. It has been reproduced by Holmes in mahogany with a tilt-top. The stand is 29″ high and 19″ wide. The suggested retail price is $225.

Brochure and price list available.

The Holmes Company
P.O. Box 1776
Wrightsville, Penn. 17368

Historic Newport Candlestand

Kittinger produces reproductions for Historic Newport as well as for Colonial Williamsburg, and a candlestand in Newport's best tradition is available. This is one which follows a design attributed to the Townsend-Goddard school of cabinetmakers. It features a columnar shaft with a spiral-fluted urn at its base. It is 22½″ high and 16″ in diameter and is made of mahogany.

Catalogue available, $4.

Kittinger Co.
1893 Elmwood Ave.
Buffalo, N.Y. 14207

Canterbury

A stand for large sheaves of music or papers, the Canterbury of the late 1700s is used today for magazines and newspapers. Thomas Sheraton claimed that it was a piece of furniture ordered by an Archbishop of Canterbury as a type of supper tray which could hold knives, forks, and plates. Whatever, the Canterbury is a handsome and useful appointment for a high-style Colonial interior.

Kittinger has produced for Williamsburg a copy of an English Sheraton piece. The squarish box is divided into three sections with a drawer below. It is fitted with casters for easy movement. The reproduction is made of mahogany and is 23″ high, 20″ long, and 15⅞″ wide. Williamsburg prices it at $705 and $730, depending on the type of finish desired.

Catalogue and price list available, $2.95.

Craft House
Williamsburg, Va. 23185

Chairs

Perhaps no piece of furniture made today owes as much to the past as this most familiar form. In the eighteenth century it reached its height as an aesthetic and functional object. A century earlier the chair was just becoming a common household item, and cabinetmakers were laying the groundwork for the veritable explosion of design that was soon to occur. English and Colonial American cabinetmakers such as Sheraton, Chippendale, Hepplewhite, and Phyfe are responsible for most of the forms with which we are comfortable today. Much later chair design is adaptive of the work of these men as well as that of noted French designers of the same period.

This is not to say that other chairmakers, both before and after the high-style eighteenth-century period, were not influential, important craftsmen. Such American figures as Benjamin Randolph, Thomas Affleck, and Jonathan Gostelowe of Philadelphia, for instance, were superb artists in the transitional period from Queen Anne to Chippendale. New York, Boston, Newport, New Haven, Hartford, Charleston, Baltimore, Albany—all these early centers of cultured life were productive of excellent workmanship. In later years, as furniture making moved West, Victorian chairmakers embroidered various revival details upon the basic eighteenth-century styles. Their work is just now coming again to public notice.

And then there is the work of the country craftsman—from the very earliest days. The Windsor, the ladder-back, the Shaker rocker, the Boston rocker, the arrow-back side chair, the Hitchcock painted slat-back have become American classics. Today they are more popular than at any time in the past. If solidly made, they are just as useful as they were yesterday.

Arrow-Back Arm and Side Chairs

A form of Windsor, the chair is marked by its use of arrow-shaped spindles (three or more). This is a nineteenth-century form which persisted in popularity through much of the more elaborate Victorian period. The spindles or splats curve backward in a graceful manner, and both legs and crossbars are ringed in the manner of bamboo. The seat in these reproductions has been scooped out, thereby adding to the chairs' comfort and authenticity.

Catalogue available.

Nichols & Stone
Gardner, Mass. 01440

Balloon-Back Side Chair

The Victorian balloon-back is really nothing more than an upholstered Windsor with added detail. The back is formed from a continuous piece of wood in a graceful loop. Magnolia, America's largest supplier of reproduction Victorian furniture, hand-carves these chairs, applies the fabrics, and hand-tufts them. There is a wide selection of materials to choose from. Priced at $139.95.

Catalogue available.

Magnolia Hall
726 Andover
Atlanta, Ga. 30327

Chippendale Side Chair

Two English straight chairs in the Governor's Palace and in the Wythe House at Williamsburg serve as models for this Georgian reproduction. Made of mahogany, it is relatively simple in design, displaying intricate carving only in the back splat. The seat is fitted with a hair pad cushion and may be upholstered in several different fabrics, including muslin or top grain leather. The purchaser may supply his own fabric at the muslin cost. Prices for the chair upholstered in muslin start at $745 and climb to leather at $786.

Catalogue and price list available, $2.95.

The Craft House
Williamsburg, Va. 23185

Edmondston-Alston House Side and Armchairs

These reproductions of Sheraton-style chairs are made for the Historic Charleston Foundation by Madison

170

Square Furniture. Handmade and hand-decorated abroad, they are authentic pieces for early nineteenth-century homes. Both the side and armchairs have cane seats. The colors are black, gold, and terra-cotta, and the material is European hardwood. Side chair, $395; armchair, $450.

Catalogue available with price list.

Historic Charleston Reproduction Shop
105 Broad Street
Charleston, S.C. 29401

Hitchcock Rush-Seat Side Chairs

Lambert Hitchcock's painted chairs are almost as well known today as they were originally in the second

L. HITCHCOCK.

quarter of the nineteenth century. The black slat-back side chair with painted decoration is one of the classics of American cabinetwork. The open, maple chair with slats in the back and a rush seat was an established form in America during the eighteenth century; Hitchcock elaborated on this. The back has a turned crest rail with an enlarged center portion. Both it and the wide slat are stencilled as is the front of the upward-curved seat. Hitchcock's chair company, which ceased business in the 1840s, was revived in 1946 in the same location.

Brochure available.

The Hitchcock Chair Co.
Riverton, Conn. 06065

Crested Victorian Armchairs

Magnolia Hall has reproduced two ornately carved mahogany lounge chairs which they call Mr. and Mrs. Hunnicut chairs. One is designed for a woman; the slightly larger, for a man. Both are made with arch frames and decoration in the rose and leaf design. Each is tufted by hand and is built with innercoil seats. Price for each, $239.95.

Catalogue available.

Magnolia Hall
726 Andover
Atlanta, Ga. 30327

Louis XV Fauteuil

Chairs made in France during the mid-eighteenth century could be masterpieces of graceful movement. Such is the case with the model for this reproduction produced by Maslow. *Fauteuil* is a French term for an armchair of the open form. The chair comes with a down cushion.

Descriptive price list available.

Louis Maslow and Son, Inc.
D & D Building
979 Third Ave.
New York, N.Y. 10022

Louis XVI Side Chair and Fauteuil

Classical motifs entered the French cabinetmaker's style book during the Louis XVI period. These are evident in the legs and base of the seat in both side and armchair. The backs are simple cane mirrors, a form that would reappear in Victorian furniture.

Descriptive price list available.

Louis Maslow and Son, Inc.
D & D Building
979 Third Ave.
New York, N.Y. 10022

Queen Anne Side and Armchairs

It is hard to conceive of a chair more beautiful. The Queen Anne style is one in which American craftsmen excelled in the early- to mid-eighteenth century. The curves are gentle, the backs are carved in a manner to suggest that one piece of wood has been used. There were a number of superb cabinetmakers working in the Queen Anne style in Philadelphia, and cabinetmaker Robert Whitley has focused on their achievements for a series of reproductions. Although primarily a restorer of antique furniture, Whitley will undertake commissions for new work. His illustrated catalogue will convince you of his understanding and mastery of the art of chair making.

The Robert Whitley Studio
Laurel Road,
Solebury, Penn. 18963

Lillian Russell Side and Armchairs

Davis categorizes its Victorian furniture as the Lillian Russell line after the famed soprano of the Gilded Age. As well stuffed as Miss Russell, the chairs feature comfortable padding on back and seat. The backs are the familiar mirror shapes crowned with cresting. These are rather delightful, carefully-carved pieces.

Catalogue available.

Davis Cabinet Company
Box 5424
Nashville, Tenn. 38106

Victorian Side and Armchairs

Maslow produces two Victorian chairs that would suit almost any mid-nineteenth-century interior. These are handsomely carved and upholstered medallion-back seats reminiscent of a Louis XV design as well as that of the Renaissance Revival.

Descriptive price list available.

Louis Maslow & Son, Inc.
D & D Building
979 Third Ave.
New York, N.Y. 10022

Ladder-Back Side and Armchairs

The ladder-back is another form of the slat-back which more closely approximates a stepladder. Berea's craftsmen make two models with finely-turned wood and

corn-shock or Sudan-grass seats. These are made of cherry, walnut, or mahogany, and are priced from $150 to $175.

Catalogue and price list available.

Berea College
Student Craft Industries
Berea, Ky. 40403

The Windsor

This is the American classic. First made in this country in Philadelphia around 1725, it differs in several degrees from its English cousin. Chief of these is the back which in American fashion is made up almost entirely of spindles; English models were usually made with a pierced center splat between spindles. Illustrated is what Nichols & Stone call a "knee-hole desk chair." It is designed to be used in those places where

pulling up a chair is difficult if not impossible—as between dining table side legs or a desk with a small opening. Other Windsors are more elaborate in their use of turned and splayed or raked legs and arms.

Catalogue available.

Nichols & Stone
Gardner, Mass. 01440

Captain's Chair

Meant for use on shipboard, the captain's chair has found its way into the home. It is a particularly sturdy, comfortable object, useful for the home office or din-

ing room. With seats larger than that of the standard chair, captain's chairs feature turned spindles and a solid-strip back which projects up just enough for good support. Nichols & Stone is just one of many manufacturers of this type of seating. Be wary, however, of the many badly constructed models found frequently on the market.

Catalogue available.

Nichols & Stone
Gardner, Mass. 01440

Corner Chair

This is an angled chair used before a desk or, naturally, in a corner. It is sometimes called a "roundabout

chair." The Williamsburg model by Kittinger is reproduced from a Philadelphia example, c. 1750–1775. It has a horseshoe-shaped arm rail which is raised slightly in the center and two vase-shaped splats which are flanked by turned supports. The seat is upholstered. The hair pad cushion may be covered with muslin ($655) or leather ($692), or you may supply your own fabric for upholstering at the muslin price.

Catalogue and price list available, $2.95.

Craft House
Williamsburg, Va. 23185

Rattan Chair

Chairs of this sort have been used inside and outside the house for many years. Fortunately, they are still

available during this age of aluminum and plastic. Superior makes a handsome chair which is especially appropriate for homes situated in such areas as the Gulf states. This is a fan armchair. It is equipped with a polyfoam or Kodel-wrapped polyfoam cushion with zippered cover.

Catalogue and price list available.

Superior Reed & Rattan Furniture Co., Inc.
500 West 52nd St.
New York, N.Y. 10019

Wing Chairs

One sits in a wing chair, not on. The sides, or "wings," enclose the sitter, protecting him from cold drafts or even snoopy occupants of the same room. There is probably no greater pleasure than that of sinking back into such a comfortable chair with a good book or the newspaper. The style itself dates from the reign of Charles II (1660–1685). It was quickly adopted here, and has become an American classic. Those in the earliest styles, such as Queen Anne and early Chippendale, are the most attractive as the arms extend only to the wings and give the appearance of having been made of one piece.

Queen Anne Wing Chair

Williamsburg offers a very handsome piece which reproduces in every respect a 1750 chair found in their collections. It is made of mahogany, and features well-formed cabriole legs and turned stretchers. This is a most expensive reproduction which costs anywhere from $1,000 to $1,458, depending on the kind of fabric wanted for the upholstery, finish on the piece itself, and material desired for the cushion.

Catalogue and price list available, $2.95.

Craft House
Williamsburg, Va. 23185

Chippendale Wing Chair

Ernest Lo Nano specializes in wing chair reproductions. One is based on a Philadelphia ball-and-claw-footed antique. This is one of the largest chairs he makes, with a width of 39″. The front legs feature elaborately carved knees. The chair is made of mahogany.

Brochure and prices available upon request.

Ernest Lo Nano
South Main St.
Sheffield, Mass. 01257

Chests

These are among the simplest and most basic of furniture forms. From them are built a number of other objects such as chests-on-chests, and chests of drawers. Since medieval times they have been used as objects in which to store clothing, bedding, and valuables. They have also served as benches on which to sit, and, positioned at the foot of the bed, they can serve the same purpose today. A chest is usually made of wood and has a hinged lid.

Blanket Chests

The Shakers made a beautifully simple chest for the storage of woolens and blankets. Tills at each inside end provide room for the placement of smaller items.

This reproduction from the Guild of Shaker Crafts is copied from a New Lebanon, New York, piece. It measures 40½″ long, 18½″ deep, and 23″ high and is made of pine or cherry. Price, $215.

Catalogue and price list available.

Guild of Shaker Crafts
401 W. Savidge
Spring Lake, Mich. 49456

Butler's Chest

From Historic Charleston's William Gibbes House comes this unusual walnut and burl Queen Anne chest. The top opens, as per the illustration, for use as a serving surface. Silver may be stored in the top drawer which is felt-lined and partitioned. The piece is 21″ wide, 21″ deep, and 37⅛″ high. It is made in England by hand by the cabinetmakers of Stebbing. Price, $1,700.

Catalogue and price list available.

Historic Charleston Reproductions Shop
105 Broad St.
Charleston, S.C. 29401

Dry Sinks

Such country, Victorian-style antiques are becoming scarce. They have become so popular for use as bars that even the scruffiest old pine objects are commanding high prices. Dry sinks are convenient receptacles for bottles, and the storage space below is useful for other purposes. Few, if any, are being used in the original manner—as kitchen sinks for the washing of dishes. They don't seem to be particularly appropriate pieces for the living room or front parlor; better to keep them in the kitchen or foyer where they can at least be employed for additional storage.

Berea's craftsmen produce a rather expensive dry sink in cherry ($715) or mahogany or walnut ($800); perhaps they would be willing to custom-make one in pine for a lower price. It is a handsome piece measuring 42″ wide, 18″ deep, and 44″ high, and is fitted with fine hardware.

Catalogue and price list available.

Berea College
Student Craft Industries
Berea, Ky. 40403

Typical of the commercially-produced dry sinks is that available from Ephraim Marsh. It may be just right for your purpose. The sink, illustrated here, is made of "maple solids and veneers." This model is somewhat smaller than that manufactured by Berea, but the cost, $159, puts it into a completely different category.

Catalogue and price list available.

Ephraim Marsh Co.
Box 266
Concord, N.C. 28025

Rockers

Every old house should be furnished with at least one rocking chair. There are few people who do not find the back-and-forth movement of such a chair pleasurable; it is certainly a piece of furniture enjoyed by children. Rockers, of course, are but chairs fitted with "rockers" or curved pieces of wood attached to the legs. The form first appeared in America in the early 1700s as a piece of farmhouse furniture. The Boston rocker, evolved from the Windsor chair, is probably the favorite type, and it was introduced in the 1840s.

Bentback Rocker

Robert Whitley's design is authentic in many ways. It is an original statement, not a copy. It surely derives from a tradition of chairmaking mastered in America, but it is also extremely contemporary in feeling and

a slight bend in the spindles meant to fit the body contour. Nichols & Stone claim that their chair will last for generations, and from the description of how they are produced, they indeed might hold up for a long period of time.

Catalogue available.

Nichols & Stone
Gardner, Mass. 01440

Gliding Rocking Chair

Platform-based rockers became popular during the Victorian era; they would *not* slide away across the floor when rocked with vigor. The gliding rocker illustrated here was patented in 1856. It looks a bit like a chair of torture, but the manufacturer claims that it is "an exhilarating sensation. . . . As you shift your weight gently, the chair glides back and forth in the most restful of motions." It surely is an American contraption worthy of an early Rube Goldberg. Priced at $299.95.

Catalogue available.

Magnolia Hall
726 Andover
Atlanta, Ga. 30327

execution. The seat, arms, and back are shaped with great care to fit the human body. The rocker is both functional and aesthetically pleasing—an ideal combination in any period.

Catalogue available.

The Robert Whitely Studio
Laurel Road
Solebury, Penn. 18963

Boston Rocker

Here is *the* American classic. It has a "saucer" seat and

Ladder-Back Rocker

Four-slat ladder-back chairs with rockers joined in the legs are probably among the earliest of rocker designs. Thomas Moser offers rockers with and without arms in cherry and walnut. Seat are made of one-half-inch natural splint that is woven in a herringbone pattern. These are most workmanlike clean reproductions.

Catalogue available.

Thomas Moser, Cabinet Maker
Cobb's Bridge Road
New Gloucester, Me. 04260

Settles

The settle was once a truly gargantuan piece of furniture made of oak. Freestanding or built into the wall, it was used for seating and storage. Presumably the high back hood protected the medieval homesteader from cold drafts if not the unfriendly protestations of unruly serfs. Since the seventeenth century the settle has been made of lighter woods and its size somewhat reduced. It surely belongs in an early Colonial kitchen or foyer of suitably large proportions.

A hooded pine settle is offered by D. R. Millbranth. This is equipped with a center armrest which folds up so that you have access to storage space underneath the hinged seat. The piece is 63″ wide, 58″ high, and 19″ deep. Unfinished, it sells for $425; with antique finish, $445.

Inquiries invited.

D. R. Millbranth, Cabinetmaker
P.O. Box 321
Gaithersburg, Md. 20760

Cane Farm's pine settle is based on one found in the Metropolitan Museum from the late 1600s. It, too, is hooded, but there is no armrest or storage space below the seat. The makers suggest that it be used in front of the fire, but you might block off the view, not to speak of the heat, from everyone else. It is 51″ wide and 64½″ high.

Literature available.

The Cane Farm
Rosemont, N.J. 08556

Congress Hall Clerk's Stool

This handsome reproduction is of a Windsor stool found in Congress Hall, Independence National Historical Park, Philadelphia. As pictured, it is three legged with a bar across for resting the feet. It is 30¾" tall and would be useful in a kitchen, if not in a library or informal office. Price, $95.

Brochure available.

The Holmes Co.
Box 1776
Wrightsville, Penn. 17368

Stools

These are extremely handy pieces of furniture. They may be used for resting tired feet and legs or just for sitting upon. Meant for the use of one person, unlike a bench which will hold two or more, the stool is highly portable and usually light in construction. It may be used in front of the fireplace or drawn up next to a chair to place papers on. In earlier days stools served as chairs since the latter objects were rather meagerly distributed. The forms from the seventeenth and eighteenth centuries with which we are most familiar have legs which follow in design those of chairs of the same period.

Footstool

Thomas Moser's footstool is an extremely simple hardwood piece 12" high by 17" deep by 19" wide. It is open on all four sides and has a top of one-half-inch natural splint which is woven in a herringbone pattern. This has been sealed, and the maker claims that it can be cleaned with a damp cloth, an important point for a stool meant for the feet.

Catalogue available.

Thomas Moser, Cabinet Maker
Cobb's Bridge Road
New Gloucester, Me. 04260

William and Mary Stool

This heavy open stool is appropriately made of walnut with heavily turned legs and stretchers. The top is of brown suede which has been attached with brass tacks of alternating small and large sizes. It is a handsome piece for either an early Colonial home or one following the very late Victorian vogue for the Tudor Gothic. Price, $80.

Literature available.

Sarreid, Ltd.
P.O. Box 3545
Wilson, N.C. 27893

or

Uniquities
Marketplace
2400 Market St.
Philadelphia, Penn. 19103

Tables

Within this category of furniture only small pieces are considered. Antique dining tables of various periods are relatively plentiful, and it is unlikely that a good reproduction will cost any less. More difficult to find are the smaller, special-use pieces such as corner and tea tables, as well as particular forms such as the gate-leg and Louis XIII occasional pieces, which are hoarded by museums and private collectors.

Corner Tables

This one-legged corner table is an English rarity dating in style from 1720. The top, of course, is triangular and the graceful leg with pad foot is decorated with scrolls and a carved shell and pendant bellflowers. It could be most usefully placed in a foyer or entrance hall. The height is 30″, width 22¼″, and depth 16″ at center. Price, $600 to $640 according to the finish desired.

Catalogue and price list available, $2.95.

Craft House

Williamsburg, Va. 23185

Gate-Leg Table

Nicholas's William and Mary gate-leg table is one of the handsomest reproductions available today. The turnings and stretchers are beautifully worked. It is made

with a double gate to support two leaves. This piece is custom-made and requires two months for completion. It is 30½″ high, 60″ wide, and 50″ deep when open. Price, $1,400.

Literature available.

Nicholas, Cabinet Maker
684 Starin Ave.
Buffalo, N.Y. 14223

Louis XIII Table

Such a table is rarely to be found on the antiques market today. The first half of the seventeenth cen-

tury was not a great period for cabinetmaking in France. The furniture is somewhat pedestrian and rectilinear in form, one not dissimilar to that of the Pilgrim Century. The legs of this and of many other tables of the period, however, are handsomely turned in a spiral fashion, thereby rendering the whole piece a distinctly interesting one.

Catalogue available.

Louis Maslow & Son, Inc.
D & D Building
979 Third Ave.
New York, N.Y. 10022

Night Tables

Included in Davis's Lillian Russell Victorian furniture line is a one-drawer night table on a four-legged base.

The pedestal is in the form of an inverted lyre. The drawer is fitted with a wooden pull. The table is 17″ wide, 14″ deep, and 28″ high.

Catalogue available.

Davis Cabinet Co.
Box 5424
Nashville, Tenn. 38106

A small table of this sort can be used in many ways, and beside the bed is one of them. The choice of aesthetically-pleasing night or end tables is today extremely limited. This table is, of course, far removed from the enclosed washstands (with removable tray tops) of the late eighteenth century and later which served as repositories for nightly needs. This is just a simple jack-of-all-trades table, handsome enough to fit in almost anywhere. It is a reproduction of an eighteenth-century piece found in Independence National Historical Park's Congress Hall, Philadelphia. It measures 29½″ wide, 19½ deep, and 28¾ high. Price, $185.

Brochure available.

The Holmes Co.
Box 1776
Wrightsville, Penn. 17368

Chippendale Tea Table

Tea tables become fashionable in America in the mid-1700s, just when the Chippendale style was gaining in popularity. Historic Charleston Reproductions has

turned to one such piece which stands in the music room of the National Russell House. This has been copied by the English cabinetmakers at Stebbing in what is termed flame mahogany. As illustrated, the table is a tilt-top with a pie-crust edge and birdcage mount. It is 33″ in diameter and 27½″ high. Price, $840.

Catalogue and price list available.

Historic Charleston Reproductions Shop
105 Broad Street
Charleston, S.C. 29401

Robert Whitley also makes a Chippendale pie-crust tea table. It is based on a Philadelphia piece, c. 1760-1780, of unusual beauty. The shaft is carved with fluting and a suppressed ball. The knees of the cabriole legs are carved with acanthus-leaf decoration. This table is 29½″ in diameter and stands 27¼″ high.

Catalogue available.

The Robert Whitley Studio
Laurel Road
Solebury, Penn. 18963

Tear-Drop Table

Magnolia's marble-topped oval table would do justice to any mid-Victorian parlor. The base is of heavy scroll-cut mahogany. Four tear-drop carvings are found on the apron of the top and in carvings below. A rose-and-leaf design is hand carved on the apron as well. The table is 26½″ tall. Price, $129.95.

Catalogue available.

Magnolia Hall
726 Andover
Atlanta, Ga. 30327

Trestle Table

The two elders and two eldresses who made up the ministry of the Shaker order in Enfield, Connecticut, dined from a table of this design. It is a small one, 27″ wide by 50″ long by 24½″ high, and yet another example of the fine design sense which all Shakers seemed to enjoy. The table is made from select hardwoods. Price, $260.

Catalogue and price list available.

Guild of Shaker Crafts
401 W. Savidge Street
Spring Lake, Mich. 49456

Umbrella Stands

Where to hang the dripping umbrella? An antique English stand has been reproduced by Madison Square

Furniture for Historic Charleston. It is decorated with brass pineapple finials and contains a black metal drip pan. The original is found in the front hall of the Edmonston-Alston House. Price, $110.

Catalogue and price list available.

Historic Charleston Reproductions Shop
105 Broad St.
Charleston, S.C. 29401

Washstands

From the mid-1700s on, special pieces of furniture were fashioned for use in bedrooms. Called wash-stands, they were built in both a closed, rectangular fashion approximating that of a night table, or as a corner, triangular piece. Sometimes a hole was cut in the top shelf for a basin. With the introduction of indoor plumbing, their utility has become limited. They do serve, however, as a convenient place on which to rest personal effects of various sorts.

Corner Washstand

This triangular object is that which was most commonly found in nineteenth-century bedrooms. It has

three shelves, the second of which has a drawer attached. Resting on three legs, it will fit back in a corner quite nicely. The stand is 25½″ wide, 17½″ deep, and 38½″ high. Price, $182.

Catalogue and price list available.

Ephraim Marsh Co.
Box 266
Concord, N.C. 28025

Shaker Washstand

From a "retiring room" of one of the Canaan families in New Lebanon, New York, comes a square pine box with cupboard below. A simple rail encloses the top on three sides. Attached to the side is a brush and towel holder. The reproduction is available in cherry or pine and is priced at $235.

Catalogue and price list available.

Guild of Shaker Crafts, Inc.
401 W. Savidge St.
Spring Lake, Mich. 49456

Furniture Designs and Kits

If you are gifted at all in woodworking or have a friend who tries his hand at cabinetmaking, be sure to investigate the number of companies offering furni-

ture kits and designs. Some of these manufacturers or designers have created exciting and attractive objects. Good reproductions, as everyone knows, are quite expensive, and there are considerable savings to be made in the do-it-yourself area if it is one that is feasible for you.

The Bartley Collection

This company, in association with the Henry Ford Museum and Greenfield Village, has assembled a handsome collection of objects which are available in kit form. They may also be purchased ready-assembled. According to the Henry Ford Museum, the Bartley people are "determined to make these pieces generally available at modest prices [and] have not compromised on quality. To accomplish this, they have provided *exact reproductions in kit form.* Instructions are explicit and easy to follow. Clamps, varnishes, sandpaper, and all things necessary to complete these outstanding additions to your home are provided."

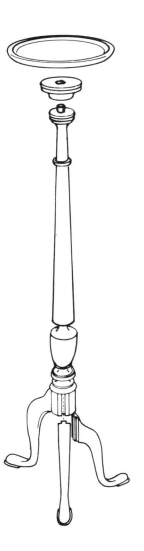

Among the kits offered by Bartley are reproductions of a seventeenth-century joint stool in solid oak or cherry, illustrated here, and a candlestand available in Honduras mahogany or cherry. The stool kit is priced at $75; the stand at $45. These are modest, small projects that upon successful completion might lead to more ambitious undertakings.

Illustrated and priced catalogue available, $1.

The Bartley Collection, Ltd.
747 Oakwood Ave.
Lake Forest, Ill. 60045

Cohasset Colonials

This is a superb supply house for the Colonial old-house buff. In addition to furniture kits, the company offers lighting fixtures, fabrics, paints, and hardware. As with Bartley, there has been a serious attempt to offer only true copies of museum-quality antiques. Cohasset has drawn examples from the Wadsworth Atheneum, the Concord (Mass.) Antiquarian Society, Fruitlands Museum, Plimoth Plantation, and Henry Ford Museum, among others.

Among the kits suitable as starter projects are a rush-seat child's chair ($18.95), a Shaker tray on a folding base ($44.95), and a night table with pine top and maple legs and drawer front ($34.95).

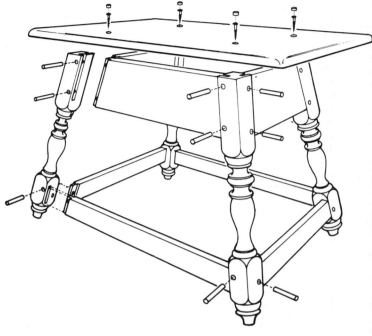

Furniture Designs

This company supplies full-size plans for woodworkers. A complete list of materials, including hardware, is included on each plan. Suggested ways of joining parts are given along with a perspective sketch of the piece when assembled. Over 150 designs are offered in the catalogue, and plans run in cost from $4 to $8.

Catalogue available, $1.

Furniture Designs
1425 Sherman Ave.
Evanston, Ill. 60201

Peerless Rattan & Reed

Cane and rush chair and stool kits are available from this company along with instruction books. They are also suppliers of other materials necessary for successful caning of seats and backs.

Brochure available.

Peerless Rattan & Reed Mfg. Co., Inc.
97 Washington St.
New York, N.Y. 10006

Other Furniture Sources

Consult List of Suppliers for addresses.

Beds

Baker, Knapp, & Tubbs
Chapman Manufacturing Co.
Davis Cabinet Co.
Guild of Shaker Crafts
The Hitchcock Chair Co.
Magnolia Hall
Ephraim Marsh Co.
Phyllis Morris Originals
Thomas Moser
Reid Classics

Benches

Baker, Knapp, & Tubbs
Craft House
Magnolia Hall
Ephraim Marsh Co.
The Hitchcock Chair Co.

Candlestands

Craft House
Guild of Shaker Crafts
The Lennox Shop
Ephraim Marsh Co.
Shaker Workshops, Inc.

Canterburies

Baker, Knapp, & Tubbs
Brewster Corp.
Chapman Manufacturing Co.

Chairs

Auffray & Co.
Brunovan, Inc.
Douglas Campbell
The Cane Farm
Guild of Shaker Crafts
Hagen International
Kenmore Furniture Co.
The Lennox Shop
Ephraim Marsh Co.
Thomas Moser, Cabinet Maker
Shaker Workshops, Inc.

Chests

Craft House
Ephraim Marsh Co.

Thomas Moser, Cabinet Maker
Nicholas, Cabinet Maker

Rockers

Berea College, Student Craft Industries
Guild of Shaker Crafts
Ephraim Marsh Co.
Shaker Workshops, Inc.

Stools

Magnolia Hall
Ephraim Marsh Co.
Nicholas, Cabinet Maker

Tables

Baker, Knapp, & Tubbs
Berea College, Student Craft Industries
The Cane Farm
Empire Furniture and Rattan Works
Gargoyles, Ltd.
The Hitchcock Chair Co.
Kaplan Furniture Co.
The Lennox Shop
Ernest Lo Nano
The McGuire Co.
Thomas Moser, Cabinet Maker
Shaker Workshops, Inc.
Superior Reed and Rattan
Townshend Furniture

Washstands

Nicholas, Cabinet Maker

Kits and Designs

Albert Constantine & Son, Inc.

drinking-cup is a copy; the gothic vase is from the design of Professor Strach. But the most beautiful of the objects contributed by Mrs. Marsh is a Fountain, which we also engrave. This work was produced expressly for the Exhibition.

The VASE, filled with artificial FLOWERS OF SILVER, is the production of STRUBE AND SON, Jewellers, and Silver and Gold Workers, of Leipsic. The Vase is an object of much delicate beauty: the flowers are not made in dies, but are the production of the artist's hand, and are accurately modelled from nature.

We saw at the establishment of Messrs. Strube much that was rare and valuable, but in this particular branch they are unrivalled.

The works of M. FALLOISE, of Liege, in wrought metals, are of the highest order of merit; the cover of a SNUFF-BOX we print on this page; and works of great ability on subsequent pages.

X Accessories

An accessory is, as per the dictionary definition, something supplementary. It is not a fundamental part of any house—old or new—yet Americans may spend more money each year for decorative accessories than they do for heating oil. Accessories are the small things which are irresistible or seem so when discovered in an antique shop, a museum store, or the corner gift emporium. A majority are probably bought on an impulse and turn up later in garage sales or the Salvation Army outlet. If purchased wisely, however, such objects can be useful tools around the house and add to a property's general attractiveness. If they are new items, they may, with age, assume the status of an antique.

In this last section of *The Old House Catalogue*, the concern is with baskets, trays, pillows, outdoor furniture, fountains, pewter, silver, china, glass, clocks, tinware, etc. The companies listed are reputable firms known for quality products that will provide more than fleeting pleasure or utility. Eliminated from the listings are many hundreds of product lines which are made up of bad copies of period objects, ephemeral items of questionable taste, and anything which reeks of synthetic fabrication. In other words, we have tried to avoid kitsch, and in the 1970s that is a full-time occupation.

The museum shop is one of the best places to look for fine accessory items. A concern for honest craftsmanship is almost always reflected in these institutions. More and more people are turning to such retail outlets for gift items for themselves and others. The shop at the Philadelphia Museum of Art, for instance, is a handsomely appointed outlet for quality glassware, stained glass, textiles, and incidental items such as wrapping paper and note cards. It is also one of the best art book shops in the area. The Philadelphia story is repeated in many other museums across North America.

A special salute is due those companies such as Robinson Iron, The Erkins Studio, and J. W. Fiske which uphold a long tradition of fine workmanship in the decorative arts. The temptation to radically change their manufacturing methods in recent years must have been a strong one; yet they have resisted the blandishments of high profit and so-called progress.

English Mercury Stick Barometers

Practical accessories, these instruments for measuring changes in atmospheric pressure also include thermometers in Fahrenheit. They are made in England and are reproductions of stick barometers from the late 1700s and early 1800s. The cases are made of solid mahogany, and all are fitted with brass fittings and

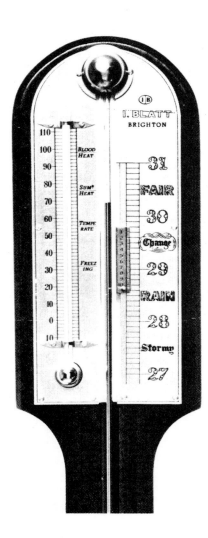

screws. There are two models to choose from, and these are priced from $125 to $175, depending on the kind of register plate (ivory or silvered brass) desired.

Literature available.

British-American Historical Arts, Ltd.
10884 Santa Monica Blvd.
Los Angeles, Calif. 90025

Hand-Woven Baskets

There are many kinds of baskets—garden, knitting, market, laundry, lunch and picnic, pie and cake, shopper's—and West Rindge produces some of the best, in ash with oak hoops and handles. Illustrated is the $5 pie and cake basket, which is priced at $10.50. It is sold with the tray. Other baskets are offered in price from $4.85 to $13.80.

Brochure available.

West Rindge Baskets, Inc.
Box 24
Rindge, N.H. 03461

Birdcages

Antique birdcages in wood and in brass are among the most imaginative and elegant of period accessories. The wrought-iron cages made by Mexico House today are of the same high quality. Particularly attractive is the model illustrated here, a circular cage with a high dome. It should put any bird in a singing mood. Price, $49.95.

Catalogue available, $1.

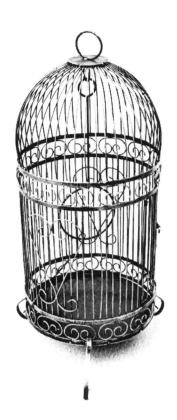

Mexico House
Del Mar, Calif. 92014

Boxes and Trays

Shaker boxes and trays are handsomely-shaped containers with a contemporary feeling. The oval nesting
boxes are the best known of these products, with side
banding that features overlapping "fingers" pointing
to the right or left. The Guild of Shaker Crafts makes
these oval boxes with maple sides and pine tops and
bottoms secured with small wooden pegs. The "fingers" point to the right. There are thirteen sizes available, from 3¼″ x 2¼″ x 1¼″ to 15″ x 11″ x 7″, at prices
ranging from $8 to $35.

Among the other containers offered by the Guild are a
dining room silver tray ($16), pine trays used for serv-
ing ($12 and $13), and a dining room deep tray, for
carrying water glasses ($29).

Catalogue available.

Guild of Shaker Crafts
401 W. Savidge
Spring Lake, Mich. 49456

China

There is little reason to choose reproduction porcelain for use at home—*unless* the new work is as fine as that done in the past. The blue and white Canton produced by Vista Alegre craftsmen working with Mottahedeh is of this quality. The drawing is accomplished; and the coloring, a luminous, true sapphire blue. A five-piece setting is priced at $60.50. There are a number of special pieces available—coffee- and teapots, a tureen and platter, pitchers, ginger jars, sugar bowl and creamer—in the same pattern. All these, along with the basic settings, have been commissioned by the Historic Charleston Foundation.

Catalogue available with price list.

Historic Charleston Reproductions Shop
105 Broad Street
Charleston, S.C. 29401

Clocks

As with china, antiques are to be preferred over reproductions. There are a number of manufacturers making copies, especially of the grandfather variety, which are crudely worked and exorbitantly priced. Avoid them. Fortunately, there are also "good guys" such as Colonial of Zeeland, Michigan, a firm that produces reproductions for the Henry Ford Museum and Greenfield Village. An example of their work is illustrated here, the Brewster and Ingraham's steeple clock with a mahogany case and an hour and half-hour strike movement. The original was made c. 1844-1852

in Bristol, Connecticut. This model is priced at $220. There are eight other clock models available, four of them tall case clocks ranging in price from $900 to $1,140.

Catalogue and price list available.

Henry Ford Museum and Greenfield Village
20900 Oakwood Blvd.
Dearborn, Mich. 48121

Regulator clocks are very precise timepieces originally produced in New England during the nine-

teenth century. Trotman carries on the tradition of fine craftsmanship with its handmade models. As the company states, "A limited quantity can be produced monthly, and quality will not be sacrificed to increase production." These long wall clocks (40″ long and 17″ wide) were often used in schools and meeting houses and today are made of pine and finished in dark walnut. Trotman imports the eight-day key-wound movement from Germany.

Brochure available.

Trotman Clock Co.
Box 71
Amherst, Mass. 01002

Replacing antique clock parts can be a difficult task. Period Hardware, however, has available brass fittings such as finials and hands. They will also restore clock faces or provide new ones from their stock. Reverse paintings on glass for various kinds of clocks can be provided as well, and these are hand painted to order.

Catalogue and price list available, $2.

Period Furniture Hardware Co., Inc.
123 Charles Street
Boston, Mass. 02114

Doorstops

Doorstops are a small touch in any old house, but very useful ones. There are some truly awful designs on the market. Ball & Ball carries better ones in solid cast and polished brass. These are cast from originals in their own collection and are priced from $34 to $40.

Catalogue available with price list, $1.

Ball & Ball
463 W. Lincoln Hwy.
Exton, Penn. 19341

Fans

Overhead fans of the Victorian variety have become more and more popular in recent years. They can be most graceful fixtures and provide more than sufficient air circulation and cooling effect for even a person used to air-conditioned comfort. Old fans salvaged from wreckers may be located in many large cities. The Windyne Company has turned to their reproduction. The basic model is based on a c.1920 ceiling fan with wooden blades. There are two sizes to choose from, 39″ or 53″ in diameter. The four blades of each are made of poplar, individually cut and hand-sanded before staining. These may be finished with a golden-oak or dark-walnut varnish. As illustrated, each fan has its own motor casing, suspension rod, and pull cord and tassel.

Literature available.

Windyne Company
Box 9091
Richmond, Va. 23225

Fountains

Cast-iron fountains for use in a patio or in a garden are handsomely produced by Robinson Iron. A few of their designs are of Spanish origin; one of these is available in a half-fountain style for use flush against a

wall. The majority of the designs, however, are nineteenth-century American. The Janney patterns for railings, gates, garden furniture, posts, fountains, etc., were the pride and treasure of Montgomery, Alabama's Janney Iron Works. Robinson is now the proud possessor of these cast-iron patterns and can reproduce any one of a number of authentic, appealing designs.

Literature available.

Robinson Iron
Robinson Road
Alexander City, Ala. 35010

Erkins' fountains are available in carved Italian stone, cast stone, and lead. Their custom-work department is also prepared to execute designs in marble and wrought iron. Of special interest are the wall bowls in cast stone and lead which provide just the right receptacle for a slow-flowing decorative wall fountain. These are offered in cast stone for $44 and $55; in lead for $35 to $400.

Catalogue available.

The Erkins Studios, Inc.
8 W. 40th St.
New York, N.Y. 10018

Gates and Fences

Elaborate wrought-iron gates, such as that illustrated here, can be found at Gargoyles. A little bit of this

goes a long way; a complete fence of such intricate work would require much time in maintenance, if not a very watchful eye. Gates and fencing of this sort are prey to the wanton destruction of the twentieth century as well as to knowledgeable thievery. If you have such a gate, be sure that it is very strongly mounted.

Catalogue available, $4.

Gargoyles, Ltd.
512 S. Third St.
Philadelphia, Penn. 19147

The House of Iron, Inc., also specializes in wrought-iron gates. Among their designs are some which are appropriate for use with fencing, if not indoors.

Literature available.

The House of Iron, Inc.
3384 Long Beach Rd.
Oceanside, N.Y. 11572

A broad selection of cast-iron components for gates and fencing is available from Tennessee Fabricating. There are designs appropriate for almost any kind of building—from French and Spanish Colonial to high American Victorian. One such group of patterns is termed Pontalba and combines scrolls, rosettes, and related wrought-iron patterns of English derivation. These were first used for New Orleans' Pontalba building in 1848.

Catalogue available, $1.

Tennessee Fabricating Co.
2366 Prospect
Memphis, Tenn. 38106

Glass

Glassware, like good china, can be found at reasonable prices in antique shops. But for far less cost and for everyday use, you may want to examine some of the reproduction lines. One of these is produced by Fostoria under license from the Henry Ford Museum and Greenfield Village. Two patterns are available. The Panelled Diamond Point is, as termed, a cut lead-crystal glass; it is available in goblets, wines, and champagnes. The Argus is a pressed pattern originally available only in clear glass. It is now made in crystal, olive green, cobalt blue, gray, and ruby. There are various kinds of goblets, tumblers, a dessert dish, and a plate. Each of the Panelled Diamond Point glasses are priced

at $8; the Argus pattern pieces range in price from $7.25 to $10.25, depending on the color and size.

Catalogue available.

Henry Ford Museum and Greenfield Village
20900 Oakwood Blvd.
Dearborn, Mich. 48121

Liberty Village is part of a complex of shops and small craft houses devoted to traditional reproduction work. A glasshouse was established several years ago and copies of South Jersey pieces are being turned out regularly. These are sold by Liberty Village and by such outlets as the shop of the Philadelphia Museum of Art. There are glasses, mugs, water pitchers, sugar bowls, creamers, and decanters. Most are made in the lily-pad design. Prices range from $15 to $42.50.

Literature available.

Liberty Village
Flemington, N.J. 08822

Gold Leaf

Metallic gilding on glass, wood, stone or marble is frequently encountered when dealing with old structures and their furnishings. M. Swift & Sons is the largest and highest quality manufacturer of gold leaf in the world; they also carry silver, aluminum, and composition or Dutch-metal leaf. Although most of these materials are used for sign decoration, they may be applied to furniture, if not certain structural elements such as columns, pilasters, and cornices.

Literature available.

M. Swift & Sons, Inc.
10 Love Lane
Hartford, Conn. 06101

Hitching Posts

You may have a real use for such a device. The horse and buggy combination is on its way back in the country as gasoline prices rise and rise. Turn to the Tennessee Fabricating Co. for authentic reproductions of Victorian posts.

Catalogue available, $1.

Tennessee Fabricating Co.
2366 Prospect
Memphis, Tenn. 38106

Kitchen Accessories

These are a dime a dozen in the gift shops across America. Most are prefectly hideous, useless objects. The exceptions are often those made in Italy or France. A number of blacksmiths, however, do produce handsome, durable objects. Stephen Parker offers several such quality pieces—the heart trivet, illustrated here; a lettuce and vegetable cutter with a maple handle; a fire broiler; and a swivel-handled toast rack to be used in the fireplace. All are of hand-forged iron.

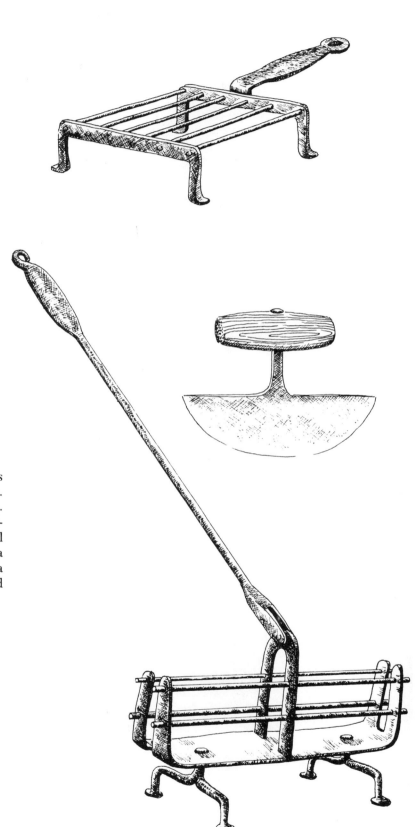

Catalogue available, $1.

Stephen W. Parker
Box 40
Craftsbury, Vt. 05826

Lawn and Porch Furniture

Cast iron will provide you with the most durable of "outdoor" furniture—whether used on an enclosed porch, a patio, or set in the lawn itself. There are many copies on the market now which are made of nothing but aluminum or other light materials. Don't bother with them. The real thing does not have to be that much more expensive. If you are seeking a base for a picnic table, for instance, think of using an old sewing machine base. It will hold almost any weight, and, besides, you can pedal as you eat.

If old cast-iron furniture is out of the question, turn to any one of several reproduction manufacturers. Gargoyles offers new cast-iron benches in the old style. These weigh anywhere from 151 to 240 pounds and are surely guaranteed to stay in place. Two models have wood seats of unfinished pine, although such other materials as redwood are available. The other two models come with wood seats and slat backs.

Catalogue available, $4.

Gargoyles Ltd.
512 S. Third St.
Philadelphia, Penn. 19147

A cast-iron settee, a chair, and a table in the traditional grapevine pattern can be purchased from Lemée's. The finish is a heavy baked white enamel. The three pieces are available as a set for $135.

Catalogue available, 35¢.

Lemée's Fireplace Equipment
Route 28
Bridgewater, Mass. 02324

Hand-forged iron table legs are available from Kenneth Lynch & Sons. These are made of wrought iron in Spanish and French designs. Lynch also specializes in cast-iron, cast-stone, and wrought-steel benches, some of which are appropriate for home use. A special catalogue, $2.50, covers these latter items.

Kenneth Lynch & Sons
Wilton, Conn. 06897

A very wide selection of furniture designs in cast iron is offered by Tennessee Fabricating. Some of these are also available in aluminum and should be avoided. Among the patterns are grape, Cajon fern, morning glory, Victorian, mountain fern, and classic garden.

Special brochure available.

Tennessee Fabricating Co.
2366 Prospect
Memphis, Tenn. 38106

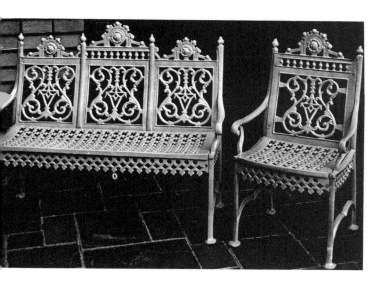

Literature available.

Reale Mirror Mfg. Co., Inc.
16-18 East 12th St.
New York, N.Y. 10003

LaBarge Mirrors have crafted a very fine Queen Anne looking glass for the Henry Ford Museum and Greenfield Village. It is a copy of a 1725 English piece with carved shell designs at top and bottom. Attached to the lower rail are two brass candle arms. Price, $398.

Mirrors

A mirror reflects more than an image; in design it is a reflection of period styles in furniture making. Reale Mirror offers more than 100 items, and each mirror is suitable for a particular period. Some contain decorative glass panels, elaborate carved frames with finials, and gold-leaf or gold-metal-leaf finish.

Catalogue and price list available.

Henry Ford Museum and Greenfield Village
20900 Oakwood Blvd.
Dearborn, Mich. 48121

Acid-etched and reverse painted mirrors are the specialties of Rococo Designs. These are all, of course, handcrafted. The acid-etched designs are particularly interesting and might be suitable for use in late-Victorian interiors. Rococo is more than willing to custom-make etched glass for front doors, windows, etc. The design illustrated here is known as Wisteria. Un-

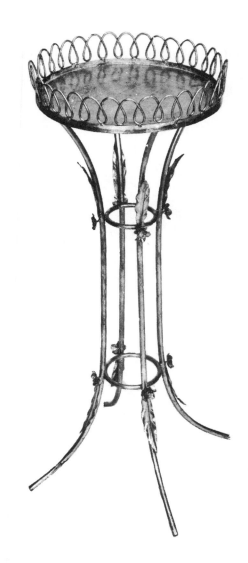

framed, the mirror is priced at $37.30; framed, from $42.30 to $49.75, depending on the kind of frame wanted (chrome, regular wood, or curly maple).

Literature available.

Rococo Designs
417 Pennsylvania Ave.
Santa Cruz, Calif. 95062

Pedestals

Pedestals may be used for sculpture, plants, or candelabra. They became popular during the late-Colonial or Federal period and enjoyed a revival again in stately late-Victorian mansions. Decorative Crafts offers thousands of items, most of them imported from Italy. A few of these are appropriate for period American homes. Italian alabaster pedestals are available, these measuring 26″, 37½″, and 39″ high. Tops are large enough to hold fairly sizeable objects. The pedestals are priced from $135 to $165. Also offered by Decora-

tive Crafts is a four-legged, wrought-iron pedestal suitable for plants. The top is defined by an open-basket scroll border. Finished in gold leaf, it stands 38″ high. Price, $125.

Literature available.

Decorative Crafts, Inc.
41 Madison Ave.
New York, N.Y. 10010

Erkins' pedestals in cast stone and carved Italian stone are suitable for the mounting of sundials. The lowest is 24″ high while the highest measures 42″. Prices run from $36 to $290.

Catalogue available.

The Erkins Studios, Inc.
8. W. 40th St.
New York, N.Y. 10018

Pewter

Pewter is probably the most popular of metals in America for decorative purposes. It has a particularly humble, hearty look, a crafted appearance. It is not false or flashy. Pewter, of course, is identified almost exclusively with Colonial interiors. By the middle of the nineteenth century the pewter industry had just about faded away. Only a few makers of britannia ware continued the pewterer's craft until the end of the century. Antique pewter can be a very handsome metal whether used in candlesticks, plates, chalices, spoons, jugs, or in other pieces. It is also very, very expensive; American pieces bring much higher prices than those made in England. If you intend to use pewter in any practical fashion, have a look at some of the better reproduction lines. There are companies active in the field that claim to make authentic pewter pieces, but these are questionable in both content and form. Those that follow are not. The new pieces, of course, are lead free.

Colonial Casting includes the following statement with all of its literature: "our products are genuine pewter.... Our pewter has the following approximate analysis with no lead added: tin, 92-93%; antimony, 6-7%; copper, 1-2%." Among the objects fashioned in real pewter are goblets, tankards, mugs, various plates, porringers, vases, and bowls. Among the most handsome are Queen Anne or scalloped-edge plates, ranging in size from 4½" to 10" in diameter. These are priced from $5.50 to $23.

Brochure available.

The Colonial Casting Co.
443 S. Colony St.
Meriden, Conn. 06450

Boston's Museum of Fine Arts has one of the finest antique pewter collections in America; their shop of-

fers extremely well-made reproductions. Illustrated is a sugar bowl based on a work by George Richardson in the early 1800s. Price, $50.

Catalogue available.

Museum Shop
Museum of Fine Arts
Boston, Mass. 02115

The Henry Ford Museum's pewter is almost as well-known as that of Boston's MFA. They have chosen Woodbury Pewterers, Inc., of Connecticut to produce their reproductions. These are exact copies of pieces by such well-known American pewterers as Ashbil Griswold, George Richardson, Rufus Dunham, Benjamin Day, and Thomas Danforth Boardman.

Catalogue available.

Henry Ford Museum and Greenfield Village
20900 Oakwood Blvd.
Dearborn, Mich. 48121

Pillows

Small throw pillows are very minor elements in any old house interior. If it were not for the fact that the Philadelphia Museum of Art shop offers such attractive designs, it would be easy to forget these textile-covered extras. Two of the beautiful designs are offered in kits: these are the crewel tiger pillow and needlepoint butterfly pillow. For do-it-yourself needleworkers, they would make handsome projects. All the designs have been adapted from works in the museum's collections.

Catalogue available.

The Museum Shop
Philadelphia Museum of Art
Box 7646
Philadelphia, Penn. 19101

Prints

There is no need to go to Paris or New York to find antique prints suitable for framing. G. B. and F. J. Manasek provide extremely handsome natural history prints from the seventeenth through the nineteenth centuries, as well as engravings in the fields of military arts and hunting. These are very reasonably priced.

The listings in their catalogue make for good reading. Why go and spend money on reproductions (usually badly printed) when such prints and engravings are available?

Catalogue and other literature available.

G. B. Manasek, F. J. Manasek
4858 S. Dorchester Ave.
Chicago, Ill. 60615

Pottery

Pottery reproductions can be used as serving dishes, ash trays, vases—ways in which you might be reluctant to use antique pieces. Bucks County's Mercer Museum is in the midst of the Pennsylvania pottery territory, and from it comes an assortment of redware. Included are a rectangular slip plate, sgraffito pie plate, crimped-edge pie plate, and deep-dish candle

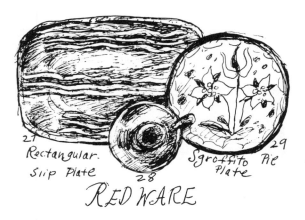

holder. Each piece is signed and dated by a local craftsman. Prices, $3.25 to $16.

Brochure available, 50¢.

Mercer Museum Shop
Bucks County Historical Society
Pine & Ashland
Doylestown, Penn. 18901

Henry Ford Museum offers a much larger selection of reproduction pottery. It includes copies of pieces made in England, Michigan, western Ohio, and Pennsylvania. Among the most handsome is a covered jar, c. 1850, in a raw umber color. Price, $37.50.

Catalogue available.

Henry Ford Museum and Greenfield Village
20900 Oakwood Blvd.
Dearborn, Mich. 48121

Silver

The Boston Museum of Fine Arts has drawn from its Pauline Revere Thayer Collection for superb pieces to be copied in silver plate and sterling. The beaker illustrated here is one such item. It was made by Paul Revere, c. 1800. The price in sterling is $75; silver plate, $14.50. The beaker stands 3 7/16″ high. The Museum Shop also offers a five-piece tea and coffee service adapted from a design by Revere. It is rendered in silver plate by Lunt Silversmith for $450.00.

Catalogue available.

Museum Shop
Museum of Fine Arts
Boston, Mass. 02115

Sundials

Kenneth Lynch & Sons specializes in sundials, among other ornamental metal appointments. Illustrated is a wall sundial, 15″ high and 11″ wide, which is made of hammered zinc or copper. The pointer is bronze and the numerals are of lead. A zinc model is priced at $50; the copper price will be furnished upon request. Lynch publishes a complete catalogue devoted to sundials, available for $2.50.

Kenneth Lynch & Sons, Inc.
Wilton, Conn. 06897

Florentine Craftsmen is probably the best-known supplier of outdoor sculpture on the East Coast. It is an important source for those who are delighted by impish fauns and satyrs. It is also a good place to look for sundials. There are at least ten models to choose from and all are of bronze. Among the unusual designs are a compass indicator and a sundial in the shape of a grape leaf. The compass design measures a foot in

diameter and sells for $60; the leaf is 8″ x 7¾″ and is priced at $35.

Catalogue available.

Florentine Craftsmen
650 First Ave.
New York, N.Y. 10016

Tinware

Antique decorative tinware is hard to find in good condition. Those pieces have disappeared into private and public collections. At the same time there is much decorated tinware or toleware on the market which is claimed to *have* age, but it has only *been* aged. Other new pieces are so inartistically stamped out and painted that you know immediately that they are recent discount store items. Fortunately the tinware produced by Sarreid Ltd. for the Henry Ford Museum is not of this sort.

Three of Sarreid's most interesting tinware items are a large oval foot bath, a bun tray, and a tin document box. The box and tray are handpainted antique ivory with a grape-and-rose design. The document box is particularly well-executed with a handmade hasp latch, double-rolled edge along lid and base, and slat-soldered corner edges. The box is priced at $66; the tray at $53; and the foot bath at $97.

Catalogue available.

Henry Ford Museum and Greenfield Village
20900 Oakwood Blvd.
Dearborn, Mich. 48121

or

Uniquities
Marketplace
2400 Market St.
Philadelphia, Penn. 19103

For those who have already taken or would like to take up the hobby of toleware painting, Craft House has available raw tin forms for many items. Among these are a deed box, coffeepot, apple tray, water pitcher, salt box, hexagonal lantern, and various candle holders. The price for a deed box, for instance, is $18; a candle holder may be priced as low as $2.70. The Craft House will send sketches of any of the items they list in stock.

Brochure available.

Craft House
1542 Main Road
Tiverton, R.I. 02878

Urns and Vases

Classical urns and vases provide much better planting beds than a wheelbarrow or—heaven help us—truck tires. Robinson has reproduced many of the cast-iron Janney patterns, which were first introduced in Montgomery, Alabama, fifteen years before the Civil War. Some of these would have delighted any landscape gardener of the 1800s who was trying to follow the lead of Alexander Jackson Downing or the creator of Central Park, Calvert Vaux.

Literature available.

Robinson Iron
Robinson Rd.
Alexander City, Ala. 35010

Erkins makes available forms in cast stone and lead which are similar to those produced by Robinson in iron. There are fluted urns as well as highly decorated containers with classical motifs or friezes. Prices run from $100 for a small pair of plain cast-stone urns to $900 for a pair of ram's-head urns.

Catalogue available.

The Erkins Studio, Inc.
8 W. 40th St.
New York, N.Y. 10018

Weather Vanes

As objects of folk art, weather vanes have assumed great popularity. They can be most fetching, imaginative objects. The presence of more than the usual directional wind indicator was probably meant to signify something about the owner's wealth or social status. Complex designs in copper and bronze were expensive to work in the nineteenth century. Only the flat tinware models were within the economic range of the average farmer.

Some of the popular castings used in the past remain today. J. W. Fiske is one of those firms which has had the good fortune to possess some of the early molds. Their vanes are made of hand-hammered copper and are finished in gold leaf. Among the most famous of the designs is trotter St. Julian with high-wheel sulky. It is 45″ long and is priced at $1,002. Less expensive vanes are available, and some of these are almost as imaginatively formed.

Brochure available.

J. W. Fiske Architectural Metals, Inc.
111-117 Pennsylvania Ave.
Paterson, N.J. 07053

E. G. Washburne also proudly claims to make new copper vanes from their original molds. There are some very handsome trotters as well as a dog and a running deer available. The dog, 33″ long, is priced at $360; the deer, $424. These prices include the full vane. The vanes are not gold leafed.

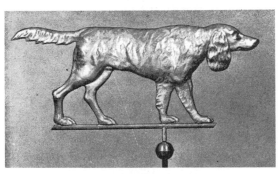

Catalogue available with price list.

E. G. Washburne & Co.
85 Andover St., Rte. 114
Danvers, Mass. 01923

Among the most accomplished of modern vane designers is Ivan F. Bailey. Among his work is the rooster illustrated here. It is a wrought-iron piece, a medium in which Bailey excels.

Literature available.

Bailey's Forge
221 E. Bay St.
Savannah, Ga. 31401

Other Sources of Supplies

Consult the List of Suppliers for addresses.

Baskets

Cane and Basket Supply Co.
Fran's Basket House
Guild of Shaker Crafts
The Vermont Country Store

Boxes and Trays

Craft House
Mercer Museum Shop
Museum Shop, Boston Museum of Fine Arts

China

Craft House
Lenox, Inc.

Clocks

Barwick Clocks, Inc.
Chapman Mfg. Co.
Craft House
Magnolia Hall
Howard Miller Clock Co.
Seth Thomas

Fans

Gargoyles, Ltd.
United House Wrecking Co.

Fountains

L. Biagiotti
European Marble Works by Puccio
Florentine Craftsmen
Kenneth Lynch & Sons, Inc.
North Salem Studios

Glass

Craft House
Lenox, Inc.
Museum Shop, Boston Museum of Fine Arts

Hitching Posts

The Erkins Studios, Inc.
Robinson Iron

Kitchen Accessories

Mercer Museum Shop

Lawn and Porch Furniture

Birmingham Ornamental Iron Co.
Louis W. Bowen, Inc.
Florentine Craftsmen
Magnolia Hall
Majestic Reproductions Co., Inc.
Trouvailles, Inc.

Mirrors

Baker, Knapp, and Tubbs

L. Biagiotti
Yale R. Burge, Inc.
Chapman Mfg. Co.
Craft House
Gargoyles, Ltd.
Magnolia Hall
Majestic Reproductions, Inc.
Mirror Fair
Phyllis Morris Originals
Museum Shop, Philadelphia Museum of Arts

Pedestals

Baker, Knapp, and Tubbs
L. Biagiotti
Chapman Mfg. Co.
European Marble Works by Puccio
Ficks Reed Co.
Keller-Scroll Inc.
Magnolia Hall
Trouvailles, Inc.

Pewter

Cohasset Colonials
Craft House
Mercer Museum Shop
North Salem Studios

Pottery

Craft House
Stangl

Silver

Craft House
Lenox, Inc.

Sundials

Craft House
Robinson Iron

Tinware

Mercer Museum Shop

Urns and Vases

Architectural Pottery
L. Biagiotti
Kenneth Lynch & Sons, Inc.

Weather Vanes

Cape Cod Cupola Co.
Kenneth Lynch & Sons, Inc.

Selective Bibliography

Historical Materials, Primary and Secondary

Benjamin, Asher. *American Builder's Companion.* 1827 edition. New York: Dover Publications, 1969.

Chippendale, Thomas. *The Gentleman & Cabinet-Maker's Director.* 3rd edition. New York: Dover Publications, 1966.

Condit, Carl W. *American Building: Materials and Techniques from the First Colonial Settlement to the Present.* Chicago: University of Chicago Press, 1968.

Cooke, Lawrence S. *Lighting in America, From Colonial Rushlights to Victorian Chandeliers.* Antiques Magazine Library. New York: Main Street/Universe Books, 1976.

Curtis, Will and Jane Curtis. *Antique Woodstoves, Artistry in Iron.* Ashville, Me.: Cobblesmith, 1975.

Downing, Andrew Jackson. *The Architecture of Country Houses.* 1850 edition. New York: Dover Publications, 1969.

Eastlake, Charles. *Hints on Household Taste.* 4th edition. New York: Dover Publications, 1969.

Eiland, Murray L. *Oriental Rugs, A Comprehensive Guide.* Greenwich, Conn.: New York Graphic Society, 1973.

Fowler, John and John Cornforth. *English Decoration in the Eighteenth Century.* London: Barrie & Jenkins, 1974.

Hamlin, Talbot. *Greek Revival Architecture in America.* New York: Dover Publications, 1963.

Hayward, Arthur H. *Colonial and Early American Lighting.* New York: Dover Publications, 1962.

Isham, Norman M. *Early American Houses and a Glossary of Colonial Architectural Terms.* Da Capo Press, 1967.

Kane, Patricia E. *Three Hundred Years of American Seating Furniture, Chairs and Beds from the Mabel Brady Garvan and Other Collections at Yale University.* Boston, Mass.: New York Graphic Society, 1975.

Lipman, Jean and Eve Meulendyke. *American Folk Decoration.* New York: Dover Publications. 1972.

Little, Nina Fletcher. *American Decorative Wall Painting: 1700–1850.* New York: E. P. Dutton & Co., 1972.

Little, Nina Fletcher. *American Decorative Wall Painting: 1700–1850.* New York: E.P. Dutton & Co., 1972.

Loth, Calder and Julius Toursdale Sadler, Jr. *The Only Proper Style, Gothic Architecture in America.* Boston: New York Graphic Society, 1975.

Loth, Calder and Julius Toursdale Sadler, Jr. *The Only Proper Style, Gothic Architecture in America.* Boston: New York Graphic Society, 1975.

Maass, John. *The Victorian Home in America.* New York: Hawthorn Books, 1972.

Montgomery, Florence M. *Printed Textiles, English and American Cottons and Linens 1700–1850.* A Winterthur Book. New York: The Viking Press, 1970.

Morrison, Hugh. *Early American Architecture.* New York: Oxford University Press, 1952.

Mumford, Lewis. *The Brown Decades: A Study of the Arts in America, 1865–1895.* New York: Dover Publications, 1955.

Mumford, Lewis. *Sticks and Stones: A Study of American Architecture and Civilization.* 2nd revised edition. New York: Dover Publications, 1955.

Pettit, Florence H. *America's Indigo Blues, Resist-Printed and Dyed Textiles of the Eighteenth Century.* New York: Hastings House, n.d.

Pettit, Florence H. *America's Printed and Painted Fabrics, 1600–1900.* New York, Hastings House, 1970.

Pierson, William H., Jr. *American Buildings and Their Architects: The Colonial and Neoclassical Style.* Garden City, N.Y.: Doubleday and Co., 1970.

Seale, William. *The Tasteful Interlude, American Interiors Through the Camera's Eye, 1860–1917.* New York: Praeger Publishers, 1974.

Vaux, Calvert. *Villas and Cottages.* 2nd edition. New York: Dover Publications, 1970.

How-To Materials, Practical Advice

Bullock, Orin M., Jr. *The Restoration Manual: An Illustrated Guide to the Preservation and Restoration of Old Buildings.* Norwalk, Conn.: Silvermine Publishers, 1966.

Communications Consultants. *Greater Wilmington Directory of Remodeling and Restoration Products and Services.* Wilmington, Del.: Author, 1976.

Devoe Paint Company. *Exterior Decoration.* Philadelphia: The Athaeneum of Philadelphia, 1976.

Directions Simplified. *How to Install a Fireplace.* Briarcliff Manor, N.Y.: Author, n.d.

Edgerton, William H., et al. *How to Renovate a Brownstone.* New York: Halsey Publishing Co., 1970.

Guitar, Mary Ann. *Property Power: How to Keep the Bulldozer, the Power Line, and the Highwayman From Your Front Door.* New York: Doubleday and Co., 1972.

Insall, Donald W. *The Care of Old Buildings Today: A Practical Guide.* New York: Crane, Russak & Co., 1972.

McKee, Harley J. *Amateur's Guide to Terms.* Rochester, N.Y.: Landmark Society of Western New York, 1970.

McKee, Harley J. *Introduction to Early American Masonry, Stone, Brick, Mortar and Plaster.* Washington, D.C.: National Trust for Historic Preservation, 1973.

McKenna, H. Dickson. *A House in the City: A Guide to Buying and Renovating Old Row Houses.* New York: Van Nostrand Reinhold, 1971.

Mercer, Henry. *The Dating of Old Houses.* Doylestown, Penn.: Bucks County Historical Society, 1926.

Moshimer, Joan. *The Complete Rug Hooker.* Boston: New York Graphic Society, 1975.

National Trust for Historic Preservation. *A Guide to State Historic Preservation Programs.* Betts Abel, ed. and comp. Washington, D.C.: Preservation Press, 1976.

Orton, Vrest. *The Forgotten Art of Building a Good Fireplace.* Dublin, N.H.: Yankee, Inc., n.d.

Osborn, Burl N. and Bernice B. Osborn. *Measured Drawings of Early American Furniture.* New York: Dover Publications, 1975.

Simpson, John W. and Peter J. Horrobin, eds. *The Weathering and Performance of Building Materials.* New York: Wiley-Interscience, 1970.

Stanforth, Deirdre and Martha Stamm. *Buying and Renovating a House in the City: A Practical Guide.* New York: Alfred A. Knopf, 1972.

Stanforth, Deirdre and Louis Reens. *Restored America.* New York: Praeger Publishers, 1975.

Stephen, George. *Remodeling Old Houses Without Destroying Their Character.* New York: Alfred A. Knopf, 1972.

Tillett, Leslie. *American Needlework, 1776–1976, Needlepoint and Crewel Patterns Adapted from Historic American Images.* Boston: New York Graphic Society, 1975.

Wall, William E. *Graining: Ancient and Modern.* Revised edition by F. N. Vaderwalker. New York: Drake Publishers, 1972.

Waring, Janet. *Early American Stencils on Walls and Furniture.* New York: Dover Publications, n.d.

Pamphlets and Booklets

American Association for State and Local History. This most national of historical agencies has supplied material of interest to restorers of old buildings for many years. Most of this information has appeared first in *History News*, the association's monthly publication. The leaflets below may be obtained by writing to the association, 1400 Eighth Avenue South, Nashville, Tenn. 37203.

Batcheler, Penelope Hartshorne. "Paint Color Research and Restoration." Leaflet No. 15.

Frangiamore, Catherine L. "Rescuing Historic Wallpaper: Identification, Preservation, Restoration." Leaflet No. 76.

Hutslar, Donald A. "Log Cabin Restorations." Leaflet No. 74.

Judd, Henry A. "Before Restoration Begins, Keeping Your Historic House Intact." Leaflet No. 67.

Stewart, John J. "Historic Landscapes and Gardens: Procedures for Restoration." Leaflet No. 80.

Thomas, James Cheston. "Restoring Brick and Stone: Some Dos and Don'ts." Leaflet No. 81.

Association for Preservation Technology. As the name indicates, this organization is a professional one concerned with historical building techniques and resources. It issues a quarterly *Bulletin* and a bimonthly newsletter, *Communiqué,* to its American and Canadian membership. Among the materials offered by the association are the following in pamphlet form:

"Early Roofing Material"
"Eighteenth-Century Heating Stoves"
"Epoxy Repair of Deteriorated Wood"
"Hardware—Cross Garnet Side & Dovetail Hinges"
"Hardware—English Iron Rim Locks"
"Hardware—Norfolk Latches"
"Linoleum Used in Restoration Work"
"Paint as a Dating Tool"
"Paint Color Research and House Painting Practice"
"The Technology of Early American Building"

These may be ordered from Mrs. Ann Falkner, Executive Secretary, APT, Box 2487, Station D, Ottawa, Ontario, Canada K1P 5W6.

Back to the City, Inc. Urban preservation is the special concern of this New York-based private organization. Most valuable to the homeowner is a manual which has been based on the proceedings of their first national conference held in New York in 1974. Entitled "Back to the City," it may be ordered from the organization at 12 East 41st St., New York, N.Y. 10017. The 78-page manual is priced at $5.

Friends of Cast-Iron Architecture. Iron buildings were neglected for many years but now are coming into favor again in both large and small cities. The new recognition is greatly due to the efforts of Friends of Cast-Iron Architecture and its indomitable chairman, Margot Gayle, author with Edmund Gillon of *Cast-Iron Architecture in New York*, available from Dover Books or the organization at 44 West 9th St., Room 20, New York, N.Y. 10011. The price is $6 postpaid.

Historic American Buildings Survey. Established in 1933 by the National Park Service to compile a perma-nent, graphic record of the country's historic buildings, HABS's aim is simply "preservation through documentation." This is accomplished by means of measured drawings, photographs, and the recording of architectural and historical data. A HABS team of architectural historians is always at work somewhere in the country. The archives are now extensive, and collections of the photographs and drawings have been gathered in numerous catalogs by state and region. In addition to these surveys, HABS also has published more general works of interest to the home preservationist.

Harley J. McKee, compiler, "Recording Historic Buildings."

James C. Massey, "The Architectural Survey."

Information regarding HABS's catalogs and records may be secured by contacting the Office of Archeology and Historic Preservation, National Park Service, Department of the Interior, Washington, D.C. 20240.

Interagency Historic Architectural Services Program. An information service, IHASP is particularly concerned with the proper maintenance and preservation of public historic properties. The type of material that they gather and disseminate may also be of interest to the private citizen. Among the pamphlets now available are:

"Basic Guidelines for the Rehabilitation of Historic Property"

"The Cleaning and Waterproof Coating of Masonry Buildings"

"Cyclical Maintenance for Historic Buildings"

"Exterior Cleaning of Historic Masonry Buildings"

"Repointing Mortar in Historic Brick Buildings"

For further information and/or to order these materials, write to: IHASP, Office of Archeology and Historic Preservation, National Park Service, United States Department of the Interior, Washington, D.C. 20240.

National Periodicals of Special Interest

American Association for Local and State History. History News, published monthly. Address: 1400 Eighth Avenue South, Nashville, Tenn. 37203.

National Trust for Historic Preservation. Historic Preservation, a quarterly magazine, and *Preservation News*, a monthly newsletter, are the two primary periodicals of this federally-chartered preservation organization. The National Trust is first with the news in depth and offers, as well, a superb book service. Information regarding these periodicals and other National Trust services may be obtained by writing the organization at 740-748 Jackson Pl., N.W., Washington, D.C. 20006.

The Victorian Society in America. Since 1966 America has had its own Victorian Society. There are now chapters in many cities and areas. Recently the society began the publication of *Nineteenth Century, a* quarterly magazine devoted to Victorian life and history, architecture and art. Also published is *The Bulletin.* For information concerning these publications as well as membership, contact The Victorian Society in America, East Washington Square, Philadelphia, Penn. 19106.

The Old-House Journal, published monthly. Address: 199 Berkeley Pl., Brooklyn, N.Y. 11217.

List of Suppliers

A

AA Abbingdon Ceiling Co.
2149 Utica Ave.
Brooklyn, N.Y. 11234

Acme Hardware Co., Inc.
150 S. La Brea Ave.
Los Angeles, Calif. 90036

Air Flow Window Systems
21 East 9th St.
New York, N.Y. 10003

Alberene Art Glass
Rt. 1, Box 226-D
North Garden, Va. 22959

Robert Allen Fabrics
25 Wells Ave.
Newton, Mass. 02159

Danny Allesandro, Ltd.
1156 Second Ave.
New York, N.Y. 10021

Allumé Handprints, Inc.
979 Third Ave.
New York, N.Y. 10021

American Abalene Decorating
   Service
33 West 17th St.
New York, N.Y. 10011

American Building Restoration,
   Inc.
9720 S. 60th St.
Franklin, Wis. 53132

American Colonies Antiques
936 N. La Cienega
Los Angeles, Calif. 90069

American Lantern
P.O. Box 280
Newport, Ark. 72112

American Needlecrafts, Inc.
979 Third Ave.
New York, N.Y. 10022

American Olean Tile Co.
1000 Cannon Ave.
Lansdale, Penn. 19446

American SERPE Corp.
716 Madison Ave.
New York, N.Y. 10021

Antique Building Supplies
979 Greenway Dr.
Xenia, Ohio 45385

Appalachian Fireside Crafts
Box 276
Booneville, Ky. 41314

Architectural Paneling Inc.
969 Third Ave.
New York, N.Y. 10022

Architectural Pottery
2020 S. Robertson Blvd.
Los Angeles, Calif. 90034

Architectural Specialties, Inc.
850 S. Van Ness Ave.
San Francisco, Calif. 94110

A. Joseph Armstrong
450 Lucky Hill Rd.
West Chester, Penn. 19380

Artform Designs Inc.
229 W. Illinois
Chicago, Ill. 60610

Artifacts, Inc.
1210 Queen St.
Alexandria, Va. 22314

Artmark Fabrics Co. Inc.
480 Lancaster Pike
Frazer, Penn. 19355

The Ash Saul Company
569 E. Ten Mile Rd.
Madison Heights, Mich. 48071

The Astrup Company
2937 W. 25th St.
Cleveland, Ohio 44113

Auffray & Co., Inc.
146 E. 56th St.
New York, N.Y. 10022

Authentic Designs, Inc.
330 E. 75th St.
New York, N.Y. 10021

Axtell Antiques
1 River St.
Deposit, N.Y. 13754

B

Bailey's Forge
221 E. Bay St.
Savannah, Ga. 31401

Baker, Knapp, & Tubbs
979 Third Ave.
New York, N.Y. 10022

A. W. Baker Restorations, Inc.
670 Drift Rd.
Westport, Mass. 02790

Baldwin Hardware Manufacturing
  Corp.
841 Wyomissing Blvd.
Reading, Penn. 19603

Ball and Ball
463 W. Lincoln Hwy.
Exton, Penn. 19341

Baltimore City Salvage Depot
213 W. Pratt S.
Baltimore, Md. 21201

B & B Needlecrafts
2277 Union Ave.
Memphis, Tenn. 38104

Bangkok Industries, Inc.
1900 S. 20th St.
Philadelphia, Penn. 19145

Barclay Fabrics Co. Inc.
7120 Airport Hwy. Box 650
Pennsauken, N.J. 08101

Barney Brainum-Shanker Steel Co.,
  Inc.
70-32 83rd St.
Glendale, N.Y 11227

Charles Barone, Inc.
114 S. Robertson Blvd.
Los Angeles, Calif. 90048

The Bartley Collection, Ltd.
747 Oakwood Ave.
Lake Forest, Ill. 60045

Bassett & Vollum, Inc.
217 N. Main St.
Galena, Ill. 61036

Bassett McNab Co.
1032 Arch St.
Philadelphia, Penn. 19107

Bedlam Brass Beds
19-21 Fair Lawn Ave.
Fair Lawn, N.J. 07410

Belaire Draperies & Fabrics
3139 Tchoupitoulas
New Orleans, La. 70115

Robert W. Belcher
1753 Pleasant Grove Dr., N.E.
Dalton, Ga. 30720

Bendix Mouldings, Inc.
235 Pegasus Ave.
Northvale, N.J. 07647

Berea College
Student Craft Industries
Berea, Ky. 40403

Bergamo Fabrics, Inc.
969 Third Ave.
New York, N.Y. 10022

Lester H. Berry
1108 Pine St.
Philadelphia, Penn. 19107

Bestwood Industries, Ltd.
P.O. Box 2042
Vancouver, B.C., Canada

L. Biagiotti
229 Seventh Ave.
New York, N.Y. 10011

The Birge Co., Inc.
390 Niagra
Buffalo, N.Y. 14201

Birmingham Ornamental Iron Co.
P.O. Box 1357
Birmingham, Ala. 35201

Blaine Window Hardware, Inc.
1919 Blaine Dr.
R.D. #4
Hagerstown, Md. 21740

Doris Leslie Blau Gallery, Inc.
15 E. 57th St.
New York, N.Y. 10022

Blenco Glass Co., Inc.
P.O. Box 67
Milton, W. Va. 25541

Jerome W. Blum
Ross Hill Rd.
Lisbon, Conn. 06351

Norton Blumenthal
979 Third Ave.
New York, N.Y. 10022

Bogart Enterprises
P.O. Box 208
Salford, Penn. 18957

Bona
2227 Beechmont Ave.
Cincinnati, Ohio 45230

Robert Bourdon
Wolcott, Vt. 05680

Richard A. Bourne Co., Inc.
Corporation St.
Hyannis, Mass. 02601

Boussac of France, Inc.
979 Third Ave.
New York, N.Y. 10022

Louis W. Bowen, Inc.
979 Third Ave.
New York, N.Y. 10022

Brass Bed Company of America
1933 S. Broadway
Los Angeles, Calif. 90007

Brewster Corportion
50 River
Old Saybrook, Conn. 06475

British-American Historical Arts,
   Ltd.
10884 Santa Monica Blvd.
Los Angeles, Calif. 90025

Bronx Window Shade & Awning
   Co., Inc.
372 E. 162nd St.
Bronx, N.Y. 10451

Carol Brown
Putney, Vt. 05346

Brunovan, Inc.
305 E. 63rd St.
New York, N.Y. 10021

Brunschwig & Fils, Inc.
979 Third Ave.
New York, N.Y. 10022

Yale R. Burge, Inc.
315 E. 62nd St.
New York, N.Y. 10021

C

Samuel Cabot, Inc.
1 Union St.
Boston, Mass. 02108

Henry Calvin Fabrics
724 Battery
San Francisco, Calif. 94111

Douglas Campbell
Denmark, Me. 04022

Cane and Basket Supply Co.
1283 S. Cochran Ave.
Los Angeles, Calif. 90019

The Cane Farm
Rosemont, N.J. 08556

Cantitoe Corners
36 W. 20th St.
New York, N.Y. 10011

The Canvas Awning Institute, Inc.
1918 N. Parkway
Memphis, Tenn. 38112

Cape Cod Cupola Co.
North Dartmouth, Mass. 02747

Constance Carol
173 Carver Rd.
Plymouth, Mass. 02360

Carrara Marble Co. of America,
   Inc.
8653 E. Garvey Ave.
Rosemead, Calif. 91770

Casella Lighting Co.
434 Brannan
San Francisco, Calif. 94107

Chapman Manufacturing Co.
481 W. Main St.
Avon, Mass. 02322

Chapulin
Rt. 1, Box 187
Sante Fe, N.M. 87501

Charterhouse Designs Ltd.
979 Third Ave.
New York, N.Y. 10022

China Seas, Inc.
149 E. 72nd St.
New York, N.Y. 10021

City Knickerbocker, Inc.
781 Eighth Ave.
New York, N.Y. 10018

Clarence House
40 E. 57th St.
New York, N.Y. 10022

Cleveland Lamp Co.
5804 Euclid Ave.
Cleveland, Ohio 44103

Cohasset Colonials
Ship St.
Cohasset, Mass. 02025

The Colonial Casting Co.
443 S. Colony St.
Meridian, Conn. 06450

Colonial Moulding and Frame Co.
  Inc.
37 E. 18th St.
New York, N.Y. 10003

Colonial Tin Craft
7805 Railroad Ave.
Cincinnati, Ohio 45243

Colonial Williamsburg
Craft House
Box CH
Williamsburg, Va. 23185

Connaissance Fabrics &
  Wallcoverings, Inc.
979 Third Ave.
New York, N.Y. 10022

Albert Constantine & Son, Inc.
2050 Eastchester Rd.
Bronx, N.Y. 10461

Continental Felt Co.
22 W. 15th St.
New York, N.Y. 10011

Coran-Sholes Industries
509 E. 2nd St.
Boston, Mass. 02127

Frederick Cooper
2545 W. Diversey Ave.
Chicago, Ill. 60647

Country Curtains
Stockbridge, Mass. 01262

Country Floors, Inc.
300 E. 61st St.
New York, N.Y. 10021

Country Salvage & Trading Co.
Rt. 4
Bridgewater Corners, Vt. 05035

Craft House
1542 Main Rd.
Tiverton, R.I. 02878

Robert Crowder Associates
8417 Melrose Place
Los Angeles, Calif. 90069

Crown Wallcovering Corp.
979 Third Ave.
New York, N.Y. 10022

D

Dana-Deck & Laminates, Inc.
Dana McBarron & Sons
Lopez, Wash. 98261

David & Dash, Inc.
2445 N. Miami Ave.
Miami, Fla. 33127

Davis Cabinet Company
Box 5424
Nashville, Tenn. 38106

Decorative Carpets, Inc.
104 S. Robertson Blvd.
Los Angeles, Calif. 90048

Decorative Crafts, Inc.
41 Madison Ave.
New York, N.Y. 10010

The Decorators Supply Corp.
3610-12 S. Morgan St.
Chicago, Ill. 60609

Decorators Wholesale Hardware
  Co.
155 E. 52nd St.
New York, N.Y. 10022

Delaware Quarries, Inc.
River Road
Lumberville, Penn. 18933

Designer Floors
444 Pleasant Valley Way
West Orange, N.J. 07052

Devoe Paint Division
Celanese Coatings
#1 Riverfront Plaza
Louisville, Ky. 40402

A. L. Diament & Co.
969 Third Ave.
New York, N.Y. 10022

Diamond K. Co., Inc.
130 Buckland Rd.
South Windsor, Conn. 06074

Dildarian, Inc.
595 Madison Ave.
New York, N.Y. 10022

Dock Street Interiors
517 Dock St.
Wilmington, N.C. 28401

Domino Patchworks
186 W. 4th St.
New York, N.Y. 10014

Betty Dowd
#15, S. 1200 E.
Salt Lake City, Utah 84102

Driwood Moulding & Millwork
  Co.
P.O. Box 1369
Florence, S.C. 29051

Duro-Lite Lamps, Inc.
17-10 Willow St.
Fair Lawn, N.J. 07410

E

E & I Oriental Co., Inc.
W-53 Century Rd.
Paramus, N.J. 07652

The 18th Century Company
Haddam Quarter Rd.
Durham, Conn. 06422

The Electric Candlelight
  Company, Inc.
1 Chelmsford St.
Chelmsford, Mass. 01824

Elegant Entries, Inc.
45 Water St.
Worcester, Mass. 01604

Elon, Inc.
964 Third Ave.
New York, N.Y. 10022

Empire Furniture Factory and
  Rattan Works
4118 Ponce de Leon Blvd.
Coral Gables, Fla. 33146

Empress Chandeliers
P.O. Drawer 2067
Mobile, Ala. 36601

William J. Erbe Co., Inc.
434½ E. 75th St.
New York, N.Y. 10021

Eriksson's Blacksmith
417 Arthurkill Rd.
Staten Island, N.Y. 10308

The Erkins Studios, Inc.
8 W. 40th St.
New York, N.Y. 10018

The Essex Forge
10 Old Dennison Rd.
Essex, Conn. 06423

F

Faire Harbour Boats
44 Captain Peirce Rd.
Scituate, Mass. 02066

Farmington Craftsmen
87-J Spring Lake
Farmington, Conn. 06032

Faultless Division, BLI
1421 N. Garvin
Evansville, Ind. 47711

Felber Studios
110 Ardmore Ave.
Ardmore, Penn. 19003

Felicity, Inc.
4005 Broadway
Knoxville, Tenn. 37917

Ferguson Fabrics, Inc.
112 N. Robertson Blvd.
Los Angeles, Calif. 90048

Ficks Reed Co.
4900 Charlemar Dr.
Cincinnati, Ohio 45227

Fine Art Wallcoverings & Fabrics,
  Inc.
979 Third Ave.
New York, N.Y. 10022

Finnaren & Haley, Inc.
1300 N. 60th St.
Philadelphia, Penn. 19151

J. W. Fiske Architectural Metals,
  Inc.
111-117 Pennsylvania Ave.
Paterson, N.J. 07503

Floorcloths Inc.
109 Main St.
Annapolis, Md. 21401

Florentine Craftsmen
650 First Ave.
New York, N.Y. 10016

Focal Point, Inc.
3760 Lower Roswell Rd.
Marietta, Ga. 30060

Folger Adam Co.
P.O. Box 688
Joliet, Ill. 60434

Henry Ford Museum and
  Greenfield Village
20900 Oakwood Blvd.
Dearborn, Mich. 48121

Maurice Franks
979 Third Ave.
New York, N.Y. 10022

Fran's Basket House
295 Rt. 10
Succasunna, N.J. 07876

Fraser Gold Carpet Corp.
919 Third Ave.
New York, N.Y. 10022

French and Ball
Main Rd.
Gill, Mass. 01376

Friedman Marble & Slate Works,
  Inc.
37-21 Vernon Blvd.
Long Island City, N.Y. 11101

Furniture Designs
1425 Sherman Ave.
Evanston, Ill. 60201

Fypon, Inc.
22 E. 24th St.
Baltimore, Md. 21218

G

Gabriel Fabrics, Inc.
979 Third Ave.
New York, N.Y. 10022

Gargoyles, Ltd.
512 S. Third St.
Philadelphia, Penn. 19147

Gaston Wood Finishes, Inc.
3630 E. 10th St.
Bloomington, Ind. 47401

Georgia Lighting Supply Co.
530 14th St., N.W.
Atlanta, Ga. 30318

Georgia Metal Products
3145 Tucker-Norcross Rd.
Tucker, Ga. 30084

Gillett Restorations
c/o Suite 420
3550 N. Central Ave.
Phoenix, Ariz. 85012

Carlo Germana
318 Hempstead Turnpike
West Hempstead, N.Y. 11552

Glass Masters Guild
621 Sixth Ave.
New York, N.Y. 10011

Glen-Gery Corp.
P.O. Box 206
Reading, Penn. 19607

Glidden-Durkee
900 Union Commerce Bldg.
Cleveland, Ohio 44115

Charles R. Gracie & Sons, Inc.
979 Third Ave.
New York, N.Y. 10022

Philip Graf Wallpapers, Inc.
979 Third Ave.
New York, N.Y. 10022

Greeff Fabrics
155 East 56th St.
New York, N.Y. 10022

P. E. Guerin, Inc.
23 Jane St.
New York, N.Y. 10014

Guild of Shaker Crafts
401 W. Savidge
Spring Lake, Mich. 49456

Gurian's
276 Fifth Ave.
New York, N.Y. 10001

Guyon, Inc.
65 Oak St.
Lititz, Penn. 17543

H

Hagen International
424 9th
Los Angeles, Calif. 90015

Hallelujah Redwood Products
39500 Comptche Rd.
Mendocino, Calif. 95460

S. Harris Co., Inc.
580 S. Douglas
El Segundo, Calif. 90245

The Harvin Co.
Waynesboro, Va. 22980

Heirloom Rugs
28 Harlem St.
Rumford, R.I. 02916

Henry Hanger Co.
450 Seventh Ave.
New York, N.Y. 10001

Heritage Lanterns
Sea Meadows Lane
Cousins Island
Yarmouth, Me. 04096

Heritage Patterns
Box 595
Mendham, N.J. 07945

S. M. Hexter Co.
2800 Superior Ave.
Cleveland, Ohio 44118

Historic Charleston Reproductions
  Shop
105 Broad St.
Charleston, S.C. 29401

The Hitchcock Chair Co.
Riverton, Conn. 06065

The Holmes Company
P.O. Box 1776
Wrightsville, Penn. 17368

Homecraft Veneer
P.O. Box 3
Latrobe, Penn. 15650

Homespun Weavers
Ridge and Keystone Sts.
Emmaus, Penn. 18049

Horton Brasses
P.O. Box 95
Nooks Hill Rd.
Cromwell, Conn. 06416

Martha M. House
1022 S. Decatur St.
Montgomery, Ala. 36104

House of Iron
3384 Long Beach Rd.
Oceanside, N.Y. 11572

House of Verde
979 Third Ave.
New York, N.Y. 10022

Howell Construction
2700 12th Ave. S.
Nashville, Tenn. 37204

John R. Hudspeth, Inc.
700 N.E. 22nd Ave.
Portland, Ore. 97232

Wm. Hunrath Co., Inc.
153 E. 57th St.
New York, N.Y. 10022

Hurley Patentee Manor
R.D. 7, Box 98 A
Kingston, N.Y. 12401

I

International Wood Products, Inc.
9630 Aero Dr.
San Diego, Calif. 92123

Iron Horse Antiques, Inc.
R.D. #2
Poultney, Vt. 05764

J

Charles W. Jacobsen
401 S. Salina St.
Syracuse, N.Y. 13201

J & R Industries
P.O. Box 4221
Shawnee Mission, Kans. 66104

Edwin Jackson, Inc.
306 E. 61st St.
New York, N.Y. 10021

William H. Jackson Co.
3 E. 47th St.
New York, N.Y. 10017

Janovic/Plaza
1291 First Ave.
New York, N.Y. 10021

Jones & Erwin, Inc.
232 East 59th St.
New York, N.Y. 10022

J. P. Enterprises
22 Lexington St.
Waltham, Mass, 02154

K

Marvin Kagan, Inc.
991 Madison Ave.
New York, N.Y. 10021

Kaplan Furniture Co.
574 Boston Ave.
Medford, Mass. 02155

Steve Kayne, Hand Forged
    Hardware
17 Harmon Place
Smithtown, N.Y. 11787

KB Moulding, Inc.
508 A Larkfield Rd.
East Northport, N.Y. 11731

Keller-Scroll, Inc.
800 N.W. 166th
Miami, Fla. 33169

Gordon Kemmet
The Studio of Etch Design
604 W. 16th St.
P.O. Box 552
Austin, Tex. 78767

Kenmore Carpet Corp.
979 Third Ave.
New York, N.Y. 10022

Kenmore Furniture Co., Inc.
156 E. 33rd St.
New York, N.Y. 10016

Kensington Historical Company
Box 87
East Ingston, N.H. 03827

Kent-Costikyan, Inc.
305 E. 63rd St.
New York, N.Y. 10022

Kentile, Inc.
979 Third Ave.
New York, N.Y. 10022

Kieffer's Pacific
2 Kansas St.
San Francisco, Calif. 94103

Kings Cabinet
622 N. LoPeer Dr.
San Francisco, Calif.

King's Chandelier Company
P.O. Box 667
Eden, N.C. 27288

Kingsworthy Foundry Co., Ltd.
Kingsworthy
Winchester, Hants SO23 7QG
England

Kittinger Co.
1893 Elmwood Ave.
Buffalo, N.Y. 14207

Klise Manufacturing Co.
601 Maryland Ave., N.E.
Grand Rapids, Mich. 49505

Koppers Co.
Forest Products Div.
188 Industrial Dr.
Elmhurst, Ill. 60126

Kristia Associates
343 Forest Ave.
P.O. Box 118
Portland, Me. 04104

L

J. & R. Lamb Studios, Inc.
151 Walnut St.
Northvale, N.J. 07647

Landmark Restorations Co.
1041 Russell Ave.
Covington, Ky. 41011

L & S Lighting Fixtures Co.
244 W. 140th
Los Angeles, Calif. 90061

Laue Wallcoverings
201 E. 56th St.
New York, N.Y. 10022

Laverne International
38 E. 57th St.
New York, N.Y. 10022

Lawrence Wallcovering Co.
1670 Weirfield
Brooklyn, N.Y. 11227

Lee/Jofa, Inc.
979 Third Ave.
New York, N.Y. 10022

Lemée's Fireplace Equipment
Route 28
Bridgewater, Mass. 02324

The Lennox Shop
1127 Broadway
Hewlitt, N.Y. 11557

or

Route 179
Lambertville, N.J. 08530

Lenox, Inc.
Prince & Meade Sts.
Trenton, N.J. 08638

Leonardo Looms, Inc.
979 Third Ave.
New York, N.Y. 10022

Leslie-Locke
2872 W. Market St.
Akron, Ohio 44313

Liberty Village
2 Church St.
Flemington, N.J. 08822

L. R. Lloyd Co.
Box 975
Uniontown, Penn. 15401

Ernest Lo Nano
S. Main St.
Sheffield, Mass. 01257

Long Associates
222 Friend
Boston, Mass. 02114

Luigi Crystal
7332 Frankford Ave.
Philadelphia, Penn. 19136

Lumpkin Stained Glass
2513 Washington St., N.W.
Huntsville, Ala. 35811

Kenneth Lynch & Sons
Wilton, Conn. 06897

M

Nancy McClelland, Inc.
232 E. 59th St.
New York, N.Y. 10022

The McGuire Co.
1201 Bryant
San Francisco, Calif. 94103

Magnolia Hall
726 Andover Dr.
Atlanta, Ga. 30327

Florence Maine
113 W. Lane (Rte. 35)
Ridgefield, Conn. 06877

Maine Line Paints
13 Hutchins St.
Auburn, Me. 14210

Majestic Reproductions Co., Inc.
222 E. 58th St.
New York, N.Y. 10022

G. B. Manasek, F. J. Manasek
4858 S. Dorchester Ave.
Chicago, Ill. 60615

Manuscreens, Inc.
979 Third Ave.
New York, N.Y. 10022

MarLe Co.
170 Sumner St.
Stamford, Conn. 06901

Ephraim Marsh Co.
Box 266
Concord, N.C. 28025

Jerry Martin Designs, Inc.
1121 Old York Rd.
Abington, Penn. 19001

The Martin-Senour Co.
1370 Ontario Ave., N.W.
Cleveland, Ohio 44113

Louis Maslow and Son, Inc.
979 Third Ave.
New York, N.Y. 10022

Mastercraft Industries
Rice Lake, Wis. 54868

Mather's
31 E. Main
Westminster, Md. 21157

Mercer Museum Shop
Bucks County Historical Society
Pine & Ashland
Doylestown, Penn. 18901

Mexico House
Del Mar, Calif. 92014

Mary Michael
1045 Park Ave.
New York, N.Y. 10028

D. R. Millbranth, Cabinetmaker
P.O. Box 321
Gaithersburg, Md. 20760

Newton Millham, Blacksmith
Bowen's Wharf
Newport, R.I. 02840

Mill Village Blacksmith Shop
Box 40
Craftsbury, Vt. 05826

Minnesota Woodworkers Supply
    Company
Industrial Blvd.
Rogers, Minn. 55374

Mirror Fair
320 E. 90th St.
New York, N.Y. 10028

Miss Kitty's Keeping Room Kolors
Turkey Run
Box 117-A, Rte. 1
Clear Brook, Va. 22624

Benjamin Moore & Co.
Chestnut Ridge Rd.
Montvale, N.J. 07645

Gates Moore
River Road, Silvermine
Norwalk, Conn. 06850

C. E. Morgan Building Products
601 Oregon St.
P.O. Box 2446
Oshkosh, Wis. 54901

Phyllis Morris Originals
8772 Beverly Blvd.
Los Angeles, Calif. 90048

Thomas Moser, Cabinet Maker
Cobb's Bridge Rd.
New Gloucester, Me. 04260

Mottahedeh & Company
225 Fifth Avenue
New York, N.Y. 10010

G. W. Mount, Inc.
576 Leyden Rd.
Greenfield, Mass. 01301

Munsell Color Products
2441 N. Calvert St.
Baltimore, Md. 21218

Museum of Fine Arts
Museum Shop
Boston, Mass. 02115

N

Nahigian Bros., Inc.
645 N. Michigan Ave.
Chicago, Ill. 60611

Nassau Flooring Corp.
242 Drexel Ave.
Westbury, L.I., N.Y. 11590

National Products, Inc.
900 Baxter Ave.
Louisville, Ky. 40204

Nesle, Inc.
151 E. 57th St.
New York, N.Y. 10022

Nettle Creek Industries
95 Madison Ave.
New York, N.Y. 10016

New Hampshire Blanket
Main St.
Harrisville, N.H. 03450

Newstamp Lantern Co.
227 Bay Rd.
North Easton, Mass. 02356

New York Flooring, Inc.
1733 First Ave.
New York, N.Y. 10028

New York Marble Works, Inc.
1399 Park Ave.
New York, N.Y. 10029

Nicholas, Cabinet Maker
684 Starin Ave.
Buffalo, N.Y. 14223

Nichols & Stone
Gardner, Mass. 01440

E. A. Nord Co., Inc.
P.O. Box 1187
Everett, Wash. 98206

Norman's of Salisbury
P.O. Drawer 799
Salisbury, N.C. 28144

North Salem Studios, Inc.
41 Cumberland Rd.
Englewood, N.J. 07631

O

Old Bennington Woodcrafters
37 West Rd.
Bennington, Vt. 05201

Old Carolina Brick Co.
Salisbury, N.C. 28144

Old Colony Curtains
Box 759
Westfield, N.J. 07090

Old-Fashioned Milk Paint Co.
Box 222
Groton, Mass. 01450

Old Smithy Shop
P.O. Box 226—Powers St.
Milford, N.H. 03055

Old Stone Mill
Adams, Mass. 01220

The Old Stove Co.
P.O. Box 7617
Dallas, Tex. 75209

Old World Moulding & Finishing,
   Inc.
115 Allen Blvd.
Farmingdale, N.Y. 11735

Old World Weavers, Inc.
136 E. 57th St.
New York, N.Y. 10022

Oriental Rug Exchange
349 N. La Cienega Blvd.
Los Angeles, Calif. 90048

Orlandini Studios, Ltd.
633 West Virginia St.
Milwaukee, Wis. 53204

The Oval Door
334 Church St.
Marietta, Ga. 30060

P

Paine and Chriscot, Inc.
1187 Second Ave.
New York, N.Y. 10021

Stephen Winslow Parker
P.O. Box 40
Craftsbury, Vt. 05826

Parma Tile Mosaic & Tile Co., Inc.
14-38 Astoria Blvd.
Long Island City, N.Y. 11102

Megan Parry
1727 Spruce
Boulder, Col. 80302

P. B. & Associates
3840 E. Washington St.
Indianapolis, Ind. 46201

Peerless Rattan & Reed Mfg. Co.,
   Inc.
97 Washington St.
New York, N.Y. 10006

I. Peiser Floors, Inc.
714 Madison Ave.
New York, N.Y. 10021

I. J. Peiser's Sons, Inc.
418 E. 91st St.
New York, N.Y. 10028

Period Brass, Inc.
P.O. Box 217
Jamestown, N.Y. 14701

Period Furniture Hardware Co., Inc.
123 Charles St.
Boston, Mass. 02114

Period Pine
P.O. Box 77052
Atlanta, Ga. 30309

Norman Perry, Inc.
P.O. Box 90
Plymouth, N.H. 03264

Persian Carpet Gallery
531 Sutter
San Francisco, Calif. 94102

Philadelphia Museum of Art
The Museum Shop
Box 7646
Philadelphia, Penn. 19101

Pierce and Stevens Chemical Corp.
P.O. Box 1092
Buffalo, N.Y. 14240

Pilgrim Glass Corp.
225 Fifth Ave.
New York, N.Y. 10010

Pittsburgh Paints
1 Gateway Center
Pittsburgh, Penn. 15222

Portland Franklin Stove Foundry,
Inc.
57 Kennebec St.
Portland, Me. 04104

Portland Willamette Co.
6804 N.E. 59th Pl.
Portland, Ore. 97218

Preservation Resource Center
Lake Shore Rd.
Essex, N.Y. 12936

Preway, Inc.
1430 2nd St., N.
Wisconsin Rapids, Wis. 54494

The Pumpkin Patch
R.D. 1, Pumpkin Hollow Rd.
Great Barrington, Mass. 01230

Q

Quaker Lace Co.
Fourth St. and Lehigh Ave.
Philadelphia, Penn. 19133

R

Rainbow Art Glass Corp.
49 Shark River Rd.
Neptune, N.J. 07753

Reale Mirror Mfg. Co. Inc.
16-18 E. 12th St.
New York, N.Y. 10003

Red Devil, Inc.
2400 Vauxhall Rd.
Union, N.J. 07083

Reed Wallcovering, Inc.
550 Pharr Rd., N.E.
Atlanta, Ga. 30305

Reid Classics
P.O. Box 8383
3600 Old Shell Rd.
Mobile, Ala. 36608

Joseph Richter, Inc.
249 E. 57th St.
New York, N.Y. 10022

Rittenhouse Carpets, Inc.
17-12 Walnut St.
Philadelphia, Penn. 19103

Robinson Iron Co., Inc.
Robinson Rd.
Alexander City, Ala. 35010

Rococo Designs
417 Pennsylvania Ave.
Santa Cruz, Calif. 95062

S

H. Sacks & Sons
144 Moody
Waltham, Mass. 02154

Salamander Glass Works
Box 264
Peterborough, N.H. 03458

The Saltbox
2229 Marietta Pike
Rohrerstown, Penn. 17603

San Francisco Victoriana
606 Natoma St.
San Francisco, Calif. 94103

George Sarkus Construction
P.O. Box 956
Syracuse, N.Y. 13201

Sarreid, Ltd.
P.O. Box 3545
Wilson, N.C. 27893

Scalamandré Silks, Inc.
950 Third Ave.
New York, N.Y. 10022

F. Schumacher & Co.
939 Third Ave.
New York, N.Y. 10022

Mrs. Eldred Scott
The Riven Oak
Birmingham, Mich. 48012

The Shade & Shutter
2305 Fairmount Ave.
Philadelphia, Penn. 19130

Shakertown Corporation
P.O. Box 400
Winlock, Wash. 98596

Shaker Workshops, Inc.
Box T
Concord, Mass. 01742

Shenandoah Manufacturing Co., Inc.
P.O. Box 839
Harrisonburg, Va. 22801

Sherwin-Williams Co.
101 Prospect Ave., N.W.
Cleveland, Ohio 44101

Shriber's Wall Papers
3222 Brighton Rd.
Pittsburgh, Penn. 15212

Shutter Modes
401 E. 163rd St.
Bronx, N.Y. 10451

Signature Floors, Inc.
979 Third Ave.
New York, N.Y. 10022

Simpson Timber Co.
900 Fourth Ave.
Seattle, Wash. 98164

Robert W. Skinner, Inc.
Bolton, Mass. 01740

The John P. Smith Co.
174 Cedar St.
Branford, Conn. 06405

Stahl & Stahl
101 Kansas
San Francisco, Calif. 94103

Stamford Wallpaper Co.
153 Greenwich Ave.
Stamford, Conn. 06902

Standard Dry Wall Products
7800 N.W. 38th St.
Miami, Fla. 33166

Stangl Pottery
Mine St.
Flemington, N.J. 08822

Stansfield's Antique Lamp Shop
Rt. 6, Box 332
Slate Hill, N.Y. 10973

Thomas Strahan Co.
150 Heard & Maple
Chelsea, Mass. 02150

Donald Streeter
P.O. Box 237
Franklinville, N.J. 08322

Stroheim & Romann
155 E. 56th St.
New York, N.Y. 10022

The Structural Slate Co.
Pen Argyl, Penn. 18072

Sturbridge Yankee Workshop
Old Turnpike
Sturbridge, Mass. 01566

Sunshine Lane
Box 262
Millersburg, Ohio 44654

Superior Reed and Rattan Furniture
   Co.
500 W. 52nd St.
New York, N.Y. 10019

M. Swift & Sons, Inc.
10 Love Lane
Hartford, Conn. 06101

T

Pete Taggett
The Blacksmith Shop
P.O. Box 15
Mount Holly, Vt. 05758

Robert Tait Fabrics
964 Third Ave.
New York, N.Y. 10022

Tennessee Fabricating Co.
2366 Prospect St.
Memphis, Tenn. 38106

Richard E. Thibaut, Inc.
204 E. 58th St.
New York, N.Y. 10022

The Paul Thomas Studio
108 E. 24th St.
Minneapolis, Minn. 55404

Thompson and Anderson, Inc.
446 Stroudwater St.
Westbrook, Me. 04092

Tolland Fabrics, Inc.
1114 First Ave.
New York, N.Y. 10021

Townhouse Restoration Company,
    Inc.
262 Herr St., Old Mid-Town
Harrisburg, Penn. 17102

Townsend Paneling
P.O. Box 916
Stuttgart, Ark. 72160

Townshend Furniture
Rt. 30
Townshend, Vt. 05353

Ernest Treganowan, Inc.
49 E. 53rd St.
New York, N.Y. 10022

Tremont Nail Co.
21 Elm St.
Wareham, Mass. 02571

Trend of the Times Fabric, Inc.
1400 Santee
Los Angeles, Calif. 90015

Norman Trigg, Inc.
763 Old Country Rd.
Westbury, N.Y. 11590

Trotman Clock Co.
Box 71
Amherst, Mass. 01002

Trouvailles, Inc.
64 Grove
Watertown, Mass. 02172

Trump & Co.
Bethlehem Pike
Flourtown, Penn. 19031

Turco Coatings, Inc.
Wheatland & Mellon Sts.
Phoenixville, Penn. 19460

Turncraft
P.O. Box 2429
White City, Ore. 97501

U

Unique Art Glass Co.
3649 Market St.
St. Louis, Mo. 63110

Uniquities
Marketplace
2400 Market St.
Philadelphia, Penn. 19103

United House Wrecking Co.
328 Selleck St.
Stamford, Conn. 06902

U.S. Cimaco Corporation
40 Orville Dr.
Bohemia, N.Y. 11716

U.S. Gypsum Co.
101 S. Wacker Dr.
Chicago, Ill. 60606

V

The Vermont Country Store
Rt. 103
Rockingham, Vt. 05101

Vermont Marble Co.
61 Main St.
Proctor, Vt. 05765

Vermont Quilts
RFD 2
South Royalton, Vt. 05068

Vermont Weatherboard Inc.
Box Y10
Wolcott, Vt. 05680

The Village Forge
P.O. Box 1148
Smithfield, N.C. 27577

Village Lantern
598 Union St.
N. Marshfield, Mass. 02059

Virginia Metalcrafters
1010 E. Main St.
Waynesboro, Va. 22980

Virtu
P.O. Box 192
Southfield, Mich. 48075

W

R. Warren Construction Co.
Rt. 2
Gardiner, Me. 04345

E. G. Washburne & Co.
83 Andover St.
Danvers, Mass. 01923

The Washington Copper Works
Washington, Conn. 06793

Washington Stove Works
P.O. Box 687
Everett, Wash. 09201

Vivian Watson Assoc.
590 Oak Lawn Plaza
Dallas, Tex.

Waverly Fabrics
58 W. 40th St.
New York, N.Y. 10018

Weblon, Inc.
5 Westchester Plaza
Elmsford, N.Y. 10523

Welsbach Lighting Products Co. Inc.
3001 E. Madison St.
Baltimore, Md. 21205

West Coast Trimmings Co.
945 Maple Ave.
Los Angeles, Calif. 90015

West Rindge Baskets, Inc.
Box 24
Rindge, N.H. 03461

The Robert Whitley Studio
Laurel Rd.
Solebury, Penn. 18963

Whittemore-Durgin Glass Co.
Hanover, Mass. 02339

I. M. Wiese, Antiquarian
Main St.
Southbury, Conn. 06488

John A. Wigen Restorations
Rt. 1, Box 281
Cobleskill, N.Y. 12043

Wilshire Fireplace
351 N. La Cienega Blvd.
Los Angeles, Calif. 90048

Wilson's Country House
P.O. Box 244
West Simsbury, Conn. 06092

Window Modes, Inc.
979 Third Ave.
New York, N.Y. 10022

Window Silhouettes
232 E. 59th St.
New York, N.Y. 10022

The Windyne Company
Box 9091
Richmond, Va. 23225

Winfield Design Associates, Inc.
2690 Harrison
San Francisco, Calif. 94110

Charles J. Winston
515 Madison Ave.
New York, N.Y. 10022

Richard W. Withington, Inc.
Hillsboro, N.H. 03244

Wood Art, Inc.
153 E. 57th St.
New York, N.Y. 10022

Wood Mosaic
P.O. Box 21159
Louisville, Ky. 40221

World Imports
530 14th, N.W.
Atlanta, Ga. 30318

The Wrecking Bar
292 Moreland Ave., N.E.
Atlanta, Ga. 30307

Y

Arthur V. Yariger, Ltd.
608 W. Commercial St.
Victoria, Tex. 77901

Ye Olde Mantel Shoppe
3800 N.E. 2nd Ave.
Miami, Fla. 33137

Williamsburg Shops

Authorized Williamsburg Shops are to be found in the following locations. All offer the same products available at the Craft House in Williamsburg. As noted throughout the text of *The Old House Catalogue*, such licensed manufacturers as Bates Fabrics, Virginia Metalcrafters, Josiah Wedgwood & Sons, F. Schumacher and Co., The Harvin Co., Kittinger Co., Folger Adam Co., Martin-Senour, and Katzenbach and Warren, among others, are represented in the Williamsburg reproduction and gift collections.

*B. Altman & Company
361 Fifth Avenue
New York, New York 10016

H. Feinberg's
705 Market Street
Wilmington, Delaware 19899

*G. Fox & Company
960 Main Street
Hartford, Connecticut 06115

Gardberg's Furniture Company
28 South Florida Street
Mobile, Alabama 36606

The Golden Rooster
1206 Perimeter Mall
4400 Ashford Dunwoody Road
Atlanta, Georgia 30346

*The Wm. Hengerer Company
465 Main Street
Buffalo, New York 14203

*The Higbee Company
Public Square
Cleveland, Ohio 44113

*Joseph Horne Company
Penn and Stanwix
Pittsburgh, Pennsylvania 15222

*Jacobson Stores, Inc.
16500 Oakwood Boulevard
Allen Park, Michigan 48101

*Marshall Field & Company
111 North State Street
Chicago, Illinois 60690

O'Neill & Bishop
Suburban Square
Ardmore, Pennsylvania 19003

+Rich's, Inc.
Lenox Square
3393 Peachtree Road, N.E.
Atlanta, Georgia 30326

The Treasure House, Inc.
120 East Front Street
Burlington, North Carolina 27215

*John Wanamaker Philadelphia, Inc.
13th & Market Streets
Philadelphia, Pennsylvania 19101

*Woodward & Lothrop
10th & 11th, "F" & "G," N.W.
Washington, D.C. 20013

Scheduled to open November 8, 1976:
*D. H. Holmes Company, Ltd.
819 Canal Street
New Orleans, Louisiana 70160

*and most branches
+Lenox Square, Birmingham and Cumberland
 branches only

General Index

A

Acid-etched mirrors, 202
Aladdin lamps, 110–111, 115
Aluminum leaf, 198
American Association for Local
  and State History, 215
Anchor bars, 73
Andirons, 70–71, 83
Appliqué, 46–47
Architectural styles, four basic,
  illustrated: Colonial, early,
  12–14; Colonial, late, 15–17;
  Victorian, early, 18–20; Vic-
  torian, late, 21–23
Armchairs, 169–176
Ash dumps, 72
Ash pit cleanout doors, 72
Association for Preservation
  Technology, 214
Awning hardware, 52
Awnings, 120, 140

B

Back to the City, Inc., 214
Ball feet, 63
Balusters, 47, 48, 49
Bar locks, shutter, 62
Barn hinges, 55
Barn siding, 49
Barometers, English mercury
  stick, 192
Baseboards, 42, 43–44
Baskets, hand-woven, 192, 208
Bathroom fixtures, 62
Batting, cotton, 137
Bayberry candles, 101
Beam hooks, 56
Beams, hand-hewn, 29, 38
Bed coverings, 120–121, 140
Bed hangings, 120, 121–122
Bed hardware, 63
Beds, 164–167, 189
Bedspreads, 121, 140
Beeswax electric candles, 102
Bellows, 71, 83
Benches, 167, 189, 200

Bentback rockers, 178–179
Betty lamps, 103, 108, 116
Beveled-edge rim locks, 59
Birdcages, 192
Blacksmiths, 52, 102
Blanket chests, 177
Blankets, 121
Bolts: door, 52, 53, 60; shutter,
  61–62
Boot scrapers, 61
Boots, stovepipe, 78
Borders, 48, 89
Boston rockers, 179
Bows, 47
Boxes, 193, 209–210
Brackets: architectural, 44–45, 49;
  hardware, 53, 66
Braided rugs, 94–95
Braids, 133–134
Brand dogs, 70–71
Brass beds, 164–165
Brasses, furniture, 65–66
Brick flooring, 86
Bricks, antique, 29–30, 86
Brocade, 137
Broilers, fire, 199–200
Brooks, Joshua, House, 12–14
Brooms, hearth, 82
Burners, lamp, 115
Butler's chests, 177–178
Butler's tray hinges, 64
Butterfly strap hinges, 55

C

"Cabbage rose" carpets, 91
Cambric, black, 137
Campaign chest hardware, 66
Candelabras, 101, 116
Candleholders, 102–103, 115, 116
Candles, 101–102
Candle sconces, 114
Candle snuffers, 115
Candlestand kit, 187
Candlestands, 102–103, 167–168,
  189
Candlesticks, 103–105, 116–117
Candle trays, 115
Canopy beds, 121–122, 165–166
Canterburies, 168–169, 189

Canvas floorcloths, 91, 94
Capitals, 47
Captains's chairs, 175
Card table hinges, 64
Carpeting, 91–93, 97
Carriage lanterns, 113
Cartouches, 47
Casters, 63
Castings, hardware, 62
Catches, 64–65
Caryatids, 47
Casings, 43, 49
Ceiling cornices, 46
Ceiling fixtures, 116
Ceilings: ornamental plaster, 30,
  38, 45, 49; steel, 30–31, 38, 45
Centers, ceiling, 45, 49
Ceramic flooring, 86–87
Chair kit, 188
Chair rails, 42, 45, 49
Chairs, 169–177, 178–180, 189
Chair seat kit, 131–132
Chair tapes, 136
Chandeliers, 100–101, 105–107,
  117
Chest lifts, 66
Chests, 177–178, 189
Child's chair kit, 187
Chimney breasts, 72
Chimneys, lamp, 115
Chinaware, 194, 210
Clapboards, 35
Cleanout doors, 72
Clinch nails, 60
Cliveden, 15–17
Clock hinges, 64
Clock parts, 195
Clocks, 194–195, 209
Coal scuttles, 78–83
Coat and hat hooks, 56
Collars, stovepipe, 78
Colonial architecture, illustrated:
  early, 12–14; late, 15-17
Colonial rim locks, 59
Corbels, 44, 49
Cord, upholsterer's, 137
Corner chairs, 175–176
Corner tables, 182–183
Corner washstands, 186
Cornices, 42, 45–46, 49
Cotton batting, 137
Coverlets, 121